U0576643

清代外務部
中外關係檔案史料叢編
——中美關係卷

·中國第一歷史檔案館 北京大學 澳大利亞拉籌伯大學 編·

第六册·國際會議

中華書局

目 錄

逕啟者、昨接准本國外部來文並本國

大伯理璽天德降諭一道、以美國從前置買魯伊阿那之地再越

一年即係百年之期、本國人欲記念此置買之事、因擬設一

天下賽寶會、聚集天下所有製造之物、與百工技藝土產

礦務材木海味珍品、為美國人素所大為羨慕者、茲奉外部

囑為轉達

貴部貴王大臣本國

大伯理璽天德切請

貴國政府、將以上所列各項、凡為中國所產者、請派官數員、

諭知商民、預為備辦各物、屆時隨同運赴會所、中國如允運

送本國、甚為欣悅、甚盼即以

貴國政府允行作復俾本國

大伯理璽天德與美國人民同深欣慰可也謹將所奉

降諭及外部所致原文照繕附送即請

貴王大臣查照是荷此布順頌

日祉 附送洋文並 降諭及外部原文

名另具 八月二十八日

康格

No. 29$.

LEGATION OF THE UNITED STATES OF AMERICA,
PEKIN, CHINA.

Oct. 8th. 1901.

Your Highness and

Your Excellencies:-

I have the honor to transmit herewith a copy of a despatch which I have just received from the State Department at Washington and of a Proclamation by the President of the United States, contained therein, announcing the intention to celebrate the one hundredth anniversary of the purchase of the Louisiana territory by the United States. The celebration is to take the form of an internationalexposition of arts, manufactures, industries, and the products of the soil, mine, forest and sea.

This celebration is one in which the American people take great interest, and I am directed to say to Your Highness and Your Excellencies that the President of the United States extends a hearty invitation to the Government of China to participate in the exposition, and will have great pleasure in learning that Your Government accepts this invitation and will appoint Commissioners to arrange for a proper display of the resources of China.

I have the honor to express the hope that Your Highness and Your Excellencies will give the matter your early consideration and return a favorable reply, which will afford great gratification to the President and the people of the United States.

I avail myself of this occasion to renew to Your Highness and Your Excellencies the assurance of my highest consideration.

E.E. and M.P. of the

United States.

To His Highness, Prince Ch'ing, President, and
Their Excellencies, the Ministers of the
Board of Foreign Affairs.

清代外務部中外關係檔案史料叢編──中美關係卷 第六冊·國際會議

[LOUISIANA PURCHASE EXPOSITION.]

—

By the President of the United States of America.

A Proclamation.

WHEREAS notice has been given me by the Louisiana Purchase Exposition Commission, in accordance with the provisions of Section 9 of the Act of Congress, approved March 3, 1901, entitled "An Act To provide for celebrating the one hundredth anniversary of the purchase of the Louisiana territory by the United States by holding an international exhibition of arts, industries, manufactures, and the products of the soil, mine, forest, and sea in the city of St. Louis, in the State of Missouri," that provision has been made for grounds and buildings for the uses provided for in the said Act of Congress:

Now, therefore, I, WILLIAM McKINLEY, President of the United States, by virtue of the authority vested in me by said Act, do hereby declare and proclaim that such International Exhibition will be opened in the city of St. Louis, in the State of Missouri, not later than the first day of May, nineteen hundred and three, and will be closed not later than the first day of December thereafter. And in the name of the Government and of the people of the United States, I do hereby invite all the nations of the earth to take part in the commemoration of the Purchase of the Louisiana Territory, an event of great interest to the United States and of abiding effect on their development, by appointing representatives and sending such exhibits to the Louisiana Purchase Exposition as will most fitly and fully illustrate their resources, their industries, and their progress in civilization.

In Testimony Whereof, I have hereunto set my hand and caused the seal of the United States to be affixed.

DONE at the City of Washington, this twentieth day of August, one thousand nine hundred and one, and of the Independence of the United States, the one hundred and twenty-sixth.

[SEAL.]

WILLIAM McKINLEY

By the President:
JOHN HAY
Secretary of State.

C I R C U L A R.

　　　　　　Department of State,

　　　　　　　　　Washington, August 22nd, 1901.

To the Diplomatic Officers

　　　　　of the United States.

Gentlemen:

　　　　I transmit herewith copies of a Proclamation issued
by the President on the 20th instant, inviting, on behalf of
the Government and the people of the United States, the Government and people of the country to which you are accredited,
to take part in the commemoration of the Purchase of the
Louisiana Territory, and event of great interest to the
United States, and of abiding effect on their development,
by holding at the City of Saint Louis, in the State of Missouri, from the 30th day of April, 1903, to the first day of
November, in that year, an international exposition of arts,
manufactures, industries, and the products of the soil,
mine, forest, and sea.

　　By this purchase, the domain of the United States was
more than doubled.　At the time of its aquisition the territory was a wilderness with not more than fifty thousand
civilized inhabitants.　From it have been formed twelf

　　　　　　　　　　　　　States.

States and twelf Territories.   These have a population of more
than fifteen millions, and their cabined wealth is estimated at Twenty billions of Dollars.   Nearly two hundred
millions of acres of land have been brought into cultivation
and made to furnish no inconsiderable portion of the world's
food supply.   The farm products for 1890 exceeded two billions of dollars in value, and the manufacture and minerals
were estimated at nearly the same sum.
          the
     It is desire of the President, speaking for people of the
United States, that all the nations of the earth, shall take
part in the proposed exposition, by appointing representatives
thereto, and by sending such exhibits as will most fitly
and fully illustrate their resourses, their industries, and
their progress in civilization.

     In communicating this invitation to the Government to which
you are accredited, you will express the pleasure which the
President will feel should that Government decide to accept
it by appointing commissioner and by further participating in
the exposition through such a display of its resources as is
contemplated.

     It is not doubted that you will endeavor, as far as
lies in your power, to promote the interests of the exposition
by lending your assistance to its duly accredited agents who

                                                  may

-3-

may present themselves to you.

At an early date further information relating to the exposition will be communicated to you for transmission to the Foreign Office.

I am, Gentlemen,

Your Obedient Servant,

John Hay.

Enclosures:

As above.

上

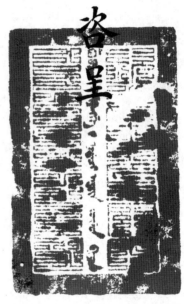

咨呈

二月廿三收

欽差大臣□□□□□□□□□□□□□□　□□□□□□□□□□□□□□□□劉　為

咨復事據江海關道袁樹勛稟稱本年正月初四日

祇奉鈞札准

外務部咨美國在散魯伊城開設賽寶會派員來

華速定辦法使商民將百工技藝各等之物預為儲

辦屆時運往赴會譯錄

酌定辦法票復並分移各關一体尊辦等

分移照辦一面函致稅務司查

稅務司好博遜復稱歷來凡遇各國開設各種賽會奉

文後如有華商願自備辦賽物來關報請出洋赴會與

賽會者本關無不准其遵章辦理並予照料免稅出口

以敦睦誼而廣見識此次美國在散魯伊城開設賽寶

會既已奉文自應仍照應辦成案辦理毋庸另議至

派員籌辦賽物等語非敢擅定除照案出示招商儗物赴會

外復請查照核轉等因前來職道伏查此案前奉憲札

業經出示曉諭各項工商人等如違反自令責罰開往

報關出口遵照向章辦理再案斷有派員之一節可否請

出使美國伍大臣酌派以便辦理並文憑亦可望

情到本大臣擬此除批此案既經該道示諭如有願赴

此會者自應照　　　理至派員一節候咨

外務部轉咨

出使伍大臣酌辦繳印發外粗應咨復為此咨呈

貴外務部謹請查照核咨施行須至咨呈者

右　咨　　呈

外 務 部

光緒貳拾捌年貳月拾肆日

美 國 之 書

譯錄銀刻請帖內之言

大美國因購得魯西亞納地方設立慶賀百年賽會總理及各董

事等敬謹恭請

大清國

大皇帝諭飭

大皇帝陛下御臨斯會並殷盼

貴國家大臣等隨同前往

總理會務巴禮德

總理會長弗蘭西　　於一千九百零二年西月三十號同簽字於散魯伊斯城

逕啟者本國明年在散魯伊斯城地方開辦賽寶會前已達知

貴部茲由該會總理人請本國

外部海大臣轉詢中國

政府該會將所刷印賽會一切議論之書運來中國分送各省

地方進口時可否准其免稅等因本大臣茲按其所請並達

貴親王查照可否免稅之處希即按照向章妥辦並希

見復是荷此泐順頌

爵祺 附洋文

名另具 四月初三日

其奏美國博覽會員巴禮總

籲懇 觀見請 旨定期由

奏 奏

署 左 侍 郎 那 宵

署 右 侍 郎 聯 六月 日 日

謹

奏

為美國特派總理博覽會大員來京籲懇

觀見

請

旨定期恭摺仰祈

聖鑒事竊臣等接准美國使臣康格函稱茲有亞

美理駕聚商南北合眾國事務全權大臣巴禮

德因美國開設散魯伊博覽會現經派為總理
之員此係記念百年大會由美國下議院商空
需用經費甚鉅巴禮德係本國特派邀請中國
赴會所過日本朝鮮等國均甚優待昨至北京

奏請
　懇代為

觀見
　屆時自應帶領入

觀成
　就其奉派前來之事務以為增加兩國友睦之

奏請
　擬應請即行入

旨定
　期等因前來日等伏查美國現議開設博覽
會特派總理之員編歷各國邀請赴會其意

頌為固執此次巴禮德來京籲懇

觀見陳明此事亙為增加睦誼之據自應請

旨定期准由美國使臣康格帶同入

觀俾遂其瞻就之忱伏候

命下臣部即知照該使臣等欽導屆期由臣等帶領

觀見所有請

旨定期

觀見緣由理合恭摺具陳伏乞

皇太后

皇上聖鑒謹

奏 光緒二十八年六月十九日奉

硃批著於本月二十二日巳正二刻觀見欽此

和會司

呈為照會事准

貴大臣照稱茲有美國總理散魯伊博覽會事務

巴禮德係本國特派來京請代為奏請

本大臣屆時自應帶領甚有名之巴欽差入

就其奉派前來之事務以為增加兩國友睦之據等

因本爵大臣於六月十九日具奏奉

旨著於本月二十二日巳正二刻觀見欽此相應恭錄照會

貴大臣轉達

貴國巴欽差欽遵屆期即由

貴大臣帶同入

也須至照會者

美康使

光緒二十八年六月　日

清代外務部中外關係檔案史料叢編——中美關係卷　第六冊·國際會議

逕啟者接准本國外部大臣來文以本國西本年九月初一至初

五日在們達那必特地方開設礦務國使會囑本大臣轉為恭請

中國政府派員赴會該會董事甚願中國派有赴會人員會中無

論於何國隨便派來之員均深願其考究美國礦務以及銷鎔之

法所有請中國赴會之請帖寄到雖遲仍應特送附送

貴親王查照自悉美國開辦此會亦於中國未曾忘記也特此

奉布即頌

爵祺附送洋文並請帖

　　名另具七月二十六日

LEGATION OF THE UNITED STATES OF AMERICA,

PEKIN, CHINA.

F.C.No. 412.   August 29th 1902.

Your Highness:

At the request of the Secretary of State, I have

the honor to communicate to Your Highness enclosed six copies of

an Official Call for the fifth Session of the International

Mining Congress which is to be held at Butte, Montana, from the Ist

to the 5th of September 1902, and to state what pleasure it would

give the Managers of the Congress if the Chinese Government could

be represented thereat by Official Delegates.

Representatives from whatever nation will be afforded every

facility for investigating some of the great American mines, mills

and smelters in operation.

This invitation, having only now come to hand, I still forward

it to Your Highness, to show that China was not forgotten in the

matter, and avail myself of this occasion to assure Your Highness

of my highest consideration.

E. H. Conger

Envoy Extraordinary and

Minister Plenipotentiary of

the United States of America.

To His Highness

Prince of Ch'ing.

SECOND ONLY IN IMPORTANCE TO A MEETING OF THE NATIONAL CONGRESS.

Official Call for Miners' Congress

E. L. Shafner, President,
Cleveland, Ohio.

Major Fred R. Reed, Vice=President,
Boise, Idaho.

Irwin Mahon, Secretary,
Carlisle, Penna.

E. C. Camp, Treasurer,
Knoxville, Tenn.

International Mining Congress

Fifth Annual Meeting

Butte, Montana

September 1, 2, 3, 4 and 5, 1902

Executive Committee

Irwin Mahon, Carlisle, Penna., Secretary.

E. L. Shafner,
Cleveland, Ohio.

Ex=Gov. L. Bradford Prince,
Santa Fe, N. M.

Maj. Fred R. Reed,
Boise, Idaho.

Col. John T. Grayson,
Baker City, Oregon.

E. C. Camp,
Knoxville, Tennessee.

Mrs. Ella Knowles Haskell,
Butte, Montana.

Local Executive Committee

Ex=Governor J. E. Rickards,
Chairman.

H. M. Patterson.

Henry Mueller.

D. J. Hennessy.

J. T. O'Brien,
Secretary.

........Official Call........

To Governors of States and Territories, Mayors of Cities, County Commissioners, Boards of Trade and all Commercial, Industrial and Mining Organizations.

The Fifth Annual Session.

of the International Mining Congress will convene in the city of Butte, state of Montana, at 10 o'clock a. m. Monday, September 1, 1902, and continue thereafter the 2d, 3d, 4th and 5th.

Great Success.

The great successs and influential effect of the four preceding assemblies, together with the wonderful expansion of the mining industry during the years 1898, 1899, 1900 and 1901, and the special importance of the subjects to be discussed and passed upon will, beyond all question, bring together a large delegation of earnest, well-informed, thinking men, insuring for the congress a most instructive and successful session.

Object.

The object of the congress is to encourage the growth and thorough development of each and every state and territory represented; to work in harmony for such national legislation as is calculated to promote the interests of the people of the nation; increase reciprocal trade between the states and territories, to discuss matters of special interest, and to formulate and decide upon plans which will bring about desired results, in the advancement of the mining industry and kindred interests.

Of the 1,500,000,000 consumers of the world 825,000,000, or more than one-half of the total, 1,500,000,000, are mainly in countries resting upon and directly opposite our Pacific sea ports and in developing American interests in home and foreign markets, it is in the fostering and maintaining of the higher advancement of our mining industry, and the encouraging of individual enterprise, that we will secure the power that will most easily, naturally and permanently build up our home and foreign trade, secure general prosperity and happiness among all classes of people, and lay a firm foundation for the success of present and future generations.

Materials of Success.

We have a territory of boundless resources and advantageous geographical position. These are but the materials of success. Success itself is an individual quality.

Agriculture.

The establishment of the agricultural department in 1889, was the creation of a beacon light to the farmer. Through the well-organized efforts of this department the products of field, farm and orchard have increased, and new markets opened up at home and abroad. So well is this department now understood and appreciated, that it is very questionable whether there is to be found in all this broad land a single individual with sufficient temerity as to even hint at a suggestion of its abrogation. Yet a department of mines and mining in its benefits will exceed in extent that of agriculture.

American Mining.

The industry of American mining is now so vast and varied and each and every year increasing so rapidly, and so much depends upon its being held clean and clear from all entangling combinations and alliances, that the immediate establishment of an independent department of mines and mining with a secretary who shall be a member of the president's cabinet, is absolutely imperative.

Statistics.

Statistics as they are now gathered on the production of metal throughout the United States, are gathered by the chief of the division of statistics of the geological survey, excepting gold and silver, and these two metals are reported on by the officials of the mint, which, in the nature of things are not, and cannot be a collection of facts covering the actual production of gold and silver.

Mining Bureau.

The mining bureau has always been added as a fifth wheel to some overcrowded bureau, or else combined with a

department whose interests were not, are not, and never will be allied to those of the mining industry, the natural consequence being that but little attention has been, or will be, paid to mining matters.

Squandered Millions.

The national government has squandered millions of money and untold energy through the separation of its scientific bureaus, and the consequent duplication of results. Similarly each state and territory is now working out its own salvation or disruption in the matter of mine administration, almost wholly without reference to what has already been accomplished in other states grappling with the same problems. Each state and territory has its own local field, but there are general questions, and many of them, which absolutely must be worked out by combined efforts, which only can be attained in justice and equity to all, under the direction of a central authority such as is desired by establishing a federal department of mines and mining.

Exploration.

By systematic exploration of our mountains, vast bodies of mineral will be brought to light, which otherwise will long remain unknown. Careful geological investigation will direct the path of the untiring prospector, save a vast amount of money and labor, now devoted to useless ends leading only to heart sores and disappointments, and increase the extent of valuable discoveries, and development to a marked degree.

State Surveys.

Few, if any, of our state surveys are complete in any sense of the word. The amount of necessary reconnoissance has been large, while the appropriation for all geological work has often been quite meager; hence the first problem which the geological surveys have had to solve, has been to make the best showing from the smallest outlay of money; naturally, therefore, the geological side had the precedence, while mining and metallurgy have suffered, and received only the crumbs from the appropriation loaf. Although intimately related, the geological and mining bent of mind are distinctive endowments, and while they may be combined, such a combination is usually conspicuous through its absence, and the attempt to combine the two under a single head has often proved destructive. A geological survey is to a mining department as a prospector to a miner—first cousin; but the very law of consanguinity forbids their marriage.

These Commercial Days.

In the mad rush of these commercial days, it is well to think of, and kindly remember the prospector and the miner. We will need their manhood as an inspiration to give the best of their lives for our country, and if we have it, it will never be said of this nation "That the ocean was dug for its grave, or the winds woven for its winding sheet, the forest for its coffin, or the mountains reared for its monument."

Mineral Exhibit.

During the session of the congress there will be a most attractive and educational display of the commercial and scientific minerals of the state of Montana, in which adjoining states and territories are urged to participate. There will be no charge for space, and every facility will be afforded, and every courtesy extended to such states and territories as are present with exhibits to display and advertise their mineral recources as they may desire.

School of Mines.

The Montana State School of Mines is taking a most active interest in the mineral display, and in connection therewith, will have an exhibition under the charge of Prof. N. R. Leonard, president of the School of Mines, some rare models covering the workings of some of the most celebrated mines of the country, which will prove interesting to all visitors, especially the scientific man.

In No Sense Partisan.

The congress will be in no sense partisan, the originators recognizing the same high patriotism in all Americans, believing all to be imbued with an equal loyalty to their country and its best interests.

Urgent Invitation.

It is therefore urged that all scientists, metallurgists, practical mining men, manufacturers of mining machinery, and all others interested in advancing the welfare of the mining industry, will attend and participate in the deliberations of this, the fifth annual session of the International Mining congress, and by the presence and advice make the proceedings of this coming assembly of so interesting and educational a character as to command favorable consideration throughout the civilized world.

Not Precious Metals Alone.

It is not the object of this congress to confine its consideration of subjects to that of mining for gold and silver and their by-products, but also that of copper, iron, coal, marble, stone, the various fire clays, asphaltum and all kindred interests in the mineral and metallic classes.

Better Recognition.

To secure better recognition of the mining industry by the national government.

Needed Changes.

To bring about needed changes in the federal mining laws.

Cultivate Acquaintance.

To cultivate acquaintance, fraternal feeling and hearty co-operation among the various mining, manufacturing transportation, commercial and labor bodies represented.

To Exchange Ideas.

To exchange practical ideas covering the various phases of the mining business; an interest embracing every branch of the mining industry, and especially to take under advisement the importance of the creation by the congress of the United States of a department to be known as the Department of Mines and Mining, thus securing a cabinet officer who represents an interest more essentially American than that of any other falling under the legislative power of our government.

Subjects and Papers.

Proposals are invited of subjects and papers on mines, mining, milling, smelting, mining machinery and all kindred topics to be embraced in a program now being prepared, and on adjournment of the congress, to be published with its proceedings in book form.

The Coming Session.

The influence of this coming session of the congress, surrounded as it will be by a multitude of problems that call for all the wisdom and experience that can be brought to bear for their solution, will be potential, and to those participating in its deliberations, or availing themselves of the results, its benefits will be immeasurable.

Rates.

Special rates will be given for the occasion, and all delegates and visitors are assured of ample accommodations, and a most cordial welcome by the citizens of Butte and state of Montana.

Delegates.

Governors of states and territories, all friendly nations, mayors of cities and towns, mining exchanges, chambers of commerce, board of trade, real estate exchanges and all commercial, trade and labor organizations, are urged to appoint representative delegates at an early date, sending their names and postoffice address of each delegate without delay to the secretary.

Representation.

Governors of states and territories, 30 delegates each.

Mayors of cities and towns, five delegates each, and one additional for each 10,000 population or fraction thereof.

Each mining bureau, five delegates each.

Each mining exchange, five delegates each.

Each chamber of commerce, five delegates each.

Each real estate exchange, five delegates each.

Each board of trade, five delegates each.

Each miners' union, five delegates each.

Each trade and labor assembly, five delegates each.

And all other commercial and business organizations, five delegates each.

Ex-Officio Delegates.

Governors of states and territories, members of the United States congress and ex-presidents of this congress, are ex-officio delegates, with all privileges of delegates except those of voting.

Entertainment of Delegates.

The local executive committee of Butte, the greatest mining and smelting camp on earth, with its hundreds of miles of underground workings, has outlined a special program and will be prepared, not only to delight all visitors with the opportunity to investigate with comfort and pleasure the practical workings of the greatest mines in the mineral world, with all classes of mining machinery, in full operation in the various mills and smelters in and around the city of Butte, but from what they see and hear, learn a lesson never to be forgotten as to the importance and actual value of the mining industry, and what its present and greater success means to the welfare and happiness of the people of this great nation.

Permanent Members.

Any person desiring to become a permanent member of this organization, can do so on payment of an annual fee of $5.00.

E. L. Shafner,
President International Mining Congress.

Irwin Mahon,
Secretary.

再查和解公斷條約我國雖已畫押尚未奉

旨批准似應由

鈞署定稿具奏先行請

旨批准寄至和國都城會所收存由彼照會各國以為將來
公斷張本查公斷衙門自設立以來畫押各國例准
派員在該衙門作為常川議員而無庸常川住署六
年為期期滿更換不給薪俸祗領虛銜掛名簿籍遇
有爭端各國可在名單內選擇議員現在歐美諸國

伍大臣信 附和解公斷條約一本

均派有定員或二員或四員不等英美等國各派四
員日本暹羅亦各派二員其所派之員不拘籍隸本
國外國大約以熟諳公法素有名望者充其選中國
似可參仿辦理酌派二員或四員為公斷衙門議員
平時並不耗費查日本所派一日本人現充公使一
美國律師現在東京當差暹羅所派一美國人現在
紐約當律師一此國人公法家不必籍隸本國現美
副外部熙路人甚公正品望素隆熟悉外交精諳公

法廷芳與之相處有素甚助中國若特派爲公斷衙門

議員彼必樂效馳驅而各國亦知楚材晉用簡派得

人不敢輕視可否借材異地之處祇候

鈞署主裁統乞

代回

邸堂

列憲是荷專此再泐祇請

勛安

伍廷芳頓首

光緒二十八年九月二十二日

又美字第九十六號

拟稿
和解公斷條約

本約畫押期限以本年十二月三十一號為止訂議各國暨全權議員寬列次序應

按本年七月二十八號會議訂定之例德意志國與斯馬加國比利時國中國丹

馬國西班牙國美利堅國墨西哥國法蘭西國英吉利國希臘國義大利國

日本國盧森不爾厄國黑山國和蘭國波斯國葡萄牙國羅美里國俄羅斯

國暹邏維國瑞羅國瑞典國瑞士國土耳其國布加夕國

大皇帝

大君主

大伯理璽天德

擬應布公法籍評是非訟立常川公斷衙門冀收成效將來受益無窮各國勛

創會之人均謂應從眾議尊崇公法俾保萬國生靈為此訂立條約所有各

國特派全權議員銜名開列於下

以上各員破此校閱全權各例託訂定之下各款

第一章　保持和局

第一條　現經議定畫押各國遇有爭端須竭力設法和商了結俾免兵

釁

第二章　和解調處

第二條　畫押各國議定如遇決裂或爭端須於用兵前審度緩急

情形特請友邦一國或數國和解或從中調處

第三條　除以上所言特請別遇和解調處外遇有兩爭端破局外

或一國或數國亦准審度緩急情形自願出場和解調處此等辦法畫

押各國酌量均謂可行雖當開戰之時仍准局外國和解調處不得視

為有傷睦誼之舉

第四條　調處國之責任即係和勸相爭之事解釋兩造嫌隙

第五條　所擬調處之法一經相爭國或調處國察明辦法實難免

從調處之責立即作罷

第六條　和解調處或由相爭國特請或係局外國自願務須商

量辦理毋得勉強

第七條　相爭國難九他國調處如未經專條訂明另有辦法不

得因此停止或遲延或按攝徵調之事暨籌備一切戰務業已開

戰如本經專條訂明后有辦法亦不得因此停止用兵

第八條 畫押各國業經商妥定有專門詢處之辦法列下如遇重大
案情有損和局相爭各國應即各舉一國由所舉國彼此座相接洽俾
得預防相爭國之絕交相爭國應將關繫爭端往來文情支即傳
此至相爭之案作為所舉之國所辦之事所舉之國自當竭力理
結如未經專條訂明另有辦法不得逾三十日期限俾竟失和所舉之
國仍應合力伺機從中轉圜議成和局

第三章 派員查究

第九條 兩國遇有爭端而於國家體面緊要利害無甚關涉如兩
國倘臣未克議結畫押名國可審度情形商定派員將此案情東公
詳細查明務期爭端易解

第十條 所派查究之員應按兩國商定專條辦理所定專條應詳
敘案情明定委員權限並查案辦法查究之前殖失訊問兩造至應

第十一條 所派查究之員如未經專條訂明另有辦法即照本約
導程式期限如未經專條訂明另有辦法即由該委員自行酌定

第三十二條 辦理

第十二條 所派查究之員應由相爭國言明給以一切利便俾得將
所查之案瀝陳清究

第十三條 所派查究之員查實文件係為查實案情不得有判斷
概畫押

第十四條 所派查究之員中報之文件係為查實案情不得有判斷
語氣至如何辦理之處概聽相爭國之便

第四章 公斷

第一節 公斷規例

第十五條 公斷之義係將兩國爭端即由該兩國所舉之員按律商
結

第十六條 凡關律法暨施行條約之爭端彼此不克商結者畫押
國認明公斷為和解最善至公之法

第十七條 公斷條約係為爭辦事件而定此類爭辦或業有成
尚無成業所定條約指一切爭端或指一類之事

第十八條 公斷條約所欲即指願從公斷者互相言明情心導照公
判語辦理

第十九條 畫押名國遇訂公約或專約言明應歸公斷外仍可於
此等約章批准之前或批准之後遇有應歸公斷辦理事件另訂公約
或專約締結歸公斷以期推廣

第二節 設立常川公斷衙門

第二十條　畫押各國因各國爭端使臣有不克商定者總為便於從速公斷起見言明設立常川公斷衙門隨時辦理該衙門應按本約內所列辦事章程辦理如相爭兩國另有專條不在此例

第二十一條　凡公斷之案該衙門一概有權辦理如相爭兩國未經訂明願歸公斷之約不在此例

第二十二條　應在和蘭都城設立萬國公所作為公斷衙門遇有公斷衙門應行會議即由該所循例知照該所存儲一切卷冊暨雜務案贖畫押各國言明將破此所討公斷條約暨公斷判語鈔稿校對無訛咨送該所再言明將有關公斷判語之律法章程文牘一律咨送該所

第二十三條　自本約批准之日起限三箇月內每國應選擇向有名望公法專家並願充公斷之人全多四員派充常川公斷衙門議員由辦公所開列名單知照畫押各國名單如有更動處亦由該所知照畫押各國所有議員可聽兩國或數國商明公選一員或數員每一員亦准兼充數國議員各議員充選以六年為限期滿亦准展限遇有告退或身故應即按章另派充補

第二十四條　畫押各國如遇多端欲請常川公斷衙門判定即在公斷衙門總名單內選擇議員如兩造未克立即商選議員應照下法辦理每造選擇兩員所選之兩員復商舉一員為總議員如仍不

合兩造可各舉一國請該兩國同公舉一員為總議員擇定議員後兩造應將該員姓名及決計願歸公斷之意知照公斷衙門至會議之期由兩造擇定名議員辦事時應享利益如出使八員例

第二十五條　曹議之處例應在和蘭都城遇有事出萬不得已或經相爭兩國允公斷人方准更換地方

第二十六條　畫押各國遇有另案專辦公斷事件和蘭都城辦公所准其借用該所地方暨辦事員役即未經畫押各國或業經畫押與未經畫押之國遇有爭端兩造商明願歸公斷衙門辦理係為亦可推廣按章辦理

第二十七條　畫押各國之內如兩國或數國遇有爭端事將決裂畫押各國應行文該國勸請歸常川公斷衙門判核此條畫押各國之責任所以畫押各國勸請導照本約歸常川公斷衙門辦理為保和起見相爭之國應得視為美意

第二十八條　本約批准至少已有九國之數速即在和蘭都城設立常川辦事公會該公會各員以畫押各國駐和公使兼充而以和蘭外部大臣為會總其萬國辦公所應由公會開設即歸該公會管轄稽查該公會應將設立公斷衙門之事知照各國將來即辦該衙門之事並詳定該衙門辦事章程暨一切應有章程判決該衙

門雜務兼操辦公所員役聽陵之權明定薪俸工資稽核用項會議時

總須有議員五人方為合例所議之事以從眾為斷該公會應議定

重程知照畫押各國並每年將公斷衙門案件辦案情形以及用項彙

報一次

第二十九條　辦公所少經費畫押各國按照萬國郵政公所章程由

各國分認

第三十條　茲為推廣公斷起見畫押各國商定下開各款以資辦

理相爭之國如另有重程不在此例

第三十一條　相爭國遇案願歸公斷應員畫押文憑詳敘案情明

第三十二條　凡遇案件可由兩造公同任意選擇一員或數員或即在

常川公斷衙門議員中選擇如兩造未先立即商選議員應照下法

辦理每造選擇兩員所選之兩員商舉一員為總議員如所舉之

總議員意見不合兩造可各舉一國請該兩國會同公舉一員為總議員

仍不各兩造可各舉一國請該兩國另選一員為總議員

第三十三條　如所舉議員係某國之君或某一方少主公斷法應由

此君或此主核奪

第三十四條　總議員為各議員之首領如無總議員即由選定各議

員俱舉一員為首領

第三十五條　議員如遇身故或告退或無論何事見阻應接重另

派充補

第三十六條　議案之處應由兩造擇定若副即在和蘭都城會議

一經擇定遇有事出萬不得已或經兩造商允公斷人方准更換地

方

第三十七條　兩造有權派名專員前赴議業處俾兩造接洽事歟

議業處接洽並兩造名員暨律師向議業處伸爭保本國權利

第三十八條　應用何國語言文字由議業處擇定

第三十九條　辦理公斷分為二事曰訴陳曰辯論所謂訴陳者將本

案全卷或刻稿與鈔稿由兩造派員送交議業處各員暨對實國送交

之件應按照末約第四十九條議業處所定程式期限辦理所謂辯論

者係將此案情節向議業處口說發明

第四十條　兩造之一所有呈出文件理各知照對質國

第四十一條　凡辯論案情須聽首領督率所有辯論必須議業核定

由兩造商允方准宣布辯論之時由首領所派之員當面宣錄講

業作證

第四十二條　訴陳文件業已停止接收而兩造之一尚有續陳文件如

本經對質國允許議案處當即卻還

第四十三條 倘兩造中之委員或參議聲請查核繕陳文件議案處應即明白知照對質國亦可索取此項文件斟酌辦理

第四十四條 議業處可向兩造委員索取不論何項文件並令詳細講解如該員不允應即寫條由備案

第四十五條 兩造所派委員暨參議准其向議業處申說維持本業之意

第四十六條 所派委員暨參議可將業情出手常例之外反意料不及等處申說發明惟一經議業判定不得再行駁詰

第四十七條 議業處各員有權訊問業情於委員暨參議並參將業中疑難情節明白申說當辯論時議業處各員所有訊問之語指駁之詞並不作為該名員確實見解

第四十八條 准議業處按照相爭國所具交憑並與此業相關之條約暨萬國公法大意酌以核定業情

第四十九條 議業處之權係酌奪全業辦法孟定兩造結業之程

第五十條 兩造委員暨參議一經將業情明白申說並交出該業證據議業處首領應即曉諭停止辯論

第五十一條 議業處公同定業務須秘判決之法以從眾為斷如議員中有一員未克允從應即寫條情由備案

第五十二條 從眾公斷判語應即寫條由各議員畫押此業即作為未定

第五十三條 公斷判語既定對眾宣讀兩造委員暨參議等均應在座

第五十四條 公斷判語業已宣讀並經繕送兩造此判語即作定讞毋得再有後言

第五十五條 兩造准於三十日內將公斷判定發仍可覆勘必須查出此業緊要別情致定業判語有關礙而議業處暨對質國均未知悉者方可准聲請覆勘如欲覆勘而未經專條訂明另有辦法應仍請原判此業之議業處聲勘議業處查明果有應行覆勘之事情節屬實方可准如所請開辯覆勘至覆勘期限文憑內應預先發明

第五十六條 公斷判語推員立文憑之兩造應其恪遵兩造如因條約意見不合聲公斷而此約係數國公同訂定者兩造應將所具關係公斷之文憑知照在約各國並准在約各國參入此業所有公斷判語必入之國亦應一體恪遵

第五十七條 兩造名認兩費全議業處公費由兩造均攤分認

第五十八條　本約應從速批准存儲和蘭都城每次送到批准之件

應立收據並將此次收據鈔稿錄對無訛由駐使轉遞在簷各國

第五十九條　其入保和會而未經畫押之國將來如願遵從本約准

其補支知照和蘭政府聲明遵從之意和蘭政府當據此轉告詞議

各國

第六十條　凡未入保和會之國亦准入約惟應如何辦理入約之處當

由訂議各國接洽商定

第六十一條　業經訂議之國將來如不願遵從本約准其備文知照和

蘭政府聲明不願遵從之意即據此轉告訂議各國自接知

照之日起以一年為限侯限滿從方許免其遵從所請不願遵從者概指

此備文知照之一國而言

為此各國全權議員在本約上畫押蓋印為憑一千八百九十九年七月二

十九號訂於和蘭都城原稿一分存儲於和蘭政府並案卷處鈔稿校

對無訛由駐使轉遞訂議各國

比利時國畫押

奧斯馬加國

德意志國

白滿那邦耳

羅日葉

中國　　　　　　戴崌

丹馬國畫押　　　畢勤

西班牙國畫押　　特迭仰　余呂確　巴益

美利堅國畫押　　勞福　懷得　紐爾　馬漢　克羅介　米葉　秩尼勤　布爾汝　畢務爾　恭斯登

墨西哥國畫押

法蘭西國畫押

英吉利國

希臘國畫押　　　德利牙尼

義大利國

日本國

盧森不爾應國

黑山國畫押　司塔勤

和蘭國畫押　喀爾訥拜克

　　　　　濮爾杜塔勤

　　　　　阿寒爾

　　　　　拉金森

　　　　　米亞利喀可汗多無勤

波斯國畫押　馬塞多

葡萄牙國畫押　多爾訥拉司

　　　　　　色利爾

羅美里國畫押　卑勤振曼

　　　　　　巴畢紐

俄羅斯國畫押　司塔勤

塞爾維國　巴西利

暹羅國畫押　奴瓦特

瑞典那威國畫押　威徐達

瑞士國　畢爾特

土耳其國　司坦秀弗

布加力國畫押　黑薩恵弗

清代外務部中外關係檔案史料叢編——中美關係卷 第六冊·國際會議

二品銜左參議陳□

花翎二品銜左參議□

花翎二品銜左丞瑞□

花翎二品銜右逸顧□

花翎二品銜右參議紹□

　　　　　　　　旨
　　　　　　　　簡

權算司

呈為劄行事查美國將於西歷一千九百零四年即中歷光緒

三十年在散魯伊斯城開設萬國博覽會本年六月間其總理

會務巴大臣親至中國敦請赴會現距開會之期不過年餘自

應及早派員以便布置一切赴會事宜此次擬請

派正監督一員並由本部揀派副監督二員惟副監督二員內

應用稅務司一員派充此任尤以美國人為合宜相應劄行總

稅務司即於各關稅務司美國人中擇一精細妥實之員開具

銜名迅速申復本部以憑奏明派往可也須至劄者

右劄花翎頭品頂戴太子少保銜總稅務司赫　准此

光緒二十八年十月　　　　日

欽加太子少保銜花翎頭品頂戴二等第一寶星總稅務司赫德為

申復事奉到十一月初一日

鈞劄內開查美國將於西歷一千九百零四年即中

歷光緒三十年在散魯伊斯城開設萬國博覽會本

年六月間其總理會務巴大臣親至中國敦請赴會

現距開會之期不過年餘自應及早派員以便佈置

一切赴會事宜此次擬請

旨簡派正監督一員並由本部揀派副監督二員惟副監

督二員內應用稅務司一員派充此任尤以美國人

為合宜相應劄行總稅務司即於各關稅務司美國

人中擇一精細妥實之員開具銜名迅速申復本部

以憑奏明派往等因奉此遵即於現任稅務司中揀

得雙龍三等第一寶星三品銜東海關稅務司柯爾

樂人美國尚屬精細妥實該員在關已閱二十二載光

緒十五年間曾派赴廣西龍州辦理開關事宜歷任

龍州蒙自思茅拱北東海等關稅務司均能措置裕

如且該員籍隸美國南界恰係現將設會之方派充

此差甚屬相宜合由 總稅務司備文將該員銜名開呈

查核如

貴部以為堪勝斯任並希於奏明時再為奏請

賞加二品銜以示尊崇而昭鄭重所有遵

飭選舉稅務司並籲懇

恩施各緣由理合一併呈請

鑒查施行須至申呈者

右　申　呈

欽命全權大臣便宜行事總理外務部事務和碩慶親王

光緒貳拾捌年拾壹月初叁日

具奏美國散魯伊斯城賽會請派

正副監督並飭南北洋大臣籌經費由

奏

奏

署左侍郎那　十一月　日

署右侍郎聯　十一月初　日　奏

謹

奏

旨簡

為美國散魯伊斯城舉行賽會請

派正監督屆時前往暨由臣部酌派副監督先期布

置赴會事宜恭摺仰祈

聖鑒

事竊查美國將於一千九百零四年即中曆光緒三

十年在散魯伊斯城開設萬國博覽會此會因

用資模仿實於通商之中隱寓勸工之意聞美國

區分類別排列會場俾各國之人咸得較其精良

泰西崇尚工商賽會之設在羅致各國物產工藝

允准簡派大員往襄盛會欽遵在案臣等伏查

答敕

觀並

蒙

准當於六月二十二日由臣等會同美國使臣康格

旨允

帶領入

觀見

經臣部奏明奉

會到京後與臣等會晤籲懇

間其總理會務大臣巴禮德前來中國敦請赴

會慶賀係美國立國以来極為重大之事本年六

記念美國由法人購得魯西亞那地方已及百年設

特
旨

此次散魯伊斯賽會其國家撥給該會鉅款以贊

其成各國均特派大員赴會蓋因此舉與交涉邦

交顯有關係而於商務尤為有益中國物產甲

於全球徒以工藝未興商情渙散此諸各國實

不逮現當整飭庶政之時適美國有此大會亞

應加意講求期於工商諸務有所裨益曾詢美

國使臣康格各國派往員數大率用正副監督三

人者居多臣等公同商酌所有正監督一員應請

簡派此後一切赴會事宜統歸該員主持仍俟開

會屆期再行前往至應派副監督查有候選

道黃開甲才具幹練熟悉商情東海關稅務司

美國人柯爾樂精細妥實在華多年均堪派充

隨同正監督辦理該副監督等應令先行前往

將度地建屋陳設貨物各事宜預為經營布置其

赴會一切用款所費不貲並應籌備以資撥用臣

等查出使經費一款從前借撥過多近年出入相

抵巳覺支絀實難再撥賽會經費而籌款不易臣

等亦所深悉惟賽會一事內可維持商務外可

聯絡邦交雖當庫藏奇絀之時不得不勉為其

難力顧大局應請

南北洋通商大臣迅即妥為籌款奏明辦理一面（及有商務者亦宜督措）

解交該監督等應用以重會務並由南北洋大臣咨

會各省督撫出示勸諭工商人等或挾貲前往專事

考求或辦貨同行兼圖貿易悉由該監督等妥為照料以仰體

飭下

考求或辦貨同行兼圖貿易悉由該監督等妥為照料以仰體

朝廷

鼓勵工商之至意所有請

旨簡派正監督暨由昌等酌派副監督前赴美國賽會並

飭籌備經費各緣由理合恭摺具陳伏乞

皇太后

皇上

聖鑒訓示謹

奏

光緒二十八年十二月初七日具奏　全日奉

硃批著派溥倫為正監督餘依議欽此

奏為美國散魯伊斯城舉行賽會請

旨簡派正監督屆時前往暨由臣部酌派副監督先期

布置赴會事宜恭摺仰祈

聖鑒事竊查美國將於西歷一千九百零四年卽中國

光緒三十年在散魯伊斯城開設萬國博覽會此

會因記念美國由法人購得魯西亞那地方已及

百年設會慶賀係美國立國以來極為重大之事

本年六月開其總理會務大臣巴禮德前來中國

敦請赴會到京後與臣等會晤籲懇

觀見經臣部奏明奉

旨允准當於六月二十二日由臣等會同美國使臣康

格帶領入

觀並蒙

答敕允准簡派大員往襄盛會欽遵在案臣等伏查泰

西崇尚工商賽會之設在羅致各國物產工藝區

分類別排列會場俾各國之人咸得較其精良用

資模仿實於通商之中隱寓勸工之意聞美國此

次散魯伊斯賽會其國家撥給該會鉅款以費其

成各國均特派大員赴會蓋因此舉與交涉邦交

顯有關係而於商務尤為有益中國物產甲於全

球徒以工藝未與商情渙散比諸各國實有不逮

現當整飭庶政之時適美國有此大會亟應加意

講求期於工商諸務有所裨益曾詢美國使臣康

格各國派往員數大率用正副監督三人者居多

臣等公同商酌所有正監督一員應請

特旨簡派此後一切赴會事宜統歸該員主持仍俟開

會屆期再行前往至應派副監督查有候選道黃

開甲才具幹練熟悉商情東海關稅務司美國人

柯爾樂精細妥實在華多年均堪派往度地建屋

督辦理該副監督等應令先行前往將其赴會一切用

陳設貨物各事宜預為經營布置其赴會一切經

款所費不貲亟應籌備以資撥用臣等查出使經

費一款從前借撥過多近年出入相抵已覺支絀

實難再發賽會經費惟賽會一事內可維持商務

外可聯絡邦交離當庫藏奇絀之時不得不勉為

其難力顧大局應請

飭下南北洋通商大臣及有商務省分各督撫迅卽妥

為籌款奏明辦理一面解交該監督等應用以重

會務並由南北洋大臣各省督撫出示勸諭工商

人等或挾貲前往專事考求或辦貨同行兼圖貿

易悉由該監督等妥為照料以仰體

朝廷鼓勵工商之至意所有請

旨簡派正監督暨由臣等酌派副監督前赴美國賽會

並

飭籌備經費各緣由理合恭摺具陳伏乞

皇太后

皇上聖鑒訓示謹

奏

一二

榷算司

呈為咨行事光緒二十八年十二月初七日本部具奏美

國散魯伊斯城賽會請

派正副監督並

飭籌經費等因一摺奉

硃批　著派溥倫為正監督餘依議欽此相應恭錄

諭旨抄錄原奏咨行

貴正監督查照欽遵可也須至咨者　粘抄　　將軍　撫

固山貝子倫晩先　盛京將軍　閩浙總督　兩廣總督

北洋大臣　山東巡撫　湖南巡撫　湖南巡撫　廣東巡撫　廣西巡撫

南洋大臣　山西巡撫　湖北巡撫

湖廣總督　河南巡撫　廣西巡撫

四川總督　江蘇巡撫　浙江巡撫　安徽巡撫

宗人府

光緒二十八年十二月

四四

権算司

呈為照會事光緒三十八年十二月初七日本部具奏請

特派正監督一員前赴

貴國散魯伊斯城賽會並由本部擬派候選道黃

開甲東海關稅務司柯爾樂克當副監督等因奉

硃批著派溥倫為正監督餘依議欽此相應照會

貴大臣欽遵查照可也須至照會者

美康使

光緒三十八年十二月

日

權算司

呈為劄行事光緒二十八年十二月初七日本部具奏

美國散魯伊斯城賽會請

特派 正監督一員並由本部擬派候選道黃開甲東海關

稅務司柯爾樂充當副監督一摺奉

硃批 著派溥倫為正監督餘依議欽此同日又附奏派赴

賽會副監督柯爾樂請

賞加 二品銜以示優異一片奉

硃批 依議欽此相應劄行總稅務司欽遵轉飭東海關稅

務司柯爾樂遵照可也須至劄者

右劄總稅務司赫　准此

光緒二十八年十二月

敬復者赴美賽會一事現奉

鈞函以賽會一切事宜亟須預為籌畫希電飭該稅司

迅速來京以便與

正監督倫貝子隨時面商妥籌辦法等因奉此查現

值西歷正月各關應結算去歲四結收支年款稅務

司督核一切忙碌異常東海稅務司事同一律原未

便令其離任惟賽會一節實屬要事自須預為籌畫

現奉前因除遵即電令迅速來京暫駐數日以便面

商妥籌　台特佈復順頌

日祉

名另具　光緒貳拾捌年拾貳月貳拾壹日

欽差辦理商約事務大臣工部大堂呂 候補四品京堂伍 為咨呈事光緒二十八年十二月

十八日承准

貴部電開 奏派赴美賽會副監督黃開甲希飭迅即來京巧等因當經

本大臣等於二十日電復黃道開甲甚為得力既奏奉

諭旨自應飭令迅速赴京現將經手事件趕為清理准於元宵節前後趕到先

此奉聞電達

貴部在案茲已飭據該道將經手事件料理清楚即日航海入都相應給

咨交該道黃開甲親賷赴

貴部報到謹請

貴部查照施行須至咨呈者

右咨呈

外務部

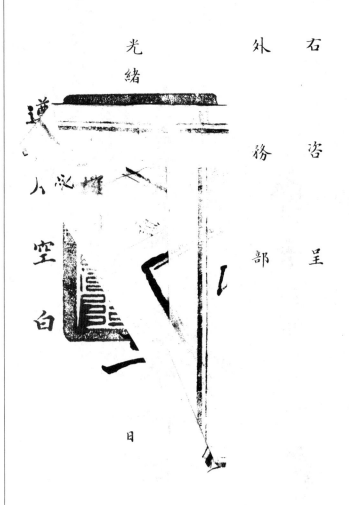

光緒　　　　年　　　月　　　日

此外務部

二月廿八日

光緒貳拾玖年貳月 貳拾捌 日

郎中黎

戶部為欽奉事北檔房審呈本部速議賽會

正監督貝子溥 奏請

飭部先行籌撥賽會經費一摺光緒二十九年二

月二十五日具奏本日奉

旨依議欽此除先行電知並抄錄正摺清單恭錄

諭旨飛咨各省查照外相應抄錄正摺清單恭錄

諭旨咨呈外務部可也須至咨呈者

外務部

右　咨　呈

咨呈

戶部謹

奏為遵

旨速議具奏恭摺仰祈

聖鑒事光緒二十九年二月二十二日軍機大臣面奉

諭旨溥倫奏賽會經費請飭部先行籌墊的款一摺著

戶部速議具奏欽此欽遵由軍機處片交到部據原

奏內稱據外務部咨具奏美國賽會請

飭各省妥籌經費一摺奉

旨依議欽此欽遵抄交等因奴才伏思此次賽會據副監

督四品卿銜候選道黃開甲東海關稅務司柯爾樂

將賽會一切用款逐加核算以現在磅價計之共

需銀七十五萬兩又據該副監督等聲稱本年三

月間即須前赴美國剋期興辦庶無貽誤請於放

洋前先行發給俾可隨定磅金免致折耗奴才籌

思再四此項經費前經外務部奏請

飭下各省分籌現尚未據報解請

飭戶部迅籌的款先行墊撥七十五萬兩以濟要需至

如何分籌歸還之處由戶部酌核奏明辦理等語臣

等伏查此次美國賽會經費本應由南北洋通商

大臣及有商務各省遵照奏案及早籌款解交該

監督應用乃現在副監督啟程在即而各省所籌

經費銀兩尚未解到自非暫由臣部代為籌墊不可

惟該監督所需經費銀至於七十五萬之多臣部

寔難全行墊給擬請先由江海關彙存浙江等七處

釐金經費餘銀項下提撥銀四十五萬交該監督領

用以濟目前之急其南北洋通商大臣及有商務各

省應行籌解此項經費即由臣部按照該監督所

奏七十五萬兩之數酌量攤派開具清單恭呈

御覽請

旨飭下各該督撫查照單開銀數迅速籌措廫全限三

月内解交江海關道收存以四十五萬兩歸還墊款

以三十萬兩交付該監督補領足數毋任稍有短欠延宕

以符奏案兩顧要需所有臣等遵

旨速議緣由理合恭摺具陳伏乞

皇太后

皇上聖鑒謹

奏

謹將攤派南北洋通商大臣及有商務各省應行籌

解美國賽會經費銀數開具清單恭呈

御覽

計開

直隸銀十萬兩

江蘇銀十萬兩

廣東銀十萬兩

四川銀十萬兩

湖北銀八萬兩

浙江銀八萬兩

江西銀四萬兩

安徽銀四萬兩

湖南銀四萬兩

山東銀四萬兩

福建銀三萬兩

以上共銀七十五萬兩務于三月內各照所派數

目解交江海關道以便分別歸還撥領

收

欽命前赴散魯伊斯賽會正監督貝勒衔圖山貝子溥

咨明事本監督前准

貴部咨稱欽奉

諭旨派令前赴美國散魯伊斯城賽會並由

二月荒日收

為

貴部奏派副監督先期前往奉

旨行令遵照在案令本監督先行剋飭華副監督四品卿衛候選道

黃開甲即日赴滬選帶工匠備辦陳設前赴美國起期興

辦至該監督到滬後定有放洋日期及隨帶工匠若干名隨後

再行咨報此項工匠人等係專為賽會建屋庇材之用一俟工

程完竣即行委遣回華其華商赴會事宜應即遵照賽

會章程辦理除照會美國欽差大臣康 據稅務司赫出

使美國大臣梁查照外相應咨呈

貴部查照可也

右洽呈

外務部

先緒貳拾玖年貳月貳拾玖日

F. O. No. 473,

LEGATION OF THE UNITED STATES OF AMERICA,
PEKIN, CHINA.

March 30th. 1903.

Your Imperial Highness:-

I have the honor to inform Your Imperial Highness that the Commandant of the United States Legation Guard proposes to send a detachment of ninety men for an outing to the Great Wall. They will leave Peking on or about April 2d. next, and will carry their shelter tents with them. They will go the first day to Hsia Ho, the second day to Nan-k'ou, the third to the Wall, the fourth back to Nan-k'ou, the fifth to the Ming Tombs, the sixth to T'ang Shan and the next will return to Peking.

The detachment is going simply for a practice march, and I trust that no objection may be made to it. I have also to request that Your Highness will notify the local officials along the route so that there may be no misunderstanding on the part of the people.

I avail myself of the opportunity to renew to Your Imperial Highness the assurance of my highest consideration.

E. H. Conger
U.S.Minister.

To His Imperial Highness, Prince of Ch'ing,

President of the Board of Foreign Affairs.

18
三月二日

欽命前赴散魯伊斯賽會正監督員勒衙圖山貝子溥　為

欽奉事本監督奏調隨員繙譯一檔於先緒

二十九年三月初五日題奏奉

硃批著照所請欽此又具奏廢寬等前往赴會一

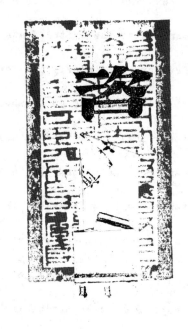

片奉

硃批知道了欽此等因相應恭錄

諭旨抄錄原奏咨呈

貴部查照可也須至咨呈者

右　咨　呈

外　務　部

光緒　　　　　　初六
　　　　　　　　　　日

奏為遵

旨辦理美國賽會事宜謹擬酌調隨員恭摺仰祈

聖鑒事竊奴才前經奉

旨派充美國賽會正監督欽此欽遵由外務部抄交

奴才遵照前來　查賽會為各國上儀赴會係

中華創舉奴才恭膺

簡命應如何黽勉將事認真經理冀副

朝廷任使之隆惟思交際為

國體所關在在均為緊要一切事務襄理必須得

人且目前開辦事宜頭緒繁多自應先事預籌

擬請酌調隨員藉資臂助奴才詳加遴選查有

內務府員外郎誠璋戶部主事彭穀孫江蘇補

用知縣祝瀛元分省補用知府程大澂候選通

判全森以上五員均能實心任事堪以隨辦賽

會事宜相應請

旨俯准交奴才差遣恭俟

命下即由奴才督飭各該員悉心經理屆期赴會一

併隨帶前往除供事另行咨調外所有奴才酌

調隨員緣由理合恭摺具陳伏乞

皇太后

皇上聖鑒謹

奏奉

硃批著照所請欽此

再賽會為通商惠工之要政中國物產素稱繁

盛自應加意維持此次美國賽會其有熟悉商

情願往赴會者未便阻其勇於任事之忱茲查

有題奏三院鄉候選道慶寬已革翰林院侍讀

學黃思永平日講求商務辦事亦能認真堪以

前往奴才為振興商務起見是否有當謹附片

具陳伏乞

聖鑒謹

奏奉

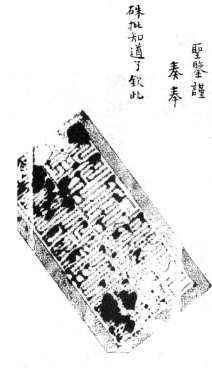

皇上聖鑒謹

奏奉

硃批著照所請欽此

再賽會為通商惠工之要政中國物產素稱繁

盛自應加意維持此次美國賽會其有熟悉商

情願往應會者未便阻其勇於往事之忱茲查

有題奏三院鄉侯選道慶寬巳革翰林院侍讀

學黃思永平日講求商務辦事亦能認真堪以

前往奴才為振興商務起見是否有當謹附片

具陳伏乞

聖鑒謹

奏奉

聖鑒謹

奏奉

硃批知道了欽此

外務部　北

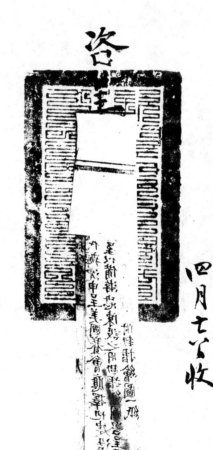

咨

四月十七收

欽差大臣辦理商洲通商事務頭品頂戴署江總督部堂兼圖書魏　為

咨請事光緒二十九年三月十一日准

代辦美日祕古國大臣沈　申呈竊查美國明年新路易舉行萬國賽會一

事前承准來文飭查會中起建房屋工程約需經費若干當經備文申復

在案現晤該會督辦及工程處總辦請其指撥相宜地段以備中國建造

房屋並派在美學生歐陽祺馳赴會場查勘地段何處最為合式旋據勘

明禀復美國新路易會場在美都西南離華盛頓三十五點鐘火車路

程勘得會場總辦公所前面正對有地方一段縱橫各一百二十五尺地基

各國已指定地段外此地最為相宜

合中國政府之意儻可指定如不

當經詢商總辦酌留此地……安

……行……聽其便筆……中各員細加詢訪僉謂此地合宜各

員意見畧谷中國休咖地名勝處所建一房屋或苑圓或園林隨意布

景最為宜稱屋內間架無論多少祇須縱橫各五六十尺即不寒傖此地專

為赴會官商游憩聚會之所至商民陳設賽會之物另分行列各以類

聚不必辟入其中如有珍異亦可在此陳設惟格於成例不能得會中

各物茶酒各品蠶絲繭綢及織成繰帛漆器磁器雕鏤象牙木器玉

欵派員暑列一表於後至會中陳設各物則礦產五金地中地上動植飛潛

查各國建造房屋約就所撥之欵三分之一以為鳩工集料之需玆就各國撥

譯漢文以備省覽應如何酌仿古今名勝屋宇建造之處聽候卓裁又

是專為各國官商游覽之處與陳設貨物之所各不相蒙特另具圖式並

近在美采購建造價當可省等情查會中章程各國建造會中房屋

雕刻精細木料繪定圖式酌帶巧匠數名來美攙合其餘粗工磚石仍就

名十據稱一層之屋約美館會事五十元兩層約十萬元三層約十二

萬五千元之譜此數是就美國料估計未免稍昂若由中國采辦

員擬等語旋招該處工程師核字樣計建造五六十尺房屋約須經費

器玩具古書古畫各種文具均為相宜懇將情形通飭各關知照又

學生歐陽祺是廣東香山縣人自備資斧來美游學已領高等學堂

文憑現在紐約專門律學肄業因使館無屆生調遣無會場書記

學生就近兼充繕譯只須酌給月薪水可免往來別需糜費等屬

切對答明晰甚有條理方今譯材難得將來如須派員來美赴會諮

兩有裨益合併陳明所有派員查勘建造賽會房屋情形理合申請察

照施行等因並圖摺到本大臣准此查中國赴美賽會已派有監督所有

會場擇地仿建屋宇及一切布置事宜自應由

賽會監督酌核辦理惟現既由

沈代辦大臣考察地勢辦法自可藉資參酌毋庸上海道候

監督至滬時呈請核辦外相

貴外務部謹請查照希即轉交

計抄摺 並繪圖壹紙

右咨呈

外務部

光緒　　　　　日

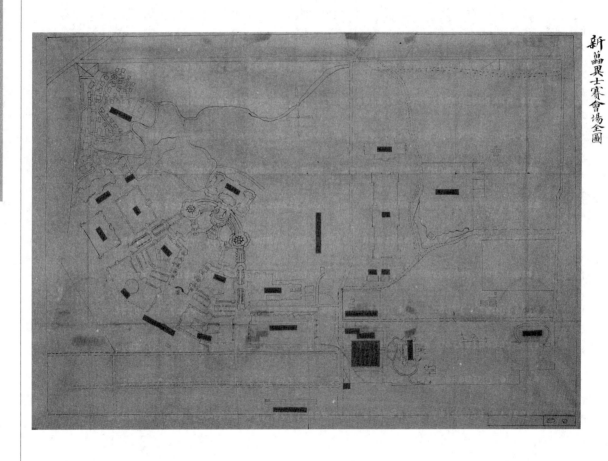

新屆異士賽會場全圖

照錄各國赴美新路易會撥款派員建造房屋表

德國先撥五十萬美圓總辦已來勘定地方仿德國古時麥定布宮
建造

法國先撥六十萬佛郎即總辦已來勘地擬仿古皇離宮建造間

法皇屆時赴會

英俄奧和意各國尚未定款

英屬坎拏大未定款已派總辦

英屬錫蘭撥款八萬擬建造茶館為錫蘭茶標準

俄擬揩西伯里亞鐵路以表工程

日本國擬撥□□□□□□□□□□□□□□□總辦已派月內可到

高麗國未民款數已派總辦撥款

波斯國擬□□□□擇地方建造

秘魯國撥□萬五千□□軍樂一部奏樂娛賓

墨西哥國撥□□□□

阿根廷國撥五十萬元總辦已到

尼加拉瓜國已派員

拉牟多國撥一萬二千圓建造

巴拉書國已派員

美政府派員專理撥款協助外另由各省督撫派員赴會

逕啟者本大臣兹接外部大臣來文囑為轉達

貴國政府現有美國軍醫會在本國巴思頓地方於西歷五月

十九二十二十一等日聚會三天該會係每年聚會一次此係第

十二次聚會請中國派陸海軍醫屆期赴會並送來英文會中大

意一紙請為轉送等因查本年議政會議定一例先准本國戶

部兵部海部大臣及海陸軍總醫官與海軍內步兵總醫官均有

附入該會之分該會係奉本國所准行故此次該會聚集國家

必為之主持中國若能准令陸海軍醫官前往本國

政府自必甚為欣悅也特此奉布即請

爵祺附送洋文並洋件

貴親王查照順頌

名另具三月十八日

F.O. No.485.

LEGATION OF THE UNITED STATES OF AMERICA,
PEKIN, CHINA.

April 14th. 1903.

Your Imperial Highness:-

I have the honor to inform Your Imperial Highness that I have
received instructions from the Department of State at Washington
directing me to make known to the Government of China the desire
of the Association of Military Surgeons of the United States to
receive official delegates representing the medical departments
of the Chinese Army and Navy at the Twelfth Annual Meeting of
the Association which is to be held at Boston, May 19, 20 and
21, 1903. I have the honor also to inclose a pamphlet setting
forth the objects of the Association. The Association is incorporated by Act of Congress, approved January 30th.1903, which-
provides that the Secretary of the Treasury, the Secretary of
War, the Secretary of the Navy, the Surgeon General of the Army
and the Surgeon General of the Navy, and the Surgeon General of
the Marine Hospital Service shall be ex-officio members of the
Association. To this extent the meeting will be under the patronage of the Government of the United States, and it will afford my Government great pleasure to learn that China will have
its military and naval departments represented at the meeting.

I avail myself of the opportunity to renew to Your Imper-

ial

(F.O. No.485)

ial Highness the assurance of my highest consideration.

E. H. Conger

Envoy Extraordinary and

Minister Plenipotentiary of

the United States.

To His Highness, Prince of Ch'ing,

President of the Board of Foreign Affairs.

大美欽差駐華便宜行事大臣康

敬啟者茲得本大臣近接本國政府來文內稱美國軍醫會向例

每年聚集一次今定於西歷一千九百零三年五月十九二十

並二十一等日在色斯頓地方舉行第十二次會議茲會

甚願中國水陸軍之各醫倣列入此會故擬請中國政府派

員屆期前往該處赴會本國政府為此諭令本大臣將

此節照會

貴國政府本大臣相應備文照會

貴親王并將該會之章程附呈其設立此會之意

旨均詳載於該章程內矣再於一千九百零三年

正月三十日該會又奉有本國議院議定之則例

洪倒內載凡本國之戶部兵部（海軍部）天侍郎並水軍陸

軍之各總醫官以及管理航海醫事之總醫官均

須萬分敦令該會人員云々據此新定（倒則此次聚會

貴國政府肯派負屆期赴會以代中國之水陸兩

軍則本國政府知之必甚願悅也須至照會

者

右

照

會

欽命總理外務部事務慶親王

西歷一千九百零三年四月拾四日

Associate Membership is open to—

1. Ex-medical officers of any of the foregoing services;
2. Other commissioned officers of the foregoing services;
3. Ex-medical officers of the Confederate service;
4. Medical officers of the services of foreign countries.

Attendance Upon Meetings not a Necessity.

While no member should deprive himself of the pleasure of attendance upon the annual meetings when practicable, such attendance is by no means essential to the enjoyment of the principal advantages of the Association. The exigencies of the public service and of professional work naturally prevent the personal engagement of many of the members in the yearly conventions, but, through papers and communications forwarded to be read in its sessions and, above all, by reading and contributing to its publications, they receive ample opportunity to participate in its work.

Insignia.

The Insignia of the Association consist of a **Badge** and a **Button**, the former to be worn with uniform, the latter for use with civilian attire.

The Badge is one of the most effective military decorations ever devised, and has been officially authorized for wearing upon the uniforms of officers, who are members of the Association, by thirty-six states, while legislation is pending which will afford it an official status in the national services.

The Button is a handsome device for the lapel of the civilian coat.

These Insignia can be obtained from the Treasurer for $10.00 and $2.00 respectively.

Applications for Membership.

In order to receive all the benefits of the Association, officers, who have not yet become members are urged to make immediate application therefor. The Secretary will furnish blank applications for membership (with spaces for the full name, rank and address), which should be mailed together with the admission fee of Five Dollars—which also includes the first year's dues—to:

THE ASSOCIATION OF MILITARY SURGEONS,
Carlisle, Pennsylvania.

ASSOCIATION OF
Military Surgeons
OF THE UNITED STATES.

President, **Brig. Gen. R. A. Blood, Surg. Gen. Mass. Vol. Militia.** | *Sec. Vice Pres.,* **Surg. Gen. W. Wyman, U.S. Marine Hospital Service.**
First Vice Pres., **Med. Dir. J. C. Wise, United States Navy.** | *Treasurer,* **Lieut. H. A. Arnold, Asst. Surg. Nat. Guard, Penna.**
Secretary and Editor, **Major James Evelyn Pilcher, Brigade Surg. U.S.V.; Capt. Ret. U.S.A.**

❦❦❦
...Statement...
1902=1903.

Expansion in Military and Naval Medicine.

Recent events have infused new life into the study and practice of military and naval medicine, surgery and hygiene. The medical officers of the twentieth century public services are making history at a rapid rate. No medical officer can afford to be distanced in the forward movements of his profession and none can afford to neglect available facilities for keeping in the van of professional progress.

Association of Military Surgeons

The Association of Military Surgeons of the United States, now in the twelfth year of its existence, was organized and has been maintained for the purpose of assisting its members to this end. The facilities afforded to-day are greater than ever. The interest of its members today is more active than ever. The influence which it exerts along the lines of its chosen field is today greater than ever.

National and International.

Its work is not confined to purely local interests, but it extends its lines of effort throughout all modern thought. At its last meeting seven foreign nations participated in its work through official delegates detailed for the purpose. At this meeting also Associate Membership was expanded to admit officers of the military and naval services of other countries, by which the field of the Association has been still more largely extended.

Objects and Aims of the Association. While the Association endeavors to promote and develop Military and Naval Medicine, Surgery and Hygiene in every possible way, it particularly aims to elevate it—

1. **By the Mutual Inspiration and Improvement** to be derived from the prompt publication, in accessible and attractive form, of the work of active practical military medical officers.

2. **By Quickening the Development of Military and Naval Medicine and Surgery,** through the constant agitation of all topics pertaining to them.

3. **By the Creation of a Living and Growing Body of Military Medical Literature,** available as a standard for permanent consultation and reference.

4. **By the Provision of an Appreciative Audience,**—not only in those members attending its meetings but in the much larger number represented in the readers of its publications,—for the presentation of advances, improvements, investigations and discoveries in Military and Naval medicine, surgery, sanitation and equipment.

5. **By Providing a Reciprocal Interchange of Views and Ideas,** between the medical officers of the national and state services, which cannot fail to be of advantage to both.

6. **By Encouraging Mutual Acquaintance between Medical Officers** and the combination with professional relations, of that social quality, which is so uniformly a stimulus to scientific growth.

7. **By Preserving a Medico-Military Esprit de Corps,** the existence of which shall insure scientific enthusiasm and unity of action in matters involving the welfare of the medical department in all military organizations.

8. **By Maintaining Military and Naval Practice as a Specialty,** well defined and clearly recognized,—which can be accomplished only by the effective organization of those interested in it.

9. **By Establishing Uniformity of Procedure** between the medical departments of the national services and the state troops, the lack of which has been found to be a fatal defect in active hostilities.

10. **By Stimulating Legislation Beneficial to the Medical Department** of both national and state military and naval establishments, and forwarding the organization of the medical staff in the various states upon a healthy basis, independent of the caprice of commanding officers.

11. **By Promoting a Constant Condition of Readiness for Duty** in the medical departments of all services, and thus providing a factor in future hostilities that will vastly reduce the suffering and diminish the mortality of the commands in which members of the Association may be engaged.

Journal of the Military Surgeons. In order to more efficiently accomplish its purposes the Association publishes a monthly Journal, which is mailed free to all its members. The *Journal of the Association of Military Surgeons of the United States* not only continues, as in the beginning, to be **the Only Military Medical Journal in the English Language,** but has also come to be generally acknowledged as well to be **the Leading Military Medical Journal in the World.**

The contents of the several numbers are varied and include many features of special interest and value.

Original Articles. During each year appear the papers read at the preceding annual meeting. The high character of these contributions is too well-known to require comment. In addition to these, other timely contributions appear from time to time. An accomplished corps of foreign medical officers contributes additional articles on foreign matters of medico-military interest.

Reprints and Translations. The Medico-Military literature of other countries is freely laid under contribution, and important contemporary articles drawn upon.

Medico-Military Index. A complete medico-military bibliography—prepared by the Librarian of the Army Medical Library—comprising the entire medico-military literature of the world, is regularly published.

Editorial Department. An aggressive and experienced staff collaborates with the Editor in presenting timely discussions, reviews, comments, and general information relative to current events of medico-military interest.

Typography and Illustration. The Journal is printed upon heavy supercalendared paper made especially for it, and is illustrated throughout the year by many fine engravings.

Membership. There are five classes of members, Active, Life, and Associate,—who are elected by the Executive Committee at any time,—and Corresponding and Honorary, who are elected by the Association at the annual meeting.

Dues. *Active* and *Associate* members pay five dollars with their application,—which includes both admission fee and dues for the present calendar year, and three dollars a year thereafter. *Life* members commute the annual dues by a payment of fifty dollars at one time.

Active Membership is open to Commissioned Medical Officers and Contract or Acting Assistant Surgeons of:—

1. The United States Army;
2. The United States Navy;
3. The United States Marine Hospital Service;
4. The National Guard and Other State Troops;
5. The United States Volunteers.

洽呈事光緒二十九年三月初五日據布政使陳璚詳奉本署督部堂札光緒二十

九年二月二十七日准

戶部電稱美國賽會經費本部奏准由直隸江蘇廣東四川各籌撥十萬兩限三月

內解滬務希照辦先電後咨戶宥等因准此飭即道照電內事理迅籌滙滬並具詳

請咨毋違等因奉此遵查川省地方連年荒歉徵解異常頒難加以去歲拳匪滋事

教案迭乘籌撫籌銅辦賑辦糧所費不貲致將各庫搜括一空約計非再有百餘萬

不能了結能否自籌不致請歇尚可知似此又紳耆人等百姓相率應北興百姓稍有師言

飭撥美國賽會經費十萬金實屬如

國體何敢朕視無論如何為難仍當籌撥民間仍懼匪捐擾亂公局亟亟亟寉聞服信股示

清代外務部中外關係檔案史料叢編——中美關係卷 第六冊·國際會議

項下免强挪湊銀二萬兩擬請發交日昇昌等號承領於光緒二十九年三月初三日

給發限令於光緒二十九年三月二十八日滙赴江海關交收掣取文批迴銷所需滙

費應請仿照借欵成案每萬兩酌給滙費九七平銀一百三十兩仍請在於貨釐項下

支給作正開報除由司繕具批迴給商承領外所有籌辦美國賽會經費又動支滙費

銀兩緣由理合具文詳請察核具

奏並咨明

戶　務　部　曁

外　務　部暨

兩江督部堂

江蘇撫部院查照等情據此本署督部堂覆核無異除察核附

奏並分咨外擬合咨呈為此咨呈

貴部謹請查照施行須至咨呈者

右呈

外　務　部

光緒　　年　　月　　日

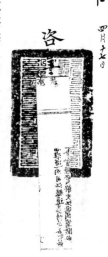

四月十七日

咨

欽差大臣辦理商約事務頭品頂戴兩江總督部堂呂 圖章 為

咨明事案查美國賽會經費前准

戶部電撥江蘇十萬兩當由寧蘇兩屬各認五萬兩寧屬應解

五萬兩係派藩運兩庫及金陵關各一萬兩支應籌防釐捐三局及

糧道各五千兩分飭遵限籌解昨據金陵關詳解一萬兩業

經分咨查照在案茲據江藩司淮運司各解銀一萬兩江糧道籌防

局各解銀五千兩先後呈報均已解交江海關備撥前來相應

咨明為此咨呈

貴外務部謹請查照施行須至咨呈者

右

咨　呈

外　務　部

光緒

拾貳

日

清代外務部中外關係檔案史料叢編——中美關係卷　第六冊·國際會議

作

四月十七日

咨明事案查美國賽會經費前准

戶部電撥江蘇十萬兩當由甯蘇兩屬各認五萬兩甯屬

應解之五萬兩係派藩運兩庫及金陵關各一萬兩支應

籌防厘捐三局及糧道谷五千兩分飭遵限籌解昨

據金陵關江藩司淮運司各解銀一萬兩江糧道籌

防局各解銀五千兩先後詳報均經分咨

貴外務部在案茲據支應局甯軍局各解銀五千兩交

江海關備撥前來查甯屬認解五萬兩業已照數解

齊相應咨明為此咨呈

貴外務部謹請查照施行須至咨呈者

右呈

外務部

光

捌日

寄直隸總督電

勘電悉賽會經費貴處現在無款

可籌自當稍緩時日再為設法撥解

至運庫應解部飭應令即速解部

毋許挪移戶冬

戶部為片呈事本部現有應發電

報一件相應抄錄電底片呈

貴部查照轉發因用印不及

逕行自片可也須至片者

右片呈

外務部

光緒貳拾玖年肆月 初貳 日

昌外 郎晏

寄直隸總督電

勘電悉審會經費貴處現在無款

可籌自當稍緩時日再為設法撥解

至運庫應解部餉應令即速解部

母許挪移戶冬

戶部為片呈事本部現有應發電

報一件相應抄錄電底片呈

貴部查照轉發因用印不及

遇行白片可也須至片者

作 四月初二日收

二品頂戴監督江南海關分巡蘇松太道為呈復事本年三月十三日奉

兵部火票遞到

戶部札北檔房紫呈本部速議賽會正監督貝子溥　奏請

飭部先行籌撥賽會經費一摺光緒二十九年二月二十五日具奏本日奉

旨依議欽此除先行電知並抄錄正摺清單恭錄

謝旨飛洛南北洋大臣直隸江蘇廣東四川湖北浙江江西安徽湖南山東福建各督撫外相應

札關一體遵照辦理其本部墊撥銀四拾五萬兩即由江海關道如數在滬撥付該監督領

用並蒙抄奏內開此次美國賽會經費本應由南北洋及有商務各省與案籌解現在

副監督啟程在即兩省所籌銀兩尚未解到非由部代墊不可擬請先由江海關彙

存浙江等七處庫金經費餘銀項下提撥銀四拾五萬兩交該監督領用其各省應籌經費

即照單開銀數限三月內解交江海關道收存以四拾五萬兩歸還墊款以三拾萬兩交

該監督補領足數並奉

溥欽憲飭將戶部墊撥銀肆拾伍萬兩交副監督收領呈報各等因到關奉此遵即

在總稅務司前此解到七處礦金還款經費積餘項下提出庫平銀肆拾伍萬兩於

三月廿九日備批治解

副監督黃　查收備用除分別呈報外理合具文呈復仰祈

憲臺俯賜鑒核為此備由呈乞

照驗施行須至呈者

右

呈

欽命全權大臣便宜行事總理外務部事務和碩慶親王

日管關巡道袁樹勛

步

欽命前赴散魯伊斯賽會正監督員勒衛圖山貝子溥　為

咨呈事本監督現有寄各省督撫電函

相應鈔錄電文咨呈

貴部即為排發可也須至咨呈者

右

咨呈

外

務

部

寄各省督撫電

審密本監督前赴散魯伊斯賽會各省

華商赴會情形業經密行貴省查照至

貴省官派赴會所運貨物件數若干計

佔地址英尺若干務於五月節前電覆即

飭副監督領向賽會董事商定庶免向隅

正監督貝子溥倫元

右八十五字

直隸

兩江

閩浙

兩廣、各總督

潮廣

四川

雲貴

江蘇
浙江
山東
安徽　江西
湖北　廣西　各巡撫
湖南
廣東
雲南

光緒二十九年四月十三日

外務部咨近來賽會風氣大開官商均有運物出口應由本商

先期赴就近海關監督處呈請發給運物執照俟所運貨物報

關出口時將此執照一併呈驗方准免稅仍隨案報明本部存

查無執照者照則納稅行令遵照辦理等因蒙此當經函致新

關德稅司查照並出示曉諭在案茲據該商人孫德源現有地

毯等件擬運赴美國散魯伊斯城賽會開單請領執照以便出

咨呈事據津海關道唐紹儀呈稱案查前蒙憲台札准

口等情前來除函

所運物件照繕清

摺咨呈

貴部謹請查照須至咨呈者

計清摺一扣

右　咨　呈

外　務　部

光緒二十九年四月二十六日

理合將該商

呈報據怒等情到本大臣據此相應將清

日

附件

清摺

謹將商人孫德源運赴美國賽會物件照繕清摺恭呈

憲鑒

計開

地毯伍張價洋貳百柒拾元

全紅小磁瓶壹箇價洋拾捌元

平金椅靠拾肆對價銀貳百拾兩

平金圓桿肆箇價銀肆拾肆兩

蝦靴肆雙價銀拾陸兩

摺絹畫拾貳塊價銀叁拾壹兩貳戔

竹胡盧叁拾箇價銀拾貳兩

平金衣料壹件價銀肆拾伍兩

共裝叁件

光緒

欽差出使美日祕國大臣梁　為

咨呈事本大臣於光緒二十九年四月十八日承准

赴會正監督貝勒銜固山貝子溥　咨開本監督先行劄飭華副監督黃開甲

即日由京赴滬選帶工匠前赴美國預為布置並照料華商運貨赴會事宜

希轉達美外部放行其華商赴會事宜應即遵照美國賽會章程辦理

等因承准此本大臣當經按照來咨事理照會美外部旋據復文允為咨行美

戶部通飭稅關優待放行其華商赴會自應遵照美戶部所定章程辦理本

大臣查接管卷內附有西歷一千九百零三年正月七號美戶部所定華人赴會

入口章程一分計共十款所擬辦法跡近瑣屑語意亦多含混大非邀請賽會
之本旨現經本大臣照會美外部轉咨駁詰以期事歸簡易便益商民亟應
先行照譯普諭赴會商民一體知悉俾免臨時觸背致多齟齬除俟接外部復
文如有損益之處再行達知外相應備文咨呈附送譯章即希
貴部先為分行轉飭曉諭赴會商民一體知悉遵章辦理庶於會事旅行兩
無窒礙為此咨呈
貴部謹請察照施行須至咨呈者附呈譯件
右
咨呈
外務部

光緒　　　　　　　　二十　　　日

美戶部定立華人來美前赴散魯伊斯賽會合章程

下

章程茲將戶部所定章程各款開列如左

第一款　凡華人來美賽會須向稅司或向委派經理禁例之官呈驗憑據指明確係承辦賽會之人或係承辦賽會人所雇用之人

第二款　凡華人來美賽會須將本人照片三分呈交入口稅司或美國委派經理此事之官任便查驗以期相符

第三款　凡華人來美前赴散魯伊斯賽會一經允准入美須直至賽場不應另到他處亦不應另作他業該華人等須於賽會收場三十日內即由原來入美之口附搭首次開行輪船或回中國或回該華人所居之國

第四款　凡華人來美賽會須向美官具立美洋五百圓保結並有可靠鋪店保其直赴賽場常川先當工業以及按章返國

第五款　凡華人按章允准來美賽會該管稅司或委派管理華人入口之

官須將來美之華人各情節開列照錄兩分一分存該口稅關一分送交戶部僑民局收存

開列情節款式如左

戶部僑民局第△號存根

何名　　何處人　　賽會某人雇用

本人照片粘貼於上

某口管理華人入口官員△△係△△處人係由承辦散魯伊斯賽會之人△△

為發給執照事照得△△官員發給執照式

△按照議院一千九百零二年四月二十九日定例雇用來美在會場作工為此

發給執照作據

管理華人入口官員△△　官銜△△　人簽名△△年△月△日發

第六款　凡華人按照定章允准來美賽會美國應派委員駐紮會場查

考嗣後若未再將章程更改須即按照下開程式開報兩分存案所派之員

應隨時查察會場華人是否遵章辦理

查察委員開報式 應備兩分第一分收留存案第二分送交僑民局總辦

傭工之人何名

傭工之人是男是女

年歲若干

來美賽會為某承辦之人雇用

在賽會充何事業

每日作業鐘數若干自某點鐘起至某點鐘止

何日到會場

何日應由會場回國

備工本人簽名

查察委員簽名

照片粘貼於上

第七款　第二款所指之照片三分管理華人入口之官應將一分送交第六

款所稱之查察會場委員粘於所開報單之上以憑考察

第八款　凡來美賽會華人如欲暫離會場必須向第六款所稱之查察委員

領票開明姓名時日各證據並聲明須於十二點鐘以內即回會場暨將領票

註銷

第九款　凡華人領票暫離會場若不按期即回應按照不准寓店美國

之例辦理所有具保款項因須充公而本人亦須遞解回國所發憑票委員

應將此事知照管理僑民入口總辦除將充公款項移送外並將該華人

照例遞解回國

第十款　賽會收場三十日後管理華人入口各官須將入口華人總數具報僑

民局總辦並將華人姓氏各節逐一開明以便查考華人果否按章回國

外務部收

駐美梁大臣致丞參信一件

與美外部商撤在華郵局及妥酌賽會
工匠事並譯送來往照會四件文粵漢鐵
路借款案現已開辦又舊館期滿已遷新館再
密陳東三省近狀與外部詳論開埠事
宜並自陳管見由　附譯件

右侍郎顧　　　　　　　　　　　月　　日
軍機大臣尚書會辦大臣瞿　　　　月　　日
軍機大臣總理外務部事務和碩慶親王　月　日
軍機大臣武英殿大學士會辦本□王　月　日
左侍郎聯　　　　　　　　　　　月　　日

光緒二十七年閏五月十九日　呂字四百十五號

敬啟者四月二十日肅布美字第四號函計邀

堂鑒頃以外國在華郵局任意擴充遞寄包件不願報稅

等事承奉

鈞咨嚼向美國政府力爭撤回在華郵局未撤以前信

封物件應報中國海關派員開看照章分別徵免以

係郵權稅課仰見

蓋謨固密燭照靡遺周勝欽佩誠當即往晤美外部海

約翰將赫總稅務司申呈各節為彼詳說並告以我

國郵政赫德專辦歷年以來迭經整頓成效昭著中
外商民無不同聲稱便各國所設郵局自應撤回以
一事權而免喧奪不謂近年分局遞有加增又復任
聽商人包件匿稅致於賠款有碍公理何存美為大
國義聞昭著若將在華郵局首先裁撤英德諸國必
能一律照行海云事隸郵部一切辦法本部實未深
悉然包件納稅一層郵章所載本大臣接收外國來
件庶經照章繳稅想應一律辦理誠以其語意圓融

似易聽受復曉以從前日本商撤外國郵局係由貴

國認許中國現今郵政較之日本當年尤為美備自

應一體照行以昭公允請一面咨商郵部一面分飭

各領事不可受人牽制託故推延以致中國稅務郵

權兩虞侵損反復推闡外部亦以為然允為咨商要

辦相機力助誠回館後即繕備洋文照會送去敦促

辦理容候接到復文一併譯漢錄呈

鈞覽竊查光緒二十三年萬國郵政聯會曾在美都會

清代外務部中外關係檔案史料叢編——中美關係卷 第六冊·國際會議

議當時我國雖未列名聯約然、

鈞署派員來美赴會所有聯會章程已得與聞況近年
推廣郵政已有成效各國設局自當撤回只以各領
事圖利攬權如廣州等處竟於租界之外任意添設
分局主權已經大碍今又包伴匿稅紊亂郵章若不
力為駁斥及早挽回在我不能杜漸而防微在彼且
將得隴而望蜀推其流極必至洋人足跡所到皆可
違約設局減價攬收則我國郵政利權陰承其害而

瞞關匾稅之案不獨見於洋商已也散魯伊斯賽會

一事前准

倫員子咨業經照會外部請將赴會工人一律優待

旋據復文以美使康格來文只有匠人並無工役須

將人數開列存案以杜冒混誠思會場房屋工程完

竣勢須派人看守照料黃副監督帶來工匠未便盡

數遣令回華此時若不聲明將來又費筆舌而且多

方詰難於體制不無少損惟人數若干未便懸擬致

有窒礙因即函告外部候屆時應留工役多少再當
酌定開單照會昨准復函已允照辦除將商辦情形
咨呈
倫貝子咨核外謹將往來照會四件譯錄附呈
鈞詧至華商赴會所帶工役散漫無稽須照戶部新章
取保領照方得登岸實緣近年賽會華人甫入美境
四出傭作以致會事毫無起色於我商務固有關礙
西東省工黨益復藉端指摘竟有不許華人來會之

議例限所以加嚴也中美立約原為禁工起見當光緒

二十年間商人學生攜有海關執照一經驗明立准

登岸嗣因工人冒充領照每被關員識破而真正商

人學生亦事留難矣近七八年來攜照到美枉被駁

回者十之八九其幸得登岸者亦必反覆推求延擱

累月商民怨苦相戒不前疊經前任照會外部駁詰

迄未轉圜誠抵金山時商董面陳苦況刻下正在力

籌駁論博訪周詢以期得當固不敢畏難而袖手旁

觀亦不欲輕舉而鹵莽從事俟駁論稍有頭緒再當

隨時奉告以紓

蓋系粵漢鐵路借票前據美國合興公司製就函請簽

名蓋印查此事載明合同自應照辦無庸另行請

示現在已經開辦按日簽名蓋印統共借票四萬五千

張計期三閱月可以畢事此間使署前任伍大臣奏

准在美國歸還款項內提撥美洋八萬圓購地與建誠

抵美接事仍未竣工舊館租約已於四月朔日期滿

房主急欲收回未便遷延致費脣舌只得遷入新館

以歸簡便今經月餘丹青土木大致楚楚而舖陳點

綴闕漏甚多尚須籌畫添充也知關

垂注合併奉

聞以上各節統乞

代回

邸堂各憲為荷肅此敬請

台安 附譯件一扣

梁誠頓首
光緒二十九年五月初八日
美字第五號

敬再密啟者東三省事近日風潮較靜俄有按約退

兵之說皆由

列憲毅力堅持故能懾服強鄰使破知難而退此邦人士

讚頌不置以為外交政策當如是此昨日美外部海

約翰談及此事謂美日請開東三省口岸台端必有

所聞前接康使來電貴國不顧開埠實為俄人所阻

本部即向俄使喀希尼詢問緣因喀堅稱並無其事

且謂俄國東方鐵路糜費億萬亦欲廣開口岸始得

使再為陳說希即函達貴國政府不論如何辦法總

請者固為東方擴商務亦即為中國保主權已燭康

遷就遼東大局將不可問美日兩國斷斷然以開埠

詭秘不類大國之行食言寒盟不卜可決貴國若稍

俄使則以未奉政府訓條為辭似此翻覆悶爍形踪

並無阻撓及至康使邀同前往貴國外部三面質明

俄使假滿已回北京本部復電康使親向查詢亦云

共享商利英國日本迭次詰問俄廷答復皆同昨聞

以開通口岸為宜中美交誼素敦故敢瀝誠相告幸

勿誤會等語誠察其詞意尚屬懇摯未便壅於

鈞聽當已允為代達伏念俄人經營東亞歷時百數十

年費財百數千萬庚子北方有事乘機竊發侵入遼

東本有久假不歸之意只以怵於公論迫於成約不

得不次第撤兵然破得政策未嘗去懷來日方長狡

謀正肆能保其必不橫挑邊釁伺間復起乎萬一有

事東三省既非通商口岸他國無從牽制加以旅連

之師鐵路之辛一呼立集防不勝防更或重略甘言

厚聯英美我無將伯之助彼作壁上之觀誠如海外

部所云大局將不可問矣竊嘗盱衡時局利害相權

以為今日不開商埠既離英日之心封豕長蛇恐無

魘足之一日今日勉開商埠縱觸強俄之怒執言使

義尚有可恃之外援如癰患然早潰則元氣猶未夫

斷進潰則創口實難收拾誠能及今俄人之氣勢未

充美日之商戰正劇東三省之人心尚固速將大東

綸音自行開埠通商各國利益均霑自必共保和局斷

不聽俄人事權獨攬致有偏枯師公法均勢之義行

外交自全之策以誠愚昧竊以為計近萬全矣至於

開埠辦法大要有三仿秦王三都成案奏請

開埠作商埠設立萬國公共租界一切事權操縱由

我此上策也允許美日開設商埠明列約款交換別

項利益此中策也另備照會允將某某等處作為通

商地方約內不為聲敘此下策也美外部有不論如

何辦法總以開埠為宜二語是其志在開通門戶共

過強俄已可概見則開埠辦法斷不強為干預碍我

主權應由

堂憲斟酌主裁轉行商約大臣婉切磋磨即照秦王三都

辦法美日亦當就範俄人尚畏公論未必能始終阻

撓獨距羣雄也事關重大

列憲自有權衡誠何敢妄參末議只以奉職覘國時值貼

危一得之愚不欲緘默用貢芻蕘上待

采擇專此密陳敬乞

代回

邸堂各憲為荷再請

台安

　　梁誠再頓首

譯件

致外部海約翰照會　光緒二十九年四月十七日

為照會事照得本大臣接准散會伊斯賽會正監督倫貝勤文稱

副監督黃開甲隨帶工匠陳設等項先期來美等因茲將來文鈔

錄附送察閱查中國與美國邦交素篤邇來文涉諸事辦理尤

為洽合是以中國政府特為竭力以助賽會盛舉此次工匠人等

來美係國家所雇傭工照來文開稱專為賽會建屋充材之用

一俟工程完竣即行妥遣回華該副監督隨帶工匠行振美境諒

貴國政府必能格外優待放行庶不失敦請赴會本意相應照會

貴外部請煩咨照戶部應如何優待之處儘速達照復以便咨呈本

國政府暨倫貝勤察核辦理須至照會者

外部海約翰來文　光緒二十九年四月二十六日
西一千九百三年五月卅二號

為照復事照得接准貴大臣本月十四號文稱散會伊斯賽會

副監督黃開甲隨帶工匠人等並陳設等項來美以助賽會

盛舉並請照復該工匠人等行振美境戶部應如何優待放

行等因本大臣准此查本衙門於貴大臣未來文以前曾接駐華

公使康格來文亦稱黃副監督隨帶工匠惟未言及中國國

家所雇傭來美賽會工人一節當將康格來文鈔送戶部大臣

查閱旋准戶部大臣本月十九號復稱嗣因康格文稱黃副

監督所帶工匠均係中國國家所派來美賽會一俟工程完

竣即行妥遣回華等語業已飭令稅關屆時放行等情第現

准貴大臣來文似屬另有別項人等來美此項人等想係意欲

始終留美賽會而戶部所措放行之工匠專為賽會建屋充材

之用一俟工程完竣即行妥遣回華不同則款待自應有別茲

承貴大臣詢問此次工匠人等行振美境應即如何優待放行一

節戶部曾請本大臣轉達貴大臣先行查明中國政府所派人
數若干方能照復若人數無多戶部當仿出使人員之例辦理
無須逐照禁工條例但中國政府應宜慎重防範不致另有
非國家雇用工匠混入其中一俟接到貴大臣來文聲明來
美人數戶部當即再行明白答復相應照會貴大臣請頒查
照須至照復者

致美外部海約翰函　光緒二十九年四月二十九日

敬啟者昨奉本月二十二號復函欣悉貴國戶部大臣擬照部函
所請屆時當准副監督黃開甲帶來之工匠一概登岸無阻
但戶部大臣意欲探悉將來擬留工匠若干名為照料國家房
屋即可諭令施行云云本大臣現接中國來牘尚未開列擬留
照料各項人數深愧未能即行函復惟本大臣十四號函所請

係專為黃副監督及工匠登岸無阻因該工匠等俟國家房
屋工程完竣即行遣送回華至時若須人看管房屋照料會
廠應留若干再將人名執役開單函請貴大臣商酌施行可
也特此布復並頌　時祉

外部海約翰復函　光緒二十九年五月初七日　一九〇三年六月二號

敬復者前接貴大臣五月二十五號來函內稱散魯伊斯賽會
副監督黃開甲隨帶工匠人等來美建造國家房屋一節本
大臣當將來函鈔錄附送戶部大臣查閱茲據戶部大臣聲
稱如中國政府欲俟工程完竣酌留工人若干屆時請即知照
以便商辦可也專此布復並頌　日祉

頭品頂戴護理浙江巡撫即補布政使司布政使翁　篯

咨呈事為照本護院于光緒二十九年四月二

十一日附片具

奏運庫滙解攤派美國賽會經費一片除俟奉到

硃批另行恭錄咨行外相應抄片咨呈為此咨呈

貴部謹請察照施行須至咨呈者

計粘抄片

外務部

右咨呈

光緒　　　　　　　日

再查准部咨議復攤派美國賠款經費一摺奉

旨依議欽此計單開浙江銀八萬兩解交江海關道撥領廿圓咨

會到浙英准電催速解壹摺浙省李儲罄洗入不敷

出洋債京餉現省直顧不遑祇可務後就急于藩

運二庫各項解欵中各撥銀二萬兩解滬此外籌實

窒礙再措經前撫臬臣誠勛電復戶部查明本籌

懇籌之欵現左一時難以用舒前先就運庫騰撥銀二萬

兩發交臬商源臺籌滙解江海關道投納由日主

藩司任內會同監運使黃祖絡具詳到滬深餘取

領滙日期咨報外理合附片具陳伏乞

聖鑒謹

奏

閏肓十岳

清代外務部中外關係檔案史料叢編——中美關係卷 第六冊·國際會議

咨呈事據津海關道唐紹儀呈稱蒙憲台札准

外務部咨近來賽會風氣大開官商運物出口應由本高先期赴就近

海關監督處呈請發給運物執照俟所運貨物報關出口時將此執照

一併呈驗方准免稅仍隨案報明本部府查奉憲批照抄著照開細稅行全遵

照辦理等因歷經遵辦在案茲經准憲鈔示津局函相催接北京電報局

來函以由京附來磁器四件轉交此次新舊總辦磁處領辛八百七十六元

此項磁器係運赴美國賽會之件請發護照一紙等因准此除函致新關

德稅司並給照外理合呈報核咨等情到本大臣據此相應咨呈

貴部謹請查照須至咨呈者

右咨呈

外務部

日

外務部

咨

咨明事光緒二十九年五月初四日據農工商
務局司道詳稱案奉撫沅札開四月十四日准
同山貝子前赴美國賽會正監督溥　電本監
督前赴散魯伯斯賽會各省華商赴會情形業

三

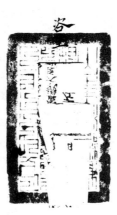

咨

咨明事光緒二十九年五月初四日據農工商
務局司道詳稱案奉撫沅札開四月十四日准
同山貝子前赴美國賽會正監督溥　電本監
督前赴散魯伯斯賽會各省華商赴會情形業

經咨行貴省查照至官派赴會所運貨物件數
若干計佔地址英尺若干務於五月節前電覆
即飭副監督預向賽會董事商定庶免向隅等
因飭即查照官商赴會情形妥籌詳報電覆等
因到局奉此查赴美國賽會貨物刻下正在製
辦之際件數多寡現尚無從估計惟陳賽貨場
所佔地址約計湏在華尺二十丈之數擬請電（見方）
覆轉飭即備華尺二十丈地址趕緊興修以便
東省官商前往陳賽並懇咨明
外務部查照立案等情到本部院據此除電覆
正監督轉飭悟辦外相應咨明為此合咨
貴部謹請查照立案施行湏至咨呈者
右
外　務　部
呈
咨

光緒二十九年五月二十日

清代外務部中外關係檔案史料叢編——中美關係卷　第六冊·國際會議

三五

抄

光緒二十九年閏五月二十五日昂字五百四九號

督辦鐵路運術江巡撫即務部政使司布政使翁

恭錄咨呈事為照本護院于光緒二十九年四

月二十一日附片具

奏運庫匯解攤派美國賽会經費一片當經抄片

咨行在案茲于本年五月十五日美弁賣回原

片奉到

硃批該部知道欽此除轉行外相應恭錄咨呈為此咨呈

貴部謹請察照欽遵施行須至咨呈者

右咨呈

外務部

光緒貳拾玖年伍月　二十九　日

上

咨呈

欽差出使美日秘古國大臣梁 為

咨呈事竊照美國戶部於西歷一千九百三年正月七日即光緒二十八年十二月初

九日定立華人來美賽會章程十款跡近瑣屑語意含混大非邀請赴會本旨

業經本大臣照會美外部轉咨駁詰並將原定章程譯送

貴部轉飭曉諭在案旋承准

赴會正監督倫貝子電咨內開外務部咨准貴大臣咨美戶部所擬華商賽

會辦法並鈔錄章程等因查章程十款跡近瑣屑自應婉辭駁詰以期便益

華商美戶部能否量為酌改歸於簡易俟有復文希速電覆等因承准此。

嗣經本大臣送次會晤美外部往復辯論始由新設之工商部於光緒二十九

年閏五月二十一日即西曆一千九百三年七月十五日將前項戶部原定章

程酌量刪改並增入華商赴會一條准美外部於閏五月二十六日照復錄送

前來本大臣查該外部來文所稱嗣後美國議院定開賽會華商意欲來

美陳設貨物者無須具保亦可不必常川在場又工商部既經改定章程則

一千九百三年正月七日戶部原定章程作廢又新增第五款載華商來

美賽會應由中國官員給照並經出口處美國公使或領事簽名此章程之第

四第九第十各款均與此項華商無涉各等語自係格外通融利便華商辦法至

於新章第三第六第七等款均有賽會僱用工人字樣則華商無庸照行已

可類推本大臣詳核新定章程十一款於華商曲示周旋而華工仍加限制自

是美國歷年成見一時斷難翻駁在彼既不失敦請赴會之本旨在我亦可

收講求商務之實效自當按照該工商部新定章程通飭曉諭商民一體

知悉凡華商來美賽會即照光緒二十年中美續約第三條辦法向中國官

員請領華洋文執照將姓名年歲籍貫身材相貌何項貿易粘貼照像一

一填註明白自由出口處美國公使或領事官簽名收執以便抵美時呈驗其

賽會華商所僱工人自應按照此次新定章程取保領照辦理儻有游歷

觀會之官紳人等可照中美續約第三款辦法領取游歷執照查驗合式自

可放行入境除電達

貴部轉行暨分別咨行外理合將美外部復文及工商部新定章程譯漢備

文咨呈

貴部轉飭曉諭俾赴會商民遵章辦理庶免抵美登岸別生齟齬於會務不

無裨益為此咨呈

貴部謹請察照施行須至咨呈者

計呈譯件一本

右　咨　呈

外　務　部

光緒二十九年陸五月　　　　　　　　　日

貝拾柒

附件

美外部覆文暨工商部改定華人來美賽會章程

照譯美外部來文　光緒二九年閏五月二十六日
西歷一千九百零三年六月二十六日

為照會事現據前大臣西□□□來文內論戶部一千九百零三年正月七號
即光緒二八年定立華人來美前往賽會所有章程業經本大臣
□□月初八日轉行核辦在案茲准工商部大臣文稱戶部所定賽會章程以為他項
華人設此限制原與本國敦請中國政府派來賽會之員無涉九中國
官商隨時來美係遵一千八百四十四年七月三號議院定例第十三款辦
理其第十三款載明本例之條款與中國出使衙官商人等為國事而來者
不相干涉其所載之文憑可作護照至其僕役人等游歷不在本例所轄之
內容請戶部所定章程係撤此意講解即如中國赴美府所派散魯伊斯2
賽會監督黃開甲日前弊而滿係在美以備佈置會場房屋
戶部尚須照文憑即能在山机開往其登岸准本部給外通融辦將

由部再次所議章程量為修通以便華美兩國議院定開審會凡

華商等款永美陳說請勅飭無稽具係六方常川往揚此協咻部新章

所藉推賣商品凡嗣年兩月卅八捐本部款訂章程飭綠附呈察閱再

此開新訂章程並非專指散齊斯審會而言日後本國凡有審會均

與律例等肉雅此稍廁陳章程一分飭知嗣大任請咨照須至

願會知單審程一件

附上飛知此華人來美審事業社

願會知單審程一件

第四十四條　大美國議院議准開辦審會來美依例第三款來美須邊此次章程

二年四月二十九號定立限禁華人入境之官亦應一律寔力奉行此條

改定以下各款辦理所派管理華人入境之官更改簡章自應作廢茲將

將一千八百零三年卅七號戶部所策審程更改簡章自應作廢茲將

改訂章程各款開列如左

第一款　凡華人來美審會須向委派管理華人入境之官呈驗憑指

附確保承辦審會之人或係為辦審會所准用之人

第二款　凡係人來美審會須將本人縣月三公且交管理華人入工之官

勅量查驗以期相符

第三款　凡華人來美賽會一經允准入境須直赴賽場不應
另到他處亦不應另作他業該華人等須於散賽會收場三十日內即由原來
入美之口附搭首次開行輪船或由中國或回該華人所居之一國

第四款　凡華人來美賽會須向美國駐管處官具立美洋五百圓係結
有可靠鋪店保其直赴賽場常川充當工業以致搭軍進國

第五款　凡各商華實業願充官商發給執照經出口赴美公堂
或備齎官發給地車程之第四第九第十各款均聰此辦理

新增

第六款　凡華人經華商管理華人入境文官須辦來美之
藥人各情第開列聰鑑兩分存此一分送交工商部管理外人

境司收存

工商部管理外人入境司第一號存根

何名　何處來　駐何東人雇用

本人照片粘貼驗真

集品管理華人入境官員發給執照

為發給執照事照得○○係○○處人由承辦○○處賽會之人○

據縣議院一千九百零二年四月二十九號定例雇用來美在會場作

工志此發給執照備據

管理賽會大臣官○六官銜○○之簽名○○年○月○日給

第七款　按縣定章凡雇來美賽會美國應派委員駐紮會場查

考嗣後若未再將章程更改即按下所開程式開報兩分存業所派

之員須隨時查察會場華人是否憑章辦理

查察委員開報式

傭工之人何名

來美賽會為某承辦之人雇用

年歲若干

傭工之人是男是女

在賽會充何事業

每日作業鐘數若干自某鐘起至某點鐘止

何日到會場

何日應由會場回國

補正處人簽名

查察委員簽名

照片粘貼於上

第八款　第二款所指之照片乃管理華人處之官將一分送之第七
款所填之查察會場委員粘於所開報單之上以憑考察

第九款　凡來美貿易華人如欲暫離會場必須向第七款所稱之查察委員
願票開明姓名將日往離辦暨開於四十八點鐘以內仍回會場暨將領
票繳銷　此款擬擴充而言其在四十八點鐘以內

第十款　凡華人領票暫離會場若不按期即回應按照不准寓居美國
之例辦理所有具保款項回須克公而本人亦須遞解回國所發憑票委員

應將此單如照管理外人入境司總辦徐將克公款項移送外並將該華
人照例遞解回國　此款擬擴充而言

第十一款　凡賽會收場三十日後籌辦華人會各官須將入口華人總數具
報管理外人入境司總辦並將華人姓氏各節逐一開明以便查考華人果否
按章回國

一千九百三年七月十五日工商部大臣萬帖由

清代外務部中外關係檔案史料叢編——中美關係卷 第六册·國際會議

廿

咨

（武戲二十九年六月二十六日繕發第三十八號）

頭品頂戴護理浙江巡撫即務布政使司布政使爲

恭錄咨呈事爲照本護院于光緒二十九年五

月十一日附片具

奏蒱庫準解推派美國賽會經費一片當經抄片

咨行在案蔴于本年閏五月初九日差弁賚回

原片奉到

硃批戶部知道欽此除轉行外相應恭錄咨呈爲此咨呈

貴部謹請察照欽遵拖行頃至咨呈者

右咨呈

外務部

光緒

日

逕啟者早數日接有海關總稅務司送來譯就華文散魯伊斯

賽會所論華人進口與帶貨赴會章程並云中國官商頗有不懌

該章之處本大臣當即電知本國外部聲明中國官商有此意見

一節茲接本國外部文囑將本國商務大臣聲復之大意云達

貴親王查照商務大臣云查該章係與中國官員無涉按美例

中國官員與其隨員跟役人等原有免其按從前所定華人

進口之禁辦理之條又按美戶部所囑管理口岸人員於中國

赴會黃副監督與其隨員跟役及其所帶在該會場蓋造華式

房屋華工均係驗有

貴國所給進美口之照毫無阻攔美國官並未另索別項進口

文憑即此可證本國戶部所定之章係與中國官及其隨員跟

役均屬無涉本年西七月一號美戶部已將管理外國人進口

一三一

岸之局、轉交商務部轄管、又稱此章程現已稍有變易之處、即

如修改章內大意、如有華商帶貨物赴會不必照原章須取保

人若干銀兩之保單亦不必按原章須時常在會場以內不得

隨便他往、惟華商前往美國必須請有

貴國所給之照、照內須聲明帶貨赴會者寔係華商、並須

有或美使館或出洋口岸美領事、於照上簽字蓋即各節而

已甚望

貴親王設法開通中國官商之疑慮、並將現所變易該章數

款補行知照可也、特佈即頌

爵祺、附送洋文

名另具七月十三日

F.O. No. 544.

Legation of the United States of America,
Pekin, China.

Sept. 4th. 1903.

Your Imperial Highness:-

I have the honor to inform Your Imperial Highness that some time since I received through the Inspector General of Customs a copy of a translation into Chinese of certain Regulations adopted by my Government, having reference to the admission of Chinese persons to the United States to take part in the Louisiana Purchase Exposition, and my attention was called to the complaint of certain Chinese merchants and officials that the Regulations appeared to them to be discourteous.

I thereupon telegraphed to the State Department at Washington, calling attention to this feeling on the part of Chinese officials and others and have now received instructions from the Department, directing me to communicate to Your Imperial Highness the substance of a report upon the subject made by the Secretary of Commerce.

The Secretary of Commerce states that the said Regulations do not affect officials of the Chinese Government, who with their body and household servants are exempted from the provisions of the Act restricting the admission of other Chinese persons to the United States. As evidence that this is the interpretation put by the Treasury Department upon the Regulations referred to he calls attention to the fact that by the instructions of the

Treasury

(F.O. No. 544)

Treasury Department Mr. Weng K'ai-kah, Assistant Commissioner of

the Chinese Government to the said Exposition, his servants, per-

sonal attendants, and the mechanics who are engaged in construct-

ing buildings for the Chinese Government on the grounds of the

Exposition, were all admitted without any other proof of their

right to land than the credentials of their Government.

Since the 1st. of July last the Bureau of Immigration has

been under the control of the Department of Commerce instead of

the Treasury Department as heretofore, and the Secretary of Com-

merce calls attention also to the modification of the Regulations

mentioned above, from which it appears that merchants desiring

to make an exhibit of their wares at the said Exposition shall

not be required to furnish bonds nor to remain continuously at

the Exposition as originally provided in the Regulations. It is

required however in order to their admission to the United States

that they shall present a certificate from their Government to

the effect that they are merchants making such a display and that

such certificate shall be visaed by the United States diplomatic

or Consular officer at the port of departure.

Trusting that Your Imperial Highness will take such steps

as may be necessary to correct the misunderstanding that has pre-

vailed with respect to these Regulations and to give publicity

to the modifications that have been made in them, I avail myself

of

(F.O. No. 544)

of the opportunity to renew to Your Imperial Highness the assurance of my highest consideration.

E. H. Conger

Envoy Extraordinary and

Minister Plenipotentiary

of the United States.

To His Imperial Highness, Prince of Ch'ing,

President of the Board of Foreign Affairs.

権算司、

呈為洛行事光緒二十九年七月十八日准駐美梁大臣

洛稱美戶部定立華人來美賽會章程十款經本

大臣迭次會晤美外部往復辯論始由新設之工商

部將前項戶部原定章程酌量高改並增入華商

赴會一條准美外部於閏五月二十六日照復錄送查

該外部來文所稱嗣後美國議院定開賽會華商

意欲來美陳設貨物者無須具保亦可不必常川在

場又工商部既經改定章程則戶部原定章程作廢

又新增第五款載華商來美賽會應由中國官員

給照並經出口處美國公使或領事簽名此章程之

第四第九第十各款均與此項華商無涉各等語自

係格外通融利便華商辦法至於新章第三第六第

七等款均有賽會僱用工人字樣則華商無庸照行已可

類推本大臣詳核新定章程十一款於華商曲示周旋

而華工仍加限制自是美國歷年成見一時斷難翻駁

在彼既不失敦請赴會之本旨在我亦可收講求商務之

實效自當按照該工部（商）新定章程通飭曉諭商民一

體知悉凡華商來美賽會即照光緒二十年中美續約

第三條辦法向中國官員請領華洋文執照將姓名

年歲籍貫身材相貌何項貿易粘貼照像一填註

明白由出口處美國公使或領事官簽名收執以便

抵美時呈驗其賽會華商所僱工人自應按照

以次新定章程取保領照辦理倘有游歷觀會

之官紳人等可照中美續約第三款辦法領取游

歷執照查驗合式自可放行合將美外部復文及

工商部新定章程譯漢咨請轉飭等因前來

查戶部初定華人赴會入口章程本近稍屬合

混本月十四日准美康使來函稱該國商務部現

將此項章程稍有變易望設法開通中國官商之

疑應並將現所變易該章數款補行知照等語當

經本部咨行在案茲准梁大臣咨稱前因相應照

錄原送該工商部新定章程咨行

貴監督查照並轉行曉諭可也須至咨者 粘抄

南北洋大臣

義賽會正監督

光緒二十九年七月

目

二 八月二〇

欽命前趕散齊伊斯寶會正監督貝勒銜圖山貝子溥　為

咨呈事　本監督現有應發各省電文二件相

應鈔錄電文咨呈

貴衙門迅為排發可也須至咨呈者

右　咨呈

外　務　部

光緒二九年八月初五日

寄　北洋大臣　盛京將軍　四川
　　湖廣總督　兩廣總督　湖北安徽
　　兩江　　　廣東浙江巡撫
　　　　　　　江蘇江西

貴省官派及商人赴美賽會貨物件數及佔地尺

寸各若干務希查明電覆以便轉剳副監督照辦

貝子溥倫歌　　右四十三字

寄　閩浙總督　福州將軍
　　山東湖南各巡撫

貴省宜派赴美賽會佔地尺寸有無更改貨物件數

已否查明有無商人前往赴會務希電覆貝子溥

倫歌　　右四十一字

欽命前遊散會伊斯貸會正監督員勒衛園山貝子溥　為

咨呈事本監督現有應寄湖南巡撫電文

一件相應鈔錄咨呈

貴部迅為排發可也須至咨呈者

　　右　咨　呈

　　外　務　部

　寄湖南巡撫電

庚電悉貴省工商大等赴會所需費用據

柯副監督查覆上等客位每名來往需美金

錢四百六十元中等三百四十下等一百三十五零用在

外在會住食每月每名最少金錢三十從豐六十

再豐百五十元等語美金一元約值華銀二兩并據

詳稱貨物水脚照尋常減輕將近一半每

噸收美金十五元者約收八元將來搭客或可從

康貝子溥倫有

光緒二十九年　八月　日

欽差大臣太子少保兵部尚書都察院右都御史辦理北洋通商事宜直隸總督部堂袁　為

咨呈事據關內外鐵路局津海關道會詳稱竊奉憲台札開准

外務部咨光緒二十九年六月十四日接比國葛署使照稱前於西歷一千

九百年在法國巴黎京城議定於西歷一千九百五年五月在美國倭生湯

地方舉行第七回萬國鐵路公會現有召集該會事宜議讓比國國家

照料一切本署大臣今接奉本國國家之命公請貴國派員前往會中會

議按照該會所訂章程如有應允昕請每年應捐該會之欵以昕派之員

多寡核計捐欵其有捐欵之數目委員一人應捐一百佛郎委員六應

山九月初七日

捐二百五十佛郎　委員三人應捐五百佛郎　委員四人應捐七百五十佛郎

委員五人應捐一千佛郎　委員六人應捐一千二百五十佛郎　委員七人應

捐一千五百佛郎　委員八人應捐一千七百五十佛郎　委員九人應捐二千

佛郎本署大臣今將該會第七回會議洋文說帖照送等因前來查該

使所請派員前往會中會議係為講求鐵路起見應否派員入會相應

抄譯說帖咨行貴大臣查照酌核辦理迅即聲復本部以便轉復比使可

也等因到本大臣准此應由關內外鐵路總局會同津海關道迅速核議

具復以憑轉咨等因奉此職道遵即會同商酌查比署使所請派員

前往會議係為講求鐵路起見現在路政關係重要各省次第興辦

亟應派員前往會議葢為講求方能獲益惟必須熟悉鐵路工程人

員始克勝任當經公同選擇查有關內外鐵路工程司候選知府詹天佑

候選同知鄺景陽在局多年辦理各路工程均極妥善堪以委派惟該

員等現以經辦要工尚未竣事擬請俟工竣後酌委一員前往會議以

期得力職道等再三商酌意見相同理合具文詳請鑒核轉咨實為

公便等情到本大臣據此除批示外相應咨呈

貴部謹請查照轉復施行須至咨呈者

右　咨　呈

外　務　部

光緒　　　　　　　　　　　　　　　日

乙　　初九日

欽命前赴散魯伊斯賽會正監督員勳衞園山貝子溥　　為

咨呈事據前工部郎中蘇錫第呈稱辦理

茶磁賽會添製綠茶等語查前准

貴部咨稱該員所請業經批准立案等語查

該郎中呈請情形與

貴部先後咨稱各節尚屬相符自應准如

所請除給札外相應咨呈

貴部查照可也須至咨呈者　計粘抄

右　咨　呈

外　務　部

光緒貳拾玖年　　月

月

具稟前 部即中炭蘇錫第為二稟請礼派

以便遵照而資保護事憲稱司員前以承重

內艱回籍旋經創辦茶磁賽會公司至善

荃等舉充公司總理稟明

外務部并蒙咨行

南洋大臣

商務大臣准予免稅在案盖以茶磁兩項

均須考究而出洋賽會之品尤宜精益

求精不得不有人專理其事當此講求

商務之時自應仰副

國家鼓舞振興之意然事艱任重未奉

札飭無所遵循且內地運貨以及將來

出洋終恐有窒礙難行之處事關賽會

大局實為中國工商之前途所繫除

經王善荃等稟明

外務部立案外所有司員辦理茶磁

賽會公司緣由理合具一稟

正監督台前即乞

恩准給札以便遵照辦理謹肅

欽命督辦鐵路總公司事務大臣太子少保前工部左堂盛 為咨呈事據鐵路總

公司參贊柯道鴻年稟稱竊奉憲台札開承准

外務部咨開接准比國萬署使照稱西歷一千九百五年五月在美國倭生湯

地方舉行第七回萬國鐵路公會公請貴國派員前往會中會議每年應捐該

會之欵以所派之員多寡校計將洋文說帖照送等因查該使所請派員前往

會議係為講求鐵路起見應否派員入會咨行貴大臣查核聲覆等因承准此

查該說帖係目關係鐵路應收之權利其多飭即查照酌核議覆等因奉此職

道遵即面稟大暑復於九月初三日奉到鈞函並電復

外務部抄稿飭將前文剋日票覆等因奉此職道遵查萬國鐵路公會之舉係

為講求推廣改良起見其說帖問題二十條無一非精益求精密益求密之意

裨益於路政者甚大各國熟諳鐵路工程尚復不憚煩勞廣徵眾慧以籌造道極登

峯中國於鐵路情形尚未窺及崔嵬會逢其適尤難視為緩圖即華人與會不

能望其獨出新意陳補救之法談整頓之方而各國既有此舉亦應志切觀光

藉充識見斷不得自甘落後有泰文明聞外國凡承辦大小鐵路公司均有派

員赴會以期集思廣益所派之員數視路之長短為定大約每路必有數員而

國家所派之員尚不在內今中國鐵路工程皆委各國之人辦理若專派華員

則洋員未免向隅沙多雖不能分身尚力求附列其名以為光寵是鐵路公會

之名集在外國視為絕大事業可想而知但既派洋員若不兼派華員似亦有

失國體且明示以中國無人啓外人輕視之心職道再四籌度雖不能仿照各

國之廣派以極少而論凡中國已經開辦鐵路如津榆盧漢粵漢正太滬甯等路

每路均派華員一人洋員一人屆期可去者去既不失大國之體而亦不至虛

糜來往川費至於派員捐數甚屬有限派員九人每年捐數不過二千佛郎克

合華銀數百兩而已事關文明義務似不宜惜此小費也是否有當伏乞察核

轉覆等情據此除俟屆期酌派華洋員司赴會外相應咨呈

貴部謹請查核施行須至咨呈者

右咨呈

外務部

光緒　　　年　　　月　　　日

清代外務部中外關係檔案史料叢編——中美關係卷 第二冊·國際會議

乚 十月初九日

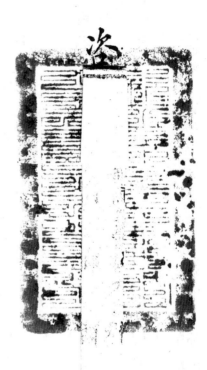

欽差辦理南洋通商事務項戴大學士督理江總督部堂□□爲

咨明事據江南商務局司道等會詳稱案奉憲台札據江南

派辦處司道申稱奉憲台批司道等詳請赴美國賽會擬懇

設立公司官商合辦由奉批以物赴賽原爲考究製造圖暢銷路

其事實重在商而不在官若以中國風氣未開必得由官提倡惟

運物赴會總須由商人自往考究方獲實益是以

出使法國孫大臣亦以宜由商家鳩設公司親運貨物往賽為言

凡事一涉官場不獨繁費且以素未諳習與其毫不相關之事

令其講究亦斷不能收實益日本由官辦物赴賽即為識者

所譏且物既不合行銷其耗費不能獲益已可概見美國相距

更為窵遠現在既由

　國家

　欽派大員前往監督論辦法各行省祇須勸導華商遴選相宜之

　貨親往比賽最為妥洽即欲官辦貨物以為先路之導亦祇

　須酌辦品樣交商帶往以試銷路今擬設公司官商合辦深慮

耗費需時有損無益且正監督來電應用地段須五月節前

電復現在公司尚無眉目計時亦慮不及不若一面勸招商家

一面酌提款項遴購樣品寄往為妥如粵中雕刻牙件閩省

漆器蘇杭綢緞蘇粵繡貨西省磁器等類皆可酌辦仰

再切實妥籌酌辦至欲設立公司廣運貨物赴美銷售儘

可俟赴賽後察看銷物情形再行斟酌也仍候

撫部院批示繳又奉

撫憲批司道等詳前事由奉批據詳赴美賽會擬官商

合辦設立公司所擬辦法均極妥協冑蘇應否合辦抑或分

辦仰即妥商會議章程呈候核奪仍候督部堂核示錄報

繳各等因奉此伏查賽會事宜本關商政前奉憲飭擬仿

日本國會辦法派員選貨赴會當由商務局轉移到處彼

因官運貨物赴會司道等有籌款用人之責自須逕由司

道等籌議具詳兹奉憲批現在公司尚無眉目不若勸招

商家酌提款項遴購樣品寄往為妥等因司道等遵即

悉心會議此後如何勸導商家設法試辦祇須体察商情酌量

詳定目下既無用人撥款之舉司道等即無從憑虛籌議江

南全省商務向由商務總局經理賽會事宜既須暫歸商家

設法試辦自應仍歸商務總局体察情形議章開辦庶期

切實而收速效除移知商務

總局遵照憲批籌議詳辦率移

蘇派辦處一体知照外合將會

核等情到本大臣據此查赴美賽會貨物件數及佔地尺寸各

若干昨准

溥監督電詢業經查案飭局會議詳辦在案據申前情合行

札催札局立即遵照批札趕速將商家如何勸招款項如何酌提

樣品如何遴購体察情形籌議一定辦法詳候核示等因到局奉

此查此案前奉憲台札飭准

美國賽會正監督溥　電詢赴美賽會貨物件數及佔地尺寸各若

干飭局會議詳辦等因奉經移會派辦處酌議稟復並申報在

案茲奉前因並准派辦處抄稿移會前來伏查運物赴賽本

為考究製造体驗銷路為推廣商務之一助憲諭其事實重

在商而不在官誠為至論自應由商人酌帶貨物前往親切

考究何物相宜足廣銷路方獲實效本司道等會同籌議擬

即遵照憲示一面出示招商令其慎選相宜貨物運往比賽如

以海路窎遠或各商合辦歸一人隨同帶往均聽其便至所帶

貨物均准向就近海關監督報明發給護照准其分別自行運往

並將由官如何保護及其中此賽此後足以行銷之利益剴切勸

導守明白曉諭第恐華商風氣未開赴賽無多一面酌籌款項由

官遴購各處著名出産合宜樣品以輔商運之不足而備應

此盛會屆時擬即寄呈

正監督溥　出洋時攜同赴會以歸一氣所有應留各貨佔地

尺寸擬請憲台先行電咨

正監督溥　預為留地百餘方尺以備一二百件之貨可以佈

置所需備辦各物款項雖庫儲支絀而現在正值振興商務自

應由本司道等設法籌撥核實動用至應否派員隨同前往觀

會以資考察屆時應候憲台酌核委派其蘇省應否合辦除侯

奉批再行遵照外所有遵飭議復赴美實會擬辦緣由是否有

當理合挈銜詳請批示並咨明

外務部

正監督　查照實為公便等情到本大臣據此除批據詳已悉侯咨

溥監督查照核辦並咨呈

外務部查照至寔蘇應否合辦旣據並詳

蘇撫部院應俟奉到批示錄報再行核奪繳印發外相應咨

明為此咨呈

貴外務部謹請查照施行須至咨呈者

右

外　　務　　部

　　　咨　　　呈

光緒貳拾陸年玖月貳拾貳

圖書

日

咨

欽命前赴散魯伊斯賽會正監督員勤銜圖山貝子溥　為

咨呈事本監督開辦賽會事宜前調供事二員

業經咨明

貴部查照在案現因公事繁多不敷差遣查有分

省縣丞彭清平堪以調充屆期放洋一併隨帶

前往相應咨朙

貴部查照存案可也須至咨呈者

右

咨呈

外務部

光緒二十九年九月　　日

二十月十五日

欽命前赴散魯伊斯賽會正監督員勒衔圖山貝子溥　　為

咨呈事據戶部主事梁用弧候選道鄧廷

鏗呈稱竊聞美國在散魯伊斯地方開設賽

會場並請中國派員招商辦貨赴該會陳賽

司員等生長粵東本省商情較為熱悉視招

集粵商創立廣業公司約鳩貲貳拾萬圓辦

俟貨到場會賽所辦各貨如翡翠玉石象牙

古玩木器絲茶繡貨及各新式物件隨赴會商

人柒拾伍名均求發給商照以免留難至貨物到

場請給美國所建賽會場內方橫約五丈作列

貨場另給中國所建亭宇內方橫約捌丈作賣

貨場惟該公司辦貨較多能否如期報關尚難

預定懇　愚札飭粵海洋關除遵照規辦章程

一律辦理外雇該公司於裝運賽會貨物到關

隨時查驗放行以便利運并乞移咨高部吏部

戶部雇作赴會人員免扣資俸理合將招商辦

貨賽會並請給札情形呈明俯求　愚准施行等

語查呈稱招商辦貨赴美賽會各節目應准

如所請札飭該員等照章前往赴會至司否准

其免扣資俸之處業經本監督啓行吏部查照

出洋賽會成案酌核辦理相應咨呈

貴部查照可也須至咨呈者

右咨呈

外務部

光緒貳拾玖年拾月

日

清代外務部中外關係檔案史料叢編——中美關係卷 第六冊·國際會議

巴 青 初 百

咨呈

咨呈事案照前准

貴部咨開美國於西歷一千九百零四年在

散魯伊斯城賽會行知各省出示勸諭工商人

等或攜貨前往專事考求或辦貨同行兼圖貿

易等因承准此當即通飭遵照並出示勸諭招

商赴會又准

前赴美國賽會正監督固山貝子溥　洛開本監督奉

旨前赴美國散魯伊斯城賽會各省華商有願籌集

資本運貨赴會者呈請轉報核辦等因准此復

經勸諭闔省商民人等籌齊運貨赴會銷售並

先電請留地華尺二十丈以便陳列嗣准

正監督溥電開各省官商赴美賽會統限於十

一月中旬報關取齊等因亦經轉飭依限齊集

各在案現據山東商務局司道詳稱此次赴美

賽會出示招商以來時通并載並無商民呈請

運貨前往其故由於東省物產有限工藝初興

並無精良品物至土產乾棗粉條之類俱係內

地食物不合外洋銷售否本年日本賽會北洋

僅派官員前往亚未攜帶貨物本司道等再四

籌商擬即仿照北洋赴會日本辦法請派委員

帶同商董赴美觀會考察一切前請留地二十

丈可否咨請通融讓於貨多省分之用等情到

本部院據此查該司道等所詳係屬實在情形

現已派委前充舊金山總領事候補道余思詒

帶同員董前往觀會專事考求商務前請留地

二十丈應請勻給別省陳列貨物之用除分咨

外相應備文咨呈為此咨呈

貴部謹請查照施行須至咨呈者

右 咨 呈

外 務 部

光緒貳拾玖年拾月拾陸日

逕啟者茲接本國外部並送到萬國律司會所出之單此會係

於一千九百零四年西九月二十九三日在散魯伊斯聚集為賽寶

會中之一事該會大意係欲商議萬國公法與海洋公法各要

事於各大國所定律例應甚關係各國於此等事各定有訊斷

與辦法之例該會甚望萬國所定者均能歸於一律又各國訊

問案件向有二本一本於該政府所定之例一本於由古以來所

傳之俗該會欲詳加查考比較此二本所開展之法本國外部

囑將此單並送

貴親王查照並云該會係美政府允為照料其用意承係

美政府所心許故囑請

貴政府屆時派員至會以為中國代表之人並請將此事布聞

各省俾凡司律之人均得知悉該會所有商定辯論之事將來

必編訂成書分送曾派人員來會之各國政府特此布達順頌

爵祉附送洋文並單一件

名另具 十月二十八日

榷算司

呈為咨行事光緒二十九年十月二十八日接准美國康使

函稱茲接本國外部送到萬國律司會所出之單此會係

於一千九百零四年西九月二十九三十日在散魯伊斯聚集

為賽寶會中之一事該會大意係欲商議萬國公法與

海洋公法各要事於各大國所定律例甚有關繫各國

於此等事各定有訊斷與辦法之例該會甚望萬國所定

者均歸一律又各國訊問案件向有二本一本於該政府所

定之例一本於古來所傳之俗該會欲詳加查考比較此二

本所開展之法本國外部囑將此單函送並云該會係

美政府允為照料其用意亦係美政府所心許故囑請

貴政府屆時派員至會以為中國代表之人並請將此

事佈聞各省俾司律之人均得知悉該會所有商定辨論

之事將來必編訂成書分送曾派人員來會之各國政府

單一件並洋文附送等因前來查中國現正講求律學自

應派員入會以期集思廣益相應將原送洋文單件一併

咨行

貴大臣查照屆期即由

貴大臣遴派妥員前赴該會以資考證並將所派之員

聲復本部以便轉達美使可也須至咨者　附件

梁大臣

欽命前赴散鸞伊斯賽會正監督員勒衔貝子溥　為

咨呈事據禮部候補員外郎瑞光呈稱竊隨

員於本年二月十四日在英京奉　出使大臣

張札開本大臣於光緒二十九年二月初九日准

倫貝子電開赴美賽會需員查有禮部員

外郎瑞光擬帶同往希飭該員束裝回華等

因奉此遵即束裝搭船內渡抵京稟到遵應

聽候差 裝好夏秋次來家父屢次患恙左

右需人適隨員脆兄瑞良升任河南布政使亦

即赴任隨員若復遠離實苦無人侍奉再四

思維叩懇垂念下情准予留京供差俾得朝

夕侍養則感沐鴻施實無既極如蒙俯允懇

乞咨行外務部王大臣吏部禮部正黃旗滿

洲都統暨出使英國大臣分別查照銷差無任

感禱之至等語查禮部候補員外郎瑞光前經

本監督電調囘葉瀾擬派濮同赴美兹據呈稱懇

予留京當差等情相應准如所請除分咨外

相應咨呈

貴部查照可也須至咨呈者

右　咨　呈

外　務　部

光緒貳拾玖年　　月

　　　　　　日

欽命前赴散魯伊斯賽會正監督員勒街圖山員子溥　為

咨呈事據戶部主事梁用弧候選道鄧廷鏗

呈稱奉劄招商辦貨赴會所辦貨物飭盡十一月

內報關等因仰見體恤商情欽感無似惟此次廣

業公司開手稍遲且辦貨物較多一時礙難如期詳

報懇恩札飭粵海洋關准該公司貨物展限十二月

底報關查驗放行赴會商人懇按名給合例執照至

所辦各貨現方陸續購辦似難預為報定應請俟報關時

以十一月廿七日

咨

統將赴會貨物件數逐項詳報以備核查實為德便等

語查華商王福泰等七十五名既據該員等呈稱均係

赴會商人應俟廣業公司赴賽貨物報明海關一律發給

護照查驗放行並飭遵照美國訂定赴會章程辦理除咨

明兩廣總督廣東巡撫粵海關監督總稅務司轉飭

粵海關稅務司發給護照外相應咨呈

貴部查照可也須至咨呈者　計赴會商人名單

右　　咨　呈

外　務　部

光緒貳拾玖年拾壹月　　　日

王福泰　王目權　箴鏡明　卸　戴　溫尚能　何元禧

何恭讓　梁宏謙　許達香　　　錦全　龍在田

劉雲棟　劉海清　陳鳳墀　陳載德　陳鴻芬　陳佐

吳錫珍　朱汝謙　朱球　李懷珍　李丹雲　李石如

李彤熙　李銘　葉瑞青　葉茂森　張國奇　張壽彭

張華　張廣漢　張世基　胡兆蘭　胡保芝　黃家政

黃雲　黃勉恩　黃德堯　黃伯鴻　賴家本　許勝

何隆　何萬順　周頌儒　龔嘉相　萬方從　呂光

錢玉恒　潘大鈞　潘新　孫念祖　楊名三　章有文

蘇志榮　沈宗驥　馮元洁　馮玉麒　周鑑　盧林

鄭昭熙　嚴福顏　謝鴻勳　黎發　黎詠裳　蔡效中

金繼光　蔣國華　伍鳳元　范得壽　羅友經　江兆年

徐仲和　董祥　唐華富

清代外務部中外關係檔案史料叢編——中美關係卷　第六册・國際會議

川青蓉

欽命前赴散魯伊斯賽會正監督員勒衔圖山貝子溥　為

咨呈事據廣西候補知縣黃翁呈稱卑職

前經具呈陳明集辦貨赴賽仰蒙給

予鈞劄在案現已購備粵產新奇器物運

赴賽場并随帶員役二十名均請給發商

照二十紙以免留難而重賽事等語 查

前據該員呈請集貲辦貨赴賽業經

批准給札并咨呈

貴部查照在案兹據呈稱現已購備粵

產器物運赴賽場随帶員役二十名均

請發給護照自應准如所請咨行總稅務

司轉飭粵海關稅務司俟該員將運賽

貨物及所帶員役報關後查驗明確發

給護照即由該員承領遵照章程前往

赴會除咨行商部兩廣總督廣東巡撫

粵海關監督并札飭該員遵照外相應

咨呈

貴部查照可也須至咨呈者

右咨呈　計赴會員役名單

外務部

光緒貳拾玖年拾壹月　　日

一總商董一員　李有濟

一副商董一員　黃信孚　梁道周　何有才　區日新

一繙譯一員　譚致遠　陳文通

一匠師二員　麥惠工　胡業勤

一同理人八員　王幹貞　廖適中　周智明　陸德恆

陳玉生　黃蓮鵬　潘士佳　李式金

一隨從三名　韓卅　趙福　馬順

止 青め

欽命前赴散魯伊斯賽會正監督員勒衙圖山貝子溥　為

咨呈事本監督現有應寄南北洋大臣柯副監

督電三件相應抄錄電底咨呈

貴部迅為排發可也須至咨呈者

右　咨　呈

外　務　部

光緒　　初肆　日

寄南洋大臣電

本監督正月中旬起程赴美希飭招商局安平或

海晏輪船屆時裝儎北駛由秦皇島赴滬再送

往日本並轉電滬道往洋務局隨帶員役祇二十人

務泛儉約是禱候電覆貝子溥倫支

寄北洋大臣電

本監督正月中旬起程赴美希飭招商局安平或

海晏輪船裝儎北駛由秦皇島赴滬並送往日本

候電覆貝子溥倫支

寄江海關造冊處稅務司賽會副監督柯爾樂電

本監督赴美請代定中曆二月中旬由橫濱開往輪船

超等艙一間員役應用頭等艙八人二等艙七人三等

艙六人候電覆貝子溥倫支

迳復者昨接

貴親王來函以接准川督電稱川省現派候補道章世恩帶同通判

祁祖彝及學生約二十人前往散魯伊斯賽會並先赴華盛頓烏約

之加告等處考查工藝添購機器訂於臘初起程請

貴親王函知本大臣轉達美國外部等因本大臣已悉所言之事轉達

本國外部矣相應函復

貴親王查照是荷此頌

爵祺附洋文

名另具十二月初四日

F.O. No.

Legation of the United States of America,
Pekin, China.

January 20th, 1904.

Your Imperial Highness:-

I have the honor to acknowledge the receipt of Your Highness'
note of the 19th. inst. informing me that you had received a telegram from the Viceroy of Szechuen, stating that Szechuen was
sending as representatives to the St Louis Exposition the Expectant Taot'ai, Chang Shih-en, who would take with him the Sub-
Prefect, Ch'i Tsu-i, and some students, about twenty in number; that they would first visit Washington, New York and Chicago, to inspect industries and purchase machinery, that they
would start about the middle of January, and tha   Viceroy
begged you to inform me, that I might transmit   elligence
to the Department of State.

I have the honor to inform Your Imperial Highness in reply
that I have already communicated the above-mentioned facts to
the Department of State.

I avail myself of the opportunity to renew to Your Imperial
Highness the assurance of my highest consideratio

Envoy Extraordinary and

Minister Plenipotentiary

Of the United States.

To His Imperial Highness, Prince of Ch'ing,
President of the Board of Foreign Affairs.

逕啟者早數日

貴大臣曾請本大臣電詢本國外部

伯理璽天德願否赴會監督　倫貝子呈遞

國書請入

觀見並允答復回書等因茲接電復云本國

伯理璽天德甚樂於　倫貝子入

觀並備回書於中國

大皇帝相應將此電複函達

　貴大臣查照是荷即頌

日祉

名另具十二月初十日

康格

清代外務部中外關係檔案史料叢編——中美關係卷 第六冊·國際會議

十二

咨

欽差出使美日祕古國大臣梁

咨呈事竊照光緒二十九年十二月十二日承准

貴部咨開光緒二十九年十月二十八日接美國康使函稱本國外部送

到萬國律司會會單定於一千九百四年九月二十八二十九三十等日在散

魯伊斯聚集商議萬國公法與海洋公法各要事囑請貴政府屆時

為

派員至會以為中國代表之人並洋文附送等因前來查中國現正講

求律學自應派員入會相應將原送洋文單件一併咨行查照屆期

遴派妥員前赴該會以資考證並將所派之員聲復以便轉達美使

等因承准此本大臣查萬國律司會在散魯伊斯大會聚議講求律

法非通曉律學曾習西例之員不足以資考究查有美署二等參贊

官周自齊三等參贊官孫士頤堪以委派屆期前赴該會除札飭外理

合備文咨呈

貴部請將擬派赴會委員銜名緣由轉達美使知照為此咨呈

貴部謹請察照施行至該員等赴會往返川資費用應請作正開銷附

入歲支案內另款造報須至咨呈者

右　咨　呈

外　務　部

光緒　　　　　　拾叁　　　日

謹

奏　為謹擬赴美國賽會正監督

救書

國書恭呈

御覽　仰祈

聖鑒　事竊臣部於先緒二十八年十二月初七日具奏請

旨簡　派前赴美國散魯伊斯城賽會正監督一摺奉

硃批　著派溥倫為正監督餘依議欽此查向章奉

命出　使大臣均先

頒給

救書　並呈遞

國　書各在案此次貝勒銜固山貝子溥倫赴美賽會

派充　正監督自應援照懇請

頒給

敕書　臣等接准美國使臣康格來函據本國外部電稱甚願

　　赴會監督入覲呈遞

國　書並備答復國書等語核其情辭甚為懇摯該監督

　　前往赴會應即先抵美國都城呈遞

國　書以通情好謹分別恭擬繕具清單進呈

御覽　伏候

命下　即由臣部繕寫滿漢文請用

御寶　容送該監督祗領呈遞所有謹擬赴美賽會監督

敕書　書緣由理合恭摺具陳伏乞

國

皇太后

皇上　聖鑒謹

奏　光緒二十九年十二月十六日具奏奉

硃批　報道了欽此

恭擬貝子溥倫赴美賽會

國書

大清國

大皇帝敬問

大美國

大伯理璽天德好中國與

貴國通好以來邦交日加親密茲因散魯伊斯城舉行百

年賽會環球物產畢萃於斯楷窺精良藉資考證

特簡貝勒銜固山貝子溥倫充赴會正監督該監督

分屬宗支留心商務經理中國商民赴會事宜必能

按照章程期臻妥洽並命該監督前赴

貴國都城親遞國書表明朕意尚冀

大伯理璽天德推誠優待俾得加意考求庶使兩國商務

日臻與盛朕有厚望焉

恭擬美國賽會正監督

敕書

皇帝

敕諭前赴美國散魯伊斯城賽會正監督貝勒衛固

山貝子溥倫朕維開物成務裕國首重厚生通商惠

工睦鄰即以善俗茲值美國散魯伊斯賽會特命

爾充赴會正監督爾其仰體朕懷志心經畫按照賽

會章程詳慎辦理所有中國商民赴會貿易者均

宜隨時保護約束俾便懋遷美洲素重商務經營

製造進步日臻該會為物產薈萃之區爾其加

意考察期於中華商業逐漸振興用副委任之

意特諭

清代外務部中外關係檔案史料叢編——中美關係卷 第六册·國際會議

廿二月廿二日

欽命前悲散會伊斯賽會正監督員勒徵圖山貝子溥　為

咨呈事准

貴部咨稱光緒二十九年十二月十六

日本部具奏謹擬赴美國賽會正監

督請

頒給

敕書

國書各一道咨送貴監督祗領欽遵辦

理等語查

貴部送到

敕書

國書各一道本監督業經敬謹領訖相應

片覆

貴部查照可也須至咨呈者

右

外　務　部

咨　呈

光緒貳拾玖年拾貳月

　日

清代外務部中外關係檔案史料叢編——中美關係卷　第六冊·國際會議

收　青七省

欽命前赴散魯伊斯賽會正監督員勒街商山具子溥　為

咨呈事光緒二十九年十二月二十七日

本監督具奏擬調東文繙譯一摺奉

旨依議欽此同日具奏慶寬等呈請開去赴美

差使一片奉

旨依議欽此欽遵由軍機處鈔交前來相應

恭錄

諭旨鈔錄原奏咨呈

貴部查照可也須至咨呈者 計鈔件

右

咨 呈

外 務 部

光緒貳拾玖年拾貳月　　　日

謹

奏為札調東文繙譯隨同出洋茶招具陳仰祈

聖鑒事竊照上年十二月間茶奉

諭命前赴美國散魯伊斯賽会自本年二月間開用

閎防以東办理京和起会一切事宜現已次苐就

結並飭令葉副監督黄開甲洋副監督招尔

乘先期赴美預為布置奴才擬擬於本年正月起程

約計開會日期擬莫程途應由太平洋赴美較

為便捷道徑日本擬隨帶翻譯一員以資通譯

查有同知銜江蘇補用知州馮國勳熟悉情形

堪以隨帶前往合併仰懇

天恩俯准奴才著遣奏候

命下即由奴才劄飭該員隨同出洋應候使臣不致

仍乞益所號奴才擬調備譯緣由理合奏摺具陳

伏乞

皇太后

皇上 聖鑒謹

奏

再據奏東三院候補選道內務府員外郎慶寬

呈稱寅戰前蒙差的赴美考察商務自應盡

心前往惟戰現已補授員外郎雖未便遠辦起程

前往赴美著使又擇分發江蘇補用直隸州知州

祝瀛元呈稱寅戰前蒙差調赴美隨員自應遵

前往惟戰現因商部東調當差刻下岁勾稽未

完了件一件未便遠辦並請開差赴美著使九

等語查慶寬祝瀛元著二員前經咨取東的

旨允

隆銘道本案前擬呈請開差赴美著使自

仰宽查情形於應請

旨隆共開差赴美著使理合附片具陳伏乞

皇太后

皇上聖鑒

此 十二月廿六

欽命前赴散魯伊斯賽會正監督員勒衔固山貝子溥　　為

咨呈事准

貴部咨稱本部收駐日楊大臣來電一

件鈔錄電底知照前來　查原電內稱

日本外部詢倫貝子何日過東隨帶

幾員是否奉

命而來以便分別接待乞電示等語 本監

督隨帶六員中歷二月初旬過東應

請

貴部電覆至所詢本監督是否奉

命而來一節本監督道經日本並未奉

命亦未自行奏明應如何電覆之處

相應咨呈

貴部酌核一併電覆楊大臣轉達日

本外部可也須至咨呈者

右 咨呈

外務部

光緒貳拾玖年拾貳月　　日

F.O. No.

LEGATION OF THE UNITED STATES OF AMERICA,
PEKIN, CHINA.

February 19th. 1904.

Your Imperial Highness:-

Acting under instructions from my Government I have the honor

to inform Your Imperial Highness that on the 24th. of December,

1903, the British Ambassador at Washington deposited in the De-

partment of State the instruments of ratification by the Govern-

ments of New Zealand, Natal, and the Cape of Good Hope of the

Universal Postal Convention signed at Washington on June 15th.

1897; and that the ratification of New Zealand is dated Nov.5th.

1901; that of Natal, October 21st. 1901; and that of the Cape

of Good Hope, October 8th. 1903.

I avail myself of the opportunity to renew to Your Imperial

Highness the assurance of my highest consideration.

Envoy Extraordinary and

Minister Plenipotentiary

of the United States.

To His Imperial Highness, Prince of Ch'ing,

President of the Board of Foreign Affairs.

List of Delegates appointed by the President of the
United States to the Universal Congress of Lawyers
and Jurists to be held at St. Louis in September,
1904.

Mr. Chief Justice Fuller,
Mr. Justice Harlan,
Mr. Justice Brewer,
Mr. Justice Brown,
Mr. Justice White,　　　　　⎬ Supreme Court of the United States.
Mr. Justice Peckham,
Mr. Justice McKenna,
Mr. Justice Holmes,
Mr. Justice Day,

Honorable Francis M. Cockrell,
Honorable John W. Daniel,
Honorable Charles W. Fairbanks,
Honorable George F. Hoar,　　⎬ United States Senate.
Honorable Alfred B. Kittredge,
Honorable John T. Morgan,
Honorable John C. Spooner,

Honorable Henry D. Clayton,
Honorable John Dalzell,
Honorable David A. DeArmond,
Honorable John J. Jenkins,　　⎬ House of Representatives.
Honorable Charles E. Littlefield,
Honorable Henry W. Palmer,
Honorable John Sharp Williams,

Honorable John Hay, Secretary of State.
Honorable L. M. Shaw, Secretary of the Treasury.
Honorable Wm. H. Taft, Secretary of War.
Honorable P. C. Knox, Attorney-General.
Honorable Wm. H. Moody, Secretary of the Navy.

Honorable Henry M. Hoyt, Solicitor-General.

Honorable John W. Foster, formerly Secretary of State, Washington, D.C.
Honorable Richard Olney, formerly Secretary of State, Boston, Mass.
Honorable John G. Carlisle, formerly Secretary of the Treasury, New
    York City, N. Y.
Honorable Elihu Root, formerly Secretary of War, New York City, N. Y.
Honorable John W. Griggs, formerly Attorney-General, New York City,
    N. Y.

Honorable Judson Harmon, formerly Attorney-General, Cincinnati, Ohio.

Honorable Wayne MacVeagh, formerly Attorney-General, Washington, D. C.

Honorable W. H. H. Miller, formerly Attorney-General, Indianapolis, Ind.

Honorable George H. Williams, formerly Attorney-General, Portland, Oreg.

Honorable Don M. Dickinson, formerly Postmaster-General, Detroit, Mich.

Honorable Benjamin F. Tracy, formerly Secretary of the Navy, New York City, N. Y.

Honorable John W. Noble, formerly Secretary of the Interior, St. Louis, Mo.

Honorable Joseph H. Choate, American Ambassador, London, England.

Honorable W. H. Pope, Associate Justice Supreme Court of New Mexico, Roswell, N. M.

Honorable Edward Kent, Chief Justice Supreme Court of Arizona, Phœnix, Ariz.

Honorable James Wickersham, United States District Judge, Eagle, Alaska.

Honorable Sanford B. Dole, United States District Judge, Honolulu, Hawaii.

Honorable Lorrin Andrews, Attorney-General, Honolulu, Hawaii.

Honorable Wm. H. Hunt, Governor of Porto Rico, San Juan, P. R.

Honorable José Severo Quinones, Chief Justice Supreme Court of Porto Rico, San Juan, P. R.

Honorable Willis Sweet, Attorney-General, San Juan, P. R.

Honorable Cayetano Arellano, Chief Justice Supreme Court of the Philippine Islands, Manila, P. I.

Honorable Luke Wright, Governor of the Philippine Islands, Manila, P. I.

Honorable L. R. Wilfley, Attorney-General, Manila, P. I.

Honorable LeBaron B. Colt, Presiding Judge Circuit Court of Appeals, Bristol, R. I.

Honorable Wm. J. Wallace, Presiding Judge Circuit Court of Appeals, Albany, N. Y.

Honorable Marcus W. Acheson, Presiding Judge Circuit Court of Appeals, Pittsburg, Pa.

Honorable Nathan Goff, Presiding Judge Circuit Court of Appeals, Clarksburg, W. Va.

Honorable Don A. Pardee, Presiding Judge Circuit Court of Appeals, New Orleans, La.

Honorable Horace H. Lurton, Presiding Judge Circuit Court of Appeals, Nashville, Tenn.

Honorable James G. Jenkins, Presiding Judge Circuit Court of Appeals, Milwaukee, Wis.

Honorable Walter H. Sanborn, Presiding Judge Circuit Court of Appeals, St. Paul, Minn.

Honorable Wm. B. Gilbert, Presiding Judge Circuit Court of Appeals, Portland, Oreg.

Mr. Chief Justice Alvey, Court of Appeals, District of Columbia.
Mr. Chief Justice Clabaugh, Supreme Court, District of Columbia.
Mr. Chief Justice Nott, United States Court of Claims.

Charles Claflin Allen, St. Louis, Mo.
James D. Anderson, Chicago, Ill.
Simeon E. Baldwin, New Haven, Conn.
Charles J. Bonaparte, Baltimore, Md.
Wm. P. Breen, Fort Wayne, Ind.
A. B. Browne, Washington, D. C.
John C. Carter, New York City, N. Y.
Holmes Conrad, Washington, D. C.
Frederic R. Coudert, New York City, N. Y.
J. M. Dickinson, Chicago, Ill.
M. F. Dickinson, Boston, Mass.
Samuel Dickson, Philadelphia, Pa.
John F. Dillon, New York City, N. Y.
Amasa M. Eaton, Providence, R. I.
G. A. Finkelnberg, St. Louis, Mo.
Francis Forbes, New York City, N. Y.
Theodore S. Garnett, Norfolk, Va.
William D. Guthrie, New York City, N. Y.
James Hagerman, St. Louis, Mo.
Alfred Hemenway, Boston, Mass.
Francis J. Heney, San Francisco, Cal.
John Hinkley, Baltimore, Md.
Wm. B. Hornblower, New York City, N. Y.
William Wirt Howe, New Orleans, La.
James H. Hoyt, Cleveland, Ohio.
John G. Johnson, Philadelphia, Pa.
Edward Q. Keasbey, New York City, N. Y.
Frank B. Kellogg, St. Paul, Minn.
Jacob Klein, St. Louis, Mo.
E. B. Kruttschnitt, New Orleans, La.
Frederick W. Lehman, St. Louis, Mo.
Charles F. Libbey, Portland, Me.
Isaac H. Lionberger, St. Louis, Mo.
Walter S. Logan, New York City, N. Y.
Alvin J. McCreery, Binghampton, N. Y.
Charles F. Manderson, Omaha, Nebr.
P. W. Meldrum, Savannah, Ga.
Rodney A. Mercur, Towanda, Pa.
Prof. John B. Moore, Columbia University, New York City, N. Y.
Charles Nagel, St. Louis, Mo.
Cortlandt Parker, Newark, N. J.
Thomas Patterson, Pittsburg, Pa.
George R. Peck, Chicago, Ill.
Wheeler H. Peckham, New York City, N. Y.
Francis Rawle, Philadelphia, Pa.

James H. Reed, Pittsburg, Pa.
John K. Richards, Cincinnati, Ohio.
Platt Rogers, Denver, Colo.
U. M. Rose, Little Rock, Ark.
George B. Rose, Little Rock, Ark.
Ferdinand Shack, New York City, N. Y.
Geo. M. Sharpe, Baltimore, Md.
Moorfield Storey, Boston, Mass.
Henry St. George Tucker, Columbian University, Washington, D. C.
George Turner, Spokane, Wash.
Frederick E. Wadhams, Albany, N. Y.
David T. Watson, Pittsburg, Pa.
Edmund Wetmore, New York City, N. Y.
Everett P. Wheeler, New York City, N. Y.
James M. Woolworth, Omaha, Nebr.
A. S. Worthington, Washington, D. C.

清代外務部中外關係檔案史料叢編——中美關係卷 第六册·國際會議

逕啟者茲接有魯意斯安納賽寶會總理人法蘭西司送來一函

請為轉送

貴親王等因相應將原函附送即希

貴親王查照檢收是荷此泐即頌

爵祉
　並洋函一件
　附送洋文

名另具正月初七日

F.O. No. 611.

Legation of the United States of America,
Pekin, China.

February 22d. 1904.

Your Imperial Highness:-

I have the honor to transmit herewith to Your Imperial Highness

a letter from Mr. David R. Francis, President of the Louisiana

Purchase Exposition, which he has requested me to forward to

Your Highness.

I avail myself of the opportunity to renew to Your Imperial

Highness the assurance of my highest consideration.

Envoy Extraordinary and

Minister Plenipotentiary

of the United States.

To His Imperial Highness, Prince of Ch'ing,

President of the Board of Foreign Affairs.

附件二

照譯美國散魯伊斯會長上

慶王爺書

慶親王鈞鑒敬啟者賽會一事副監督責任重大中國此次

特派黃開甲以充之僕與本會各員均甚欣悅黃君現已

回華往迎倫員子來美故僕乘此機會謹啟

王爺座前黃君氣象洪大人甚謙和辦理一切緊要事宜均為

得當故敝國人士無不欽佩在心士庶官高皆樂與交遊

來往凡聽其所演說者則皆喜多知中國情形於此可

見黃君此次之來美足使中美之邦交更加親密此誠

敝國人民所念切者也中國政府於整備賽會事宜一

一舉行實為僕所厚望者專肅順頌

日祉

會長弗蘭賽司謹啟

一千九百零四年正月十合由散魯伊斯發

二

四月初六日

欽命前赴散會伊斯賽會正監督員勒衙圖山貝子溥　為

咨呈事准

貴部咨接日本内田使函稱現准本國外務大

臣電開聞倫貝勒將到我國游歷業經奏明

臣電開聞倫員勒將到我國游歷業經奏明

奉旨以賓禮接待即應派員前往長崎迎迓望

將到東日期及隨員名單詢明電覆等情為此

函請轉達迅即開送以便轉電本國等因前來

本部查此事前准復文當以貴員勒隨帶六員

於中歷二月初自過東境游歷並未奉

命等語於十年十二月二十五由本部電覆駐日本楊

大臣在案兹復接准内田使函稱各節相應咨

行查照速復以憑轉復等語　本監督定於正

月拾捌日啟程赴滬再行開往長崎約計二月初

壹貳日可抵長崎所帶隨員內務府員外郎誠璋

戶部主事彭穀孫分省補用道程大澂候選通判全森

江蘇補用知縣馮國勳等五員又據副監督候選道

黃開甲電稱由美回華仍隨同本監督放洋東下

應請一併開列函覆除候由上海開往長崎日

期屆時再行電請

貴部轉達外相應咨呈

貴部查照轉覆可也須至咨呈者

右　咨呈

外　務　部

光緒叁拾年正月

　　　　日

権算司

呈為咨行事光緒三十年正月十三日本部接准美國衛

繙譯面交伯爾特蘭省承辦賽會會長來函內稱自

美國得奧賽貢之日起至一千九百零五年恰已百年故

擬特開此會以誌其事懇請中國入會相賽以助此舉

特將所刊之件附孟上呈等因前來相應照譯洋文原件

抄送

　　商部

貴部查照可也須至咨者　　附抄件

光緒三十年正月

美國伯尔特蘭省承辦賽会会長致中國外部函

敬啟者伯尔特蘭省內將於西曆一千九百零五年開場賽会自五月一號起至十月一號止今特

思並都司克拉克奉美國德羅弗尔森之命壽得此地自美國得奧賽貢之月起計至

一千九百零五年恰已百年故擬特開此会以誌其事也美國之奧賽貢國華盛頓國愛

達豪國蒙塔訥國烏克明國均在賽貢地方之內今日美國之奧賽貢國得以稱雄於太平洋其座

皆由於得此地也此次為美國公共賽会会場之大計三百三十七有餘內有失湖座

藏於北開会所用經費約須美金玉兆圓美國之母國議定入会者現已不少其奧賽

貢國則已於一千九百三年正月三十日南美總督再為官會議之免機経費美

金の十五萬元以为之倡伯尔特蘭城之户口約十二萬玉千之多該城寬為美

國商務最盛之地及包生意每年約美金一百五十兆元有條為製造廠每年所造之

物共值又不五十兆元及鋪之股本約五十兆元銀行之欵約三十兆元美國出口三麦

麵由此出口者最多每年後口卓歐亞斐南美北美为洲往來之貨物約值美金十五

兆元每年所製之木板材料共長不下の百兆美呎减可甲於天下也本会今特懇請

中國入会相賽以助此舉此事備蒙

貴國政府俯賜俾辦本会實深感激

標知本会回顧

顧問之處必所敬謹緣陳本函特為恭请

貴國入会當由美國外部代為遞送專書敬候

復雙音順頌

日祉

　　　　　会長恩考特
　　　　　総辦尔理德　会啟
　　　　　一千九百三年十月十五号由伯尔特蘭發

十二月初十日

頭品頂戴兵部侍書署理兩廣總督谷　為

呈呈事案照承准

前總理衙門咨行出使美日秘國楊大臣與美國

使署律師科士達詳酌拟定華人赴美漢洋文護

照程式咨粵照辦嗣後華人往美一體仿照所拟

程式飭由粵海關發給等因兹有商民馮壽銘鄭

煜之馮植雲林達陳贊黃兆爵林康陳調典林沛

咨

等均請照前往美國散魯伊斯城賽會稟由粵海

關驗填護照並無騙揚頂冒情弊且有股定鋪保

具結存案核與章程相符准粵海關咨請核咨前

來除咨復並照章咨行

出使美日秘國大臣駐美金山總領事查照外擬

合咨呈為此合咨

貴部謹請查照備案施行須至咨呈者

右咨　呈

外務部

九　　　　　　　　　　　　　頂印空白

十七

日

收閱廿日

商部為片置事本部現有

發南北洋太醫電各一律相

應片呈

貴部迅即排發可也須至片呈者 粘抄電

右片呈

外務部

光緒叁拾叁年正月 二十一 日

發

南洋大臣電
北洋大臣電

據駐美梁大臣電稱賽會華商護照違式殊

煩礙論請飛電各督撫嚴飭務遵前咨賽會

新章領照否則殊難登岸等語希轉飭各關

遵照商部

逕啟者茲奉本國外部來文囑將所寄之信函一件轉達

貴親王緣散魯伊斯賽寶會內另有素擅才藝婦女赴會之

塲故該會中特派出經理照料之婦數人此信函即係所派經

理之婦特備請中國婦女之函大意不過欲使天下婦女同得

進步之益並囑請

貴親王將函中大意布告中國婦女等因相應將原函附送

即希

查照是荷順頌

爵祺　附洋文並原函

名另具　正月二十二日

F.O. No.

LEGATION OF THE UNITED STATES OF AMERICA,
PEKIN, CHINA.

March 9th. 1904.

Your Imperial Highness:-

I have the honor to inform Your Imperial Highness that I have

received instructions from the Department of State, directing me

to forward to Your Highness an invitation addressed to the wo-

men of China by the Board of Lady Managers of the Louisiana Pur-

chase Exposition with a view to promoting woman's interests at

the Exposition, and I am directed to ask that Your Imperial

Highness will give it due publicity to the end that it may come

to the knowledge of the women of China.

        I avail myself of the opportunity to renew to Your Imperial

Highness the assurance of my highest consideration.

Envoy Extraordinary and

        Minister Plenipotentiary of the

        United States.

To His Imperial Highness, Prince of Ch'ing,

President of the Board of Foreign Affairs.

One Inclosure: Letter of Invitation.

Louisiana Purchase Exposition,
Board of Lady Managers.
Mrs. Daniel Manning, President.

St. Louis, Mo, January 22, 1904

Excellency:-

By an Act of the Congress of the United States the Board of Lady Managers of the Louisiana Purchase Exposition is directed to join with the other constituted authorities in commemorating the great event in the history of the United States when, a century ago, there was added to its territory a new field which today is the home of many people and where earnest and sincere women, as well as men, are laboriously working out the problems of the progress of humanity and the advancement of the race.

No single individual, no one people, no separate country can supply that full knowledge from which may be fixed the condition of mankind, its development in the industries, the arts, the sciences at the commencement of the twentieth century. The entire world must contribute to this knowledge and therefore the entire world has been invited to take part in this universal exposition and to bring hither the fruit of the lands, the products of other soils, the articles manufactured by foreign hands and evidences of the achievements of the intellect and intelligence in the higher fields of thought.

To His Excellency
The Minister of Foreign Affairs
of China.

While in gathering all these things there is no distinction made between the work of man's hand and of woman's hand, between the product of man's mind and of woman's mind, nevertheless it is the peculiar function of this Board to act as the channel through which women as individuals and as organizations may be brought into immediate communication with the Exposition at St. Louis.

It is therefore with cordiality and eagerness that we invite the women of your country to join with us in presenting to the world information of the condition, opportunities, development and promises of their sex in their own country and to exhibit at the Exposition specimens of their productions and examples of their activities, manual and mental, scientific and artistic.

And coupled with this invitation we would express the hope that we may be permitted to be of personal service to such women as may visit the Exposition in person, or to give special attention to the exhibits of such as may not be able to come.

Requesting Your Excellency's good offices to the end that due publicity may be given to the invitation in order that it may come to the knowledge of the women of your country, I beg to assure you of the high consideration with which I am

Your obedient servant

Mary Margaretta Manning

President.

敬復者美國賽會一事奉到本月二十二日

鈞函以華商護照違式飭轉致各海關遵照新章發給

等因奉此查華商赴美領照原係副監督柯爾樂逕

辦若

貴部存有護照式樣請發一分閱看為荷惟此特遵改

照式縱後去者不再違章而已經起程之商絡繹載

道又何能一一撤回補發竊以為美國邀請赴會原

以昭兩國睦誼而中國官商長途跋涉所費不貲亦

謂承此盛情勉全友誼不若一面通行各省關所有

華商未經起程者務須詳細遵照新章定式領照前

往其業經首途或已到美境者應由

貴部照知美國駐京大臣以該商等所執之照若有違

式之處斷無弊混礙難一一撤回改辦請其原諒此

情概不駮阻云云以上請不駮阻之情總稅務司已

函致康大臣未知能否辦到除電飭江海粵海兩稅

務司速將已發護照式樣送京外理合函復

鑒查可也專此佈復順頌

日祉

　　　　名另具 光緒叁拾年正月貳拾叁日

敬復者奧賽貢賽會一事奉到本月十六日

鈞函飭為查核酌復等因奉此查美國現於散魯伊斯

城開賽大會中國業派

王大臣等前往已可謂曲盡友邦之誼其奧賽貢開會

一節不若俟散魯伊斯會畢

王大臣等回京詳詢情形後再議亦不為遲除將原件

奉還外理合玉復

鈞鑒可也專此順頌

升祺

　附繳洋文章程等件

　　名另具光緒叄拾年正月貳拾肆日

榷算司

呈為照會事光緒三十年正月十九日准駐紮

貴國梁大臣電稱散魯伊斯賽會華商來美護

照違式請飛電正監督各督撫暨稅司嚴飭務遵

前咨賽會新章領照否則難於登岸等語當由

本部轉電正監督倫貝勒并咨行商部及丞致

總稅務司轉飭稅務司遵照去後茲准正監督復

電商部復咨各稱接梁大臣來電已電致各督撫

嚴飭遵照等因本部查此次

貴國邀請赴會原以重商務而昭睦誼中國官

商長途跋涉所費不貲此時改正護照式樣縱後

去者不再違章而業經起程之商人絡繹在道又

何能一一撤回補發所有華商未經起程者自當嚴

飭遵照新章定式領照前往其業經首途或已到

美境者該商等所持之照即或達式斷無弊混實

有礙難撤回改辦之處相應照會

貴大臣查照即請電達

貴外部原諒前情不致駁阻並希

見復可也須至照會者

　　美康使

光緒三十年正月

敬復者散魯伊斯賽會一事奉到本月二十六日

鈞函領悉壹是現據代辦賽會善後事宜江海關稅務

司好博遜電稱江海關所發之照均係駐滬美領事

照章應發者粵海關所發之照係平常護照由駐粵

美領事畫押蓋印者不日即將各照式寄呈等因前

來查江海既由美領事照章繕發粵海雖係平常之

照而由美領事畫押蓋印則到美被阻一節更不可

解前已將駁阻情事函達駐京康大臣據復已行知

美國外部請為查辦云 云 惟能否照允辦理則殊難

預度也專是佈復順頌

升祺

名另具 光緒叁拾年正月貳拾捌日

赫德

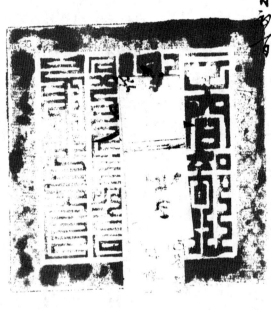

商部為咨呈事光緒三十年肆月

二十六日接准

咨稱准美㴉使函稱奉本國外部

來文囑將所寄之信一件轉達

緣散魯伊斯賽會內有素擅才

藝婦女赴會之場此信即係該會

所派經理之婦特備請中國婦女

之函並囑將函中大意布告中國

婦女等情相應咨行貴部查照

辦理等因前來除由本部咨行

南洋大臣轉飭江海關道飭知女

學堂遵照外相應咨復

貴部查照可也須至咨呈者

右咨呈

外務部

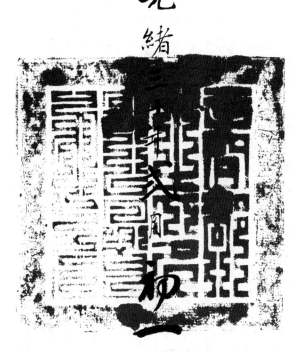

光緒三十四年二月初二日

一二月初四日

東　溥倫

　　子政務部

崇為陳報啟程日期恭摺仰祈

聖鑒事竊臣欽差前赴美國散魯伊斯賽會監督事分

恭膺

恩命派光前赴美國散魯伊斯賽會監督事分

務部意准

頒發

國書

敕書歡迎賀函等件並准

御覽先成繪造茶畫出洋

陛辭之日仰蒙

召訓開譯莫名欽感臣昌於正月十八日率同隨

帶各員由京乘火車起程美國使以康格

日本國使以內田康哉均派委機處作陪

顧為殷良振護尾訊槽乘周旋暨脫行抵天津

各國驛館津館多及北洋大及以下委多依次接見

次日登招甫局啟年輪船碇即測驗於二十三日行

抵吳淞二十四日登岸美國領事古衛日事館多

小田初筹寿之助蒡荟國領多及海關稅務司

二月初十日

日本國使以內田康哉均派委機處作陪

顧為殷良振護尾訊槽乘周旋暨脫行抵天津

各國驛館津館多及北洋大及以下委多依次接見

次日登招甫局啟年輪船碇即測驗於二十三日行

抵吳淞二十四日登岸美國領事古衛日事館多

小田初筹寿之助蒡荟國領多及海關稅務司

和衣武楷陞地方文武官商笔以催見連日宴

看宜立民委臺拿荟與各國駛爾滬領多卹許

往返轉敦誼素於二十八日仍中岑手輪挑捷

赴日本神戶橫雲籍事務拝東京候僅見隊

再由橫濱赴美空依居承陳西承沙鳥執宵

住歐美各國欽縣外窝邦承內修那車用是

蓝日上馴發信強此次赴美實信宜

中朝之邦立礙美國之覬覦雅有遠計

編音修来好以仲副

聖意寿陛之正之呉有救澤日眠理合恭摺晃陳

伏乞

皇太后

皇上聖鑒謹

奏

光緒三十年二月初十日奏

硃批知道了欽此

二月二十八日

逕啟者兹准本國外部來文囑為達知

貴親王美國書籍館會議定於散魯伊斯設立萬國書籍會、

於西本年十月十七號開會至二十二號為止此會大意係欲

聚晰各國書籍會情形並欲考究各國各經理書籍館攷閱

各國之要法美國議院書會首事人即係美國書籍館會首事

人是以該會首請政府合力請中國

政府派員前赴該書會會議中國如允派員前往該書籍館

會甚願預知所派人員若干位及係何銜名等因相應請

貴親王查照如允赴此會即希將所派員數與銜名迅速知照

是荷此泐即頌

爵祉附送洋文

名另具 二月二十一日

康格

F.C. No.

W

LEGATION OF THE UNITED STATES OF AMERICA,
PEKIN, CHINA.

April 6th. 1904.

Your Imperial Highness:-

In compliance with instructions just received from the Depart-

ment of State at Washington, I have the honor to inform Your Im-

perial Highness that the American Library Association will hold

an International Library Conference at St Louis during the week

of October 17 to 22 inclusive of the present year. The purpose

of the Conference will be to receive reports of library conditions

in the various countries represented, and to discuss certain pro-

jects connected with the management of libraries which are of in-

ternational interest and importance. The Librarian of Congress is

President of the Association and has asked the good offices of

the Department of State in endorsing and transmitting to Your

Imperial Highness' Government an invitation to be represented at

the Conference.

I am directed by the Department to extend this invitation to

the Chinese Government and to say that, should your Government

decide to send a delegation, the Association would like to receive

an early notification of the number and character of such delega-

tion

(F.O. No.   )

tion.

    I avail myself of the opportunity to renew to Your Imperial Highness the assurance of my highest consideration.

[signature]

               Envoy Extraordinary and

                     Minister Plenipotentiary of the

                        United States.

To His Imperial Highness, Prince of Ch'ing,

President of the Board Of Foreign Affairs.

          etc.   etc.   etc.

F.O. No. 688.

W

LEGATION OF THE UNITED STATES OF AMERICA,
PEKIN, CHINA.

April 6th. 1904.

Your Imperial Highness:-

In compliance with instructions just received from the Department
of State of the United States, I have the honor to inform Your
Imperial Highness that the International Congress of Military
Surgeons will be held in connection with the Universal Exposition
at St Louis from October 10 to October 15, 1904. The Congress is
to be held under the auspices of the Association of Military Surgeons of the United States, and I am directed by the Secretary of
State to extend to the Government of China on behalf of the Association an invitation to be represented at the Congress by delegates from the Chinese Army and Navy. The Association of Military Surgeons of the United States is incorporated by Act of Congress and is officially recognized by my Government, its Advisory
Board being composed of the Secretary of War, the Secretary of
the Navy, the Surgeon General of the Army, the Surgeon General
of the Navy, and the Surgeon General of the Public Health and Marine Hospital Service. I inclose two copies of a printed statement which will show the character of the Association.

My Government would learn with great pleasure of the acceptance by China of this invitation.

I

(F.O. No.   )

I avail myself of the opportunity to renew to Your Imperial Highness the assurance of my highest consideration.

Envoy Extraordinary and

Minister Plenipotentiary of the

United States.

To His Imperial Highness, Prince of Ch'ing,

President of the Board of Foreign Affairs.

清代外務部中外關係檔案史料叢編——中美關係卷 第六冊·國際會議

欽命前赴散魯伊斯賽會正監督員勳徽四員李溥　為

洽呈事據分省補用縣丞彭清平呈稱竊供事前

蒙爵憲洽調充當供事前赴美國奉准割飭在案

供事自應隨同前往以供差遣　惟　供事現因患病不

克遠行爵憲即日放洋勢難隨同前往惟有叩求

恩准咨明外務部吏部等衙門准其銷去隨赴

美國差使恭候恩准批示施行寔爲德便等語查

該供事呈稱現因患病不克赴美當差自係寔

在情形相應咨呈

外務部

右　咨　呈

貴部查照可也須至咨呈者

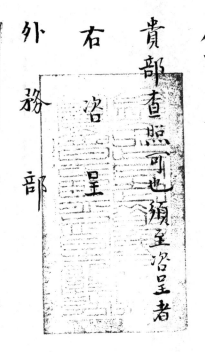

光緒叁拾年貳月　　　日

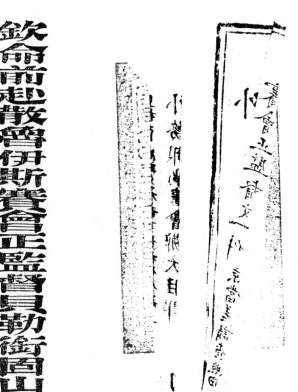

欽命前往散魯伊斯賽會正監督賞加二品銜道員吕 為

咨呈事據候選通判全森呈稱竊卑職前蒙

爵憲奏調前赴美國散魯伊斯賽會隨帶

前往奉准劄飭於正月十八日隨同爵憲由

京起程自應聽候當差以供驅使惟卑職上

年在京患病甫經痊愈滿擬隨赴美國藉資

閱歷乃行抵日本以來感受風寒觸發舊病

竊維憲恩高厚惟有竭力支持而指日登舟

深恐不習風濤病體更益加增貽悞要公實

為惶恐躊躇再四祇有叩求恩准奏明銷去

隨帶赴美差使咨明外務部吏部等衙門回

京當差恭候爵憲批准施行實為德便等

語 查該員呈稱各節委係實在情形應即

飭令回京當差 相應咨呈

貴部查照可也須至咨呈者

右 咨呈

外務部

光緒叄拾年貳月　　日

清代外務部中外關係檔案史料叢編——中美關係卷　第二册·國際會議

欽命前赴散魯爾伊斯贊會正監督員勒銜鎮山貝子溥

咨呈事本監督現有應遞

安摺二封正摺一件於三月十五日由散魯

伊斯拜發相應鈔錄奏底附帶印花咨呈

為

北

貴部代為呈遞可也須至咨呈者

右　咨呈

外　務　部

光緒叁拾年叁月　　日

奏為恭報奴才行抵散魯伊斯並擇期開會情形恭摺具陳仰祈

聖鑒事竊奴才前將行抵華盛頓城並呈遞

國書日期均經恭摺奏報在案旋於三月十二日由美京乘坐輪

車起程於十三日行抵散魯伊斯美國駐紮該處官員及總

理會務紳董登車相迎情誼殷勤僑屬該埠華商人等

奴才亦均依次接見茲美國定於三月十五日舉行開會奴才

親往致賀至中國開會日期據副監督黃開甲甲稱會場房

屋工程一律趕期蕆事副監督柯爾樂申稱海關赴會貨物

一律如數運齊江蘇廣東湖南湖北福建浙江等省官運赴

會貨物亦均陸續運到陳設奴才謹擇於三月二十日開會以重

會務而遂觀瞻伏查散魯伊斯賽會萬邦咸集品物備陳

凡足以惠工商而資考察中國地大物博而製造尚未盡振

興誠能研究精詳詢可廣開風氣奴才自應悉心經理以副

朝廷通商惠工之至意所有奴才行抵散魯伊斯並擇期開會緣由

理合恭摺具陳伏乞

皇太后

皇上聖鑒謹

奏

美國華盛頓城拜發相應抄錄

安摺二封正摺一件片一件於三月初八日由

欽命軍機營伊斯賚會正監督勒德圖山貝子溥

沿呈事本監督現有應遞　為

乙

の月廿六

奏底附帶印花洽呈

貴部代為呈遞可也須至洽呈者

右洽　　呈

外　務　部

光緒叁拾年叁月初捌　日

奏片

奏為陳報奴才行抵美京日期恭摺具陳仰祈

聖鑒事竊奴才於二月十四日由横濱口岸乘坐英公司蓋

立克輪船起程赴美業經恭摺奏報在案旋於是日開

行二十五日抵檀香山三月初三日抵舊金山美國駐

紮各該處總督等官奉其政府之命敬以

中朝敦睦

特簡宗親交際益隆欵待甚厚沿途分駐領事各員暨華商

人等奴才亦均依次接見由舊金山換坐輪車前赴美

京初八日行抵華盛頓城出使美秘古墨大臣梁誠恭

皇太后

設香案跪請

皇太后

皇上聖安並據該大臣接准美外部照會内稱定於三月

初十日往見美國總統呈遞

國書應俟禮成再行專摺奏報所有奴才行抵美京

日期謹恭摺具陳伏乞

皇太后

皇上聖鑒謹

奏

再據候選通判仝森呈稱竊職前蒙奏調赴美賽會奉

准劄飭隨同起程自應聽候當以供驅使惟上年患病

甫愈滿擬隨赴美國籍資閱歷乃行抵日本感受風寒

觸發舊病即日登舟深恐貽悞要公實為惶恐叩求奏

明銷去隨帶赴美差使咨明外務部吏部回京當差

等語　查該員呈稱沿途患病懇請給咨回京當差

係屬實在情形自應准如所請前由橫濱起程赴美恭

摺奏報業經拜發未及陳明理合補行奏陳除咨明外

務部吏部外謹附片具陳伏乞

聖鑒謹

奏

欽命前赴散會伊斯鑵會正監督員勒衙闉山貝子溥　　　　為

咨呈事本監督現有應遞

安摺二封正摺一件於三月初十日由美京

拜發相應鈔錄奏底附帶印花咨呈

貴部代為呈遞可也須至咨呈者

右咨呈　計粘單

外務部

光緒參拾年參月初十日

奏為恭報呈遞

國書日期恭摺具陳仰祈

聖鑒事竊奴才於三月初八日行抵美國華盛頓城業經

恭摺奏報在案擬出使美秩古墨大臣梁誠接

准美外部照會內稱美揔統定於三月初十日接

見是日美揔統派令副將官前來導迎並派令

外部大臣先行款待美揔統旋即接見奴才偕同

出使大臣梁誠副監督黃開甲及隨員等恭費

國書敬謹呈遞並循例謹致頌詞美揔統親目捧

領虔頌我

皇太后

奴才溥　跪

皇上

聖安奴才敬謹宣布

德音問答如儀禮成而退連日與美外部等衙門大臣及

各國駐美公使酬酢往還以崇睦誼現因散會

伊斯會期伊途奴才應即退赴會場以昭慎重一俟

行抵該處再行恭摺奏報所有奴才遞

國書日期謹恭摺具陳伏乞

皇太后

皇上

聖鑒謹

奏

清代外務部中外關係檔案史料叢編──中美關係卷 第六冊·國際會議

二 〇 月廿六

欽命前往散魯伊斯賽會正監督貝勒銜固山貝子溥

咨呈事本監督於三月初八日行抵美國華

盛頓城業經專摺奏報咨呈

貴部代為呈遞在案茲於初十日呈遞

為

國書並循例謹致頌詞由梁大臣預為代擬咨

送前來相應照錄漢文洋文各一通咨呈

貴部查照可也須至咨呈者

右　咨　呈
　　　　　　　　計漢文洋文黏單各一件

外　務　部

光緒叁拾年叁月　初十日

貴大總統本監督奉

大清國

大皇帝諭旨著將

國書親手呈遞

貴大總統本監督實深榮幸本監督行抵美境經過

各處地方均以優禮相待極為心感今蒙

貴大總統接見得以面貢謝忱近年以來

大清國深知與各國通商實為要政本監督奉

命到美係為竭力振興中美商務惟望

貴國政府推誠相助庶能日見興旺並祝

貴大總統身體康健諸事如意

貴國百姓永享太平日進富強本監督實所欣願

謹頌

逕啟者適接本國外部來文囑轉達

貴親王本年六月二十八號至七月一號在散魯伊斯賽寶會內

設一萬國學堂教法學問會係本國原有學堂會之總理人與賽

寶會內總理人合設此萬國學會寄來請中國赴此會之請帖並

所印講論此會中大意一紙囑為轉送等因、

貴國如允派員前往本國政府甚為欣悅也此沏即頌

爵祺 附洋文並請帖及所印會意一紙

名另具 三月十一

康格

逕啟者適接本國外部来文囑將請帖一紙轉送

貴國政府所請者即係請

貴政府派人赴散會伊斯會內所設之萬國修造馬路會議會定

於西本年五月十六號起至二十一號止經理該會數位人意欲

請各國著名工程師數位講論各所用集欵應用之法及用何法

造路與成路後如何歲修並欲於會場內修造各等馬路式樣俾

人閲視其修造係用最新極好之器機有工程師每日在該處講

解造馬路造法與用吧瑪油攪合砂石及煤氣油合砂石松香合

砂石各種新出造馬路之式樣並欲講解如何設法使貧苦人與

游手及犯法各等人均行作工雖此會係由民立非本國政府所

設

貴國政府如以此會為關緊要派人前往本國政府亦甚欣願茲

將寄到請帖一分函送即希

貴親王查照是荷此泐即頌

爵祺 附洋文並請帖一分

名另具三月十一日

康格

敬啟者三月初四日肅貝美字第三十號函度邀

堂釐初八日

倫貝勒抵華盛頓誠率領參隨各員及美總統所派

總管宮府大臣副將賽門赴車站迎迓以鴉靈頓大

容廬為行邸初九日賽門將總統命以電車來請

貝勒遍遊美京名勝晚間在署便飯初十日總統接

見呈遞

國書拜候各國頭等駐使總統夫人請聽樂各部院公使陪

座在署晚餐到者部院大臣上下議紳共二十六人

十一日海外部請午餐前外部福士達設茶會客數

百人履舄交錯頗極其盛旋由　誠請在可崙比亞戲

院觀劇今辰

貝勒率隨員人等乘坐專車赴散魯伊斯會場查閱

一切預備開會事宜此次

邸節駐留為日無多官紳諸人瞻望顏色無不欣歡

鼓舞引為榮幸而於我國開化之隆邦交之篤尤為

津津稱道副將賽門朝夕侍從極盡心力美總統睦

誼隆情殊可感念　誠本擬隨侍

邸駕前往會場適聞美總統將於十五日在華盛頓

行開會禮各國駐使均經東邀往觀奉

貝勒面諭屆期代為致賀毋庸隨往俟中國陳列所
告成再往行禮等因誠思連日上議院議辦新例機
局正緊亦須留心伺察隨時駁論不敢拘牽儀節致
誤事機上議院紳自接誠表理說帖之後復經福士
達諸人從中運動頗持正議將下議院所定新例屆
層挑駁大約可以轉圜矣俟有續聞當馳電飛布用慰

憲廑以上各節敬乞

代回

均安

邸堂列憲鑒察是荷專肅敬請

　　　　梁誠頓首

光緒三十年三月十二日
美字第三十一號

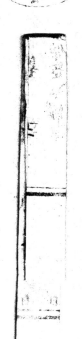

辰三月廿日

欽加太子少保銜花翎頭品頂戴二等第一寶星總稅務司赫德為

申呈事竊查美國散魯伊斯城賽會一事現據粵海

關署稅務司盧力飛詳稱前奉光緒二十九年十一

月二十八日劄開准赴美賽會正監督溥　咨稱據

戶部主事梁用弧候選道鄧廷鏗呈稱奉劄招商辦

貨赴會報關查驗放行請按名發給合例執照等語

查華商王福泰等七十五名既據該員等呈稱均係
赴會商人應俟廣業公司赴賽貨物報明海關一律
發給護照查驗放行並飭遵照美國訂定赴會章程
辦理咨請轉飭粤海關稅務司發給護照等因劄行
遵辦等因奉此本稅務司當即一面照會監督照章
發給執照七十五張一面爲鄧職員於美領事前代
爲先容旋准監督復稱赴會商人七十五名內據職
員梁用弧查悉梁宏謀等六十七名均籍赴賽僞冒
商名應即按名將照扣留以杜混冒其王福泰等八
名既係廣業公司所用赴賽商人自應按照赴美賽
會領照新章核給護照送請美領事簽名蓋印請由
督部堂轉咨　出使大臣照料登岸以符向章等因

正在酌辦間又奉

督憲訇同前因各到關嗣准美領事照稱所有赴美

之商人七十五名本領事不能照料亦不能於此項

執照上代為簽押緣此等人訪係一行之東彩承辦

一行之貨物未免令人駭異且其所備川資亦甚形

蓋澀必致竭蹶恐抵舊金山時本政府定不准其登

岸等語本稅司並聞鄧職員乘此賽會機緣有心將

此若許無用之人送赴美國且風聞該職員現時尚

不前往須俟下月方克起程云 云詳請查悉等因前

來總稅務司 覆核前情除飭該稅務司遵將王福泰

等八名請由監督核給執照並照章送請美領事簽

名蓋印給領外其餘梁宏謀等六十七名之偽商自

應一併扣除等因去訖所有冒名擬行赴美各緣由

理合備文申請

貴部鑒查並希轉洽

赴美賽會正監督知悉可也須至申呈者

右　申　呈

欽命全權大臣便宜行事軍機大臣總理務部事務顧慶親王

光緒參拾年參月拾玖日

清代外務部中外關係檔案史料叢編——中美關係卷 第六冊·國際會議

權算司

呈為咨行事光緒三十年三月二十日准總稅務司申稱竊查

美國散魯伊斯城賽會一事現據粵海關署稅務司盧力飛

詳稱前奉光緒二十九年十一月二十八日劄開准赴美賽會正

監督薄 咨稱據戶部主事梁用張候選道鄧廷鏗呈稱

奉劄招商辦貨赴會報關查驗放行請按名發給合例執

照等語查華商王福泰等七十五名呈據該員等呈稱均

係赴會商人應俟廣業公司赴賽貨物報明海關一律

發給護照查驗放行並飭遵照美國訂定赴會章程辦

理咨請轉飭粵海關稅務司發給護照等因劄行遵辦

等因奉此本稅務司當即一面照會監督照章發給執照

七十五張一面為鄧職員於美領事前代為先容旋准監督

復稱赴會商人七十五名內據職員梁用弧查悉梁宏謀

等六十七名均藉赴賽偽冒商名應即按名將照扣留

以杜混冒其王福泰等八名既係廣業公司所用赴賽商人

自應按照赴美賽會領照新章核給護照送請美領

事簽名蓋印請由督部堂轉咨出使大臣照料登岸以符

向章等因正在酌辦間又奉督憲箚開各到關嗣准

美領事照稱所有赴美之商人七十五名本領事不能照料

亦不能於此項執照上代為簽緣此等人訪係一行之東

粵承辦一行之仇貨物未免令人駭異且其所備川資亦甚

形羞澀必致竭蹶恐抵舊金山時本政府定不准其登岸

等語本稅司並聞鄧職員乘此賽會機緣有心將此若

許無用之人送赴美國且風聞該職員現時尚不前往須候

下月方可起程等因總稅務司覆核前情除飭該稅務

司遵將王福泰等八名請由監督核給執照並照章送請

美領事簽名蓋印給領外其餘梁宏謀等六十七名之偽

美領事簽名蓋印給領外其餘梁宏謀等六十七名之偽

商自應一併扣除等因申請　轉　咨前來相應咨行

貴監督查照可也須至咨者

美國賽會正監督

光緒三十年三月

外務部

大

五月初六

谘呈

谘呈事竊照前據湖南派辦美國散魯伊斯城

賽會商董稟稱現已辦齊商品請附入

兩江督部堂所派委員代為照料運赴美國賽

會並派商董朱瑞琛等四人同往等情業經分

別咨呈在案茲查朱瑞琛因病未能赴會所有

湖南賽會貨物應派商董陳琪前往禀承

正監督商同兩江委員照章陳設賽會以資攷

鏡除發給華洋文護照飭江海關道轉照駐滬

美領事簽名並分別咨行外相應咨呈為此咨請

外務部查照照會美使望切施行須至咨呈者

右咨呈

外務部

二十七　　日

清代外務部中外關係檔案史料叢編——中美關係卷 第六冊·國際會議

外務部 收 四月廿四

咨呈

頭品頂戴兵部尚書暑理兩廣總督岑 為

咨呈事案照承准

前總理衙門咨行出使美日秘國楊大臣與美國使

署律師科士達詳酌擬定華人往美漢洋文護照程

式咨粵照辦嗣後華人往美一體仿照所擬程式飭

由粵海關發給等因茲有商民梁焯材赴轅請照前

往美國散魯伊斯城賽會稟由粵海關驗填護照並

無假冒情弊且有殷實舖保具結存案核與章程相

符准粵海關咨請核咨前來除咨復并照章咨行

出使美日秘國大臣駐美金山總領事查照辦理外

擬合咨呈為此合咨

貴部謹請查照備案施行須至咨呈者

右　咨　呈

外　務　部

光緒三十年　　　　　　初八　　日

逕啟者接奉本國外部來函內稱茲有美國牙醫會與

各國牙醫會之人於瑞魯伊斯設立萬國第四次牙醫會自

西歷本年八月二十九號開會至九月三號為止本國政府

以各牙醫會欲盡心成全此會凡有牙醫之國自應請其國

牙醫會中之人屆期前來赴會囑為代請中國並送到牙醫

會單一本等因相應將該會單備函附送即希

貴親王查一照請派人員屆期前往赴會是盼此布即頌

爵祺 附送洋文並會單一本

名另具四月十三日

逕啟者茲接本國外部來函云美國監製牛乳食物等公會

在敝魯伊斯設五萬國精製飲食會以為衛生之助定於

西本年九月二十六號開會至十月一號為止即有會單

一紙閱之即可悉會中大概情形本國政府想此會於

中國係有攸關故囑將該會印送之單轉送

貴國屆期即請派員前往等因相應將所印會單備函

附送即希

貴親王查照派員辦理是盼此布即頌

爵祺 附送洋文並會單一件

名另其 四月十三日

康格

欽差出使美秘古墨國大臣梁　為

咨呈事竊照本大臣於光緒三十年四月十六日承准

貴部咨開光緒三十年二月二十日

內廷口傳現在恭繪

皇太后聖容告成交外務部祗領飭總稅司敬謹寄至美國即由赴賽會

正監督恭迎至散魯伊斯會場俾共瞻仰俟該監督觀會事畢應令

出使美國大臣轉達總統敬謹賷送美國國家等因除照會美康使

轉達美政府外相應咨行貴大臣欽遵等因承准此查本大臣前承准

貴部電咨

皇太后聖容已派沈道能虎於十九日由美國協隆洋行船名西比利亞恭奉

六月十一

北

赴美侯會畢即由貴大臣轉達總統齎送美國國家希遵照外務部

宥等因當經遵照咨呈

赴會正監督固山貝子溥並照會美外部轉美政府在案旋據金山

總領事鍾守寶稟稱四月十三日午後兩點鐘

皇太后聖容安抵該華經偕同隨員繕譯等遵札敬謹照料守衛仍由委員

沈道護送前往散魯伊斯等語茲承前因除侯會事完畢欽遵轉達

總統敬謹齎送美國國家再行

奏咨外理合備文聲覆為此咨呈

貴部謹請察照須至咨呈者

右　咨呈

外務部

光緒　　　　　　　年拾捌月　　　　　　日

知大意如允派員前往本國政府殊為欣悦等語除咨行

中國水陸各軍醫官若干位前往赴會兹將英文送閱即

萬國醫館會奉外部大臣囑代本國醫館會請貴國特派

西本年十月十號至十五號在散魯伊斯賽寶會內設一

外務部咨開光緒三十年二月二十一日准美康使函稱

清詳稱竊查前蒙憲札二月二十八日准

咨呈事據津海關道唐紹儀會同軍醫學堂候補道徐華

咨

臨

為

南洋大臣外相應將該使送來醫館會英文原件咨行查

照酌量辦理並聲復本部可也等因准此應飭津海關道

會同徐道華清督同屆守永秋妥議具復以憑核咨除分

行外合將原件札發札到該道即便查照辦理計原件仍

繳等因蒙此當經職道紹儀會同職道華清督同屆守永

秋查得北洋籌辦防疫需員較多現在醫學堂醫官及畢

業各生尚在不敷分派又軍醫學堂醫官除各軍調用外

在堂醫官無多尚須分班教授該堂各學生寔難派往美

國赴會所有遵飭查明緣由理合將奉發英文一件具文

詳送查核歸檔並請轉咨

外務部查照實為公便等情到本大臣據此查北洋醫學

堂醫官因籌辦防疫事關緊要軍醫各員亦因各軍調用

敷分派委難派往美國赴

貴部言詢察照須至咨呈者

會

右

外務部

呈

光緒　　　　　　日

奉批

閱呈 胃二十六日

奏為代進出使美國賽会正監督摺件仰祈

聖鑒事竊臣部接准前赴散魯伊斯賽会正監督

貝勒銜固山貝子溥倫本年三月初八日拜發

奏摺一封

安摺二摺又三月初十日拜發

奏摺一封

安摺二摺謹將原件恭呈

御覽哀咨代進賽会正監督摺件緣由理合恭摺具

陳伏乞

皇太后

皇上聖鑒謹

奏

具奏代進美國賽会正監督奏報抵美日期呈進國書金森詩偏多摺

片由

和

欽命前總辦散學伊斯饗會正監督員勒衛區口貝字溥

咨呈事准

貴部咨稱光緒三十年二月二十一日准美康使

函稱准本國外部來文散魯伊斯議設萬國

為

書籍會於西本年十月十七號開會至二十二號

為止此會大意係欲調查各國書籍會情形並

考究各國各經理書籍館攸關各國之要法是

以該會請中國派員前赴該書會會議中國

如允派員赴會希將所派員數與銜名迅速

知照等語相應咨行貴正監督查照會同梁

大臣就駐美使館各員內遴派數員俟萬國

書籍會開會時屆期赴會並將派出各員銜

各先復本部以便知照該使等語 查散魯伊

斯議設萬國書籍會美康使函請中國派員前

往赴會茲准

貴部咨行本監督會同出使美國大臣就駐美

使館內遴派人員屆期赴會查駐美使館繙

譯官蘇銳釗熟悉情形堪以派往赴會商諸

出使美國大臣意見相同應即會同派令該

員前往赴會除釗飭該員遵照外相應咨覆

貴部查照可也須至咨呈者

右　咨　呈

外　務　部

光緒叁拾年肆月　　弐拾柒月

清代外務部中外關係檔案史料叢編——中美關係卷　第六冊·國際會議

欽差出使美秘古墨國大臣梁　為

咨呈事竊照光緒三十年四月三十日承准

貴部咨開光緒三十年三月十一日准美康使函稱接本國外部文稱

本年六月二十八號至七月一號在散魯伊斯賽會內設一萬國學堂

教法學問會寄來請中國赴會帖一分並所印講論此會中大意一紙

屬為轉送等因相應將原送請帖暨所印講論一紙咨行查照遴派人

員屆期往赴該會並將派出該員銜名聲復本部以憑轉復康使等

因附洋文二件承准此查有駐紐約正領事官夏偕復究心教育堪以

派赴萬國教育會除札飭外理合將該員銜名備文聲復請由

貴部轉復康使爲此咨呈

貴部謹請詧照須至咨呈者

右　咨　呈

外　務　部

光緒　　　年　　月

　　　　　　叁拾　　　　　　日

欽命前赴散魯伊斯賽會正監督員勒衡图山貝子溥　為

　咨呈事　本監督會同出使美國梁大臣泰迴

皇太后聖容抵散魯伊斯會場敬謹供奉禮成拜發

安摺二封正摺一封由散魯伊斯交遞並鈔錄摺

底附送印花咨呈

貴部代為呈遞可也須至咨呈者

右　咨　呈　計鈔原奏一件印花一封

外　務　部

光緒参拾年肆月参拾日

清代外務部中外關係檔案史料叢編──中美關係卷 第六冊·國際會議

奏 底

奏為恭迎

皇
太后聖容行抵散魯伊斯供奉禮成恭摺具陳仰祈

聖鑒事竊奴才前准外務部咨稱光緒三十年二月

廿一日

內廷口傳現在恭繪

皇
太后聖容告成交外務部祇領飭總稅務司敬謹寄

美即由賽會正監督恭迎至散魯伊斯會場俾

共瞻仰候該監督觀會事畢應令出使美國大

臣轉達總統敬謹賚送美國國家等因除照會

美康使轉達美國政府外相應咨行欽遵又准

電開恭繪

奴才溥 跪

皇
太后聖容告成由總稅務司謹寄會場希即預備慶

所敬謹供奉又准電開

皇
太后聖容已派沈道能虎於三月十九日搭坐美國

協隆洋行西比利亞輪船由滬起程恭齎赴美

各等語奴才伏查恭繪

皇
太后聖容告成由外務部飭總稅務司敬謹齎送赴

美並派令前直隸通永道沈能虎由上海恭齎

一同赴美疊經咨引出使美國大臣梁誠遵照

轉達美國政府暨札飭金山總領事恭候抵埠

敬謹照料以昭慎重並由出使大臣梁誠接准

外務部各電咨先後抄送奴才遵照前來四月

十五日據金山總領事電稟

皇太后聖容安抵金山當經　奴才電咨外務部在案並

飭副監督黃開甲用柯爾樂電致鐵路公司選備

輪車恭送至散魯伊斯並照會會務總辦福蘭

西司悉心照料俾臻妥洽　奴才会同出使美國

大臣梁誠謹詣恭迎於二十九日平安引抵会場

於三十日敬謹恭奉禮成緊維我

皇太后聖德淵涵

宸懷愉暢

天心眷佑

壽考無艱地肺交通昇平有慶繪摹

日月悅傳

吁嘩於寫真瞻就

雲天俱觀

容光之必照難帝諭皇煌刻畫曾垂諸金石而堯眉

舜目觀瞻未託於瀛壖今當美國百年開會之

期恭值

聖容萬里遙頒之日

龍光載御於前警蹕之聲象譯臚歡共獻昇平之頌

合覲嘗四方以觀禮會衣冠萬國而襄儀如才

壽恭逢

盛典慶幸莫名欽

至德之光昭中外咸徵夫視福攄

徽音之巍煥追邇昏賴以蒙麻陳俟會務藏事應由

出使美國大臣梁誠轉達總統敬謹賫送美國

國家外所有奴才祗遵恭迎供奉禮成緣由謹

會同出使美國大臣梁誠合詞具陳伏乞

奏

皇上聖鑒謹

皇太后

欽差出使美秘古墨國大臣梁　為

咨呈事竊照光緒三十年四月三十日承准

貴部咨開光緒三十年三月十一日准美康使函稱接本國外部文稱本年五月十六

號起至二十一號止請貴政府派人預赴魯伊斯會內所設之萬國修造馬路會茲

將寄到請帖一分函送等因相應將原送洋文並請帖一分咨行貴大臣查照遴派

駐美使館人員屆期往赴該會並將派出該員銜名聲復本部以便轉復康使等

因承准此查西歷五月十六號至二十一號係中歷四月初二日至初七日現在會期已過

似應毋庸派員前往以昭核實而節糜費理合備文聲復為此咨呈

貴部謹請察核備案須至咨呈者

右　　咨呈

外務部

光緒　　　　初壹　　　日

五月初一

臣傅倫　　　　期

○ 柳示外務部　　　　五月初一日

奴才傅倫跪

奏為恭摺呈覽

國書日期恭摺具陳仰祈

聖鑒事竊奴才於三月初八日行抵美國華盛頓城業

經恭摺報委查夫業接生使臣墨國大民梁

誠拔派美外部此会内稱美總統定於三月而

十日接見是日美總統派令副將官前來導迎

并派令外部大臣先行款待美總統挂印接見

奴才偕同出使大臣梁誠副監督黃開甲及隨員

等恭齎

國書敬禮呈遞並循例禮致頌祝美總統祝寸推

欽遵欽我

皇太后

皇上聖躬萬福敬禮宣希

德音問答如儀稽陛而迟連日其美外部尚衙門大

臣及各國駐美公使詢知郅治現進以崇睦誼現因

敬魯伊斯會期伊迟期應行退址會屬心照慎

重一俟行抵後再行恭摺奏報臣等如期奎迟

皇上聖躬萬福敬禮宣希

德音問答如儀稽陛而迟連日其美外部尚衙門大

臣及各國駐美公使詢知郅治現進以崇睦誼現因

敬魯伊斯會期伊迟期應行退址會屬心照慎

重一俟行抵後再行恭摺奏報臣等如期奎迟

國書日期謹恭摺具陳伏乞

皇太后

皇上聖鑒謹

奏

光緒三十年五月初一日本

硃批知道了欽此

三月廿日

敬啟者四月初六日肅布美字第三十四號函度邀

臺鑒誠於初十日前往散魯伊斯會場以華商賽會陳列

貨品等事謁商

倫員子十五日隨往紐約赴美國亞洲會等處之請

紐約地方官如府尹馬克列倫等紳士如狄彪等富

商如古盧等莫不殷勤款接敬禮有加員束相邀者

凡數十處適接金山總領事電稟沈道恭奉

皇太后聖容由金起程不日可到　誠即隨

聖容奉入廳事當中懸掛時已子夜中外男女翹首瞻仰皆

率夫役數十名經歷五時之久敬將

蘭息士及各總辦執事人等均具禮服隨同　誠等督

置借用會場鐵軌三十日直送至畫院門首其時佛

聖容之所二十九日傍晚專車行抵散魯伊斯先經　誠等布

為恭奉

妥會場總理佛蘭息士等擇定美國國家畫院正廳

倫貝子馳回會場一面訂定專車前往迎迓一面商

以幸得瞻就

雲日為希有之遭逢此當經

倫貝子挈列 誠衡恭摺奏報並鈔達

冰案

倫貝子翌日赴紐約句留一日華商恭請筵宴五月

初三日乘坐法公司船前往法國哈富富海口取道回

華誠經電達 慕韓星使轉達法國外部照料一切

兵此次

倫貝子以

天潢貴胄奉使殊方雄節經臨期程怱促乃所至之處華洋
人等歡呼迎接其趨承恐後之狀愛慕依戀之誠實
為各國宗藩遊歷此邦所未曾有蓋自前年
振貝子節臨以後至今日乃復見其盛自今伊始美
國上流人士益知我國之日進文明而華人之不可
易侮論者謂王公大臣時歷外邦曲示聯絡於國際
上大有裨益誠至言也四月二十八日祇奉

堂函以前呈節畧第七條檀飛華工另訂章程應改為

飛島開禁第十條華人犯罪審實撥出為有流弊等

因具見

邱堂列憲子惠僑民詳審慎莫名欽佩前稿寄後誠亦

曾再四商榷將原稿大加刪改有較為周密者有全

行刪去者有改就圓融者有益加切實者畧擬約稿

為十一款前開之第七款年數人數一語已經刪去

惟逕言開禁檀島或可商量飛島恐難辦到蓋檀島

紳民志在地利亟盼華工入口代為關治飛島紳民

意圖自立深忌華人闌入礙彼利權內情既已迥殊

方針所以大異也第十條原礙美國主權巻查光緒

二十四年議辦交犯條約案內曾有此款美外部未

經允議連年金檀等處募民猖獗枉殺良善許告官

長非設法籍制不可過息故不得已姑為是說識逆

計美國政府未必允行業已全條刪去此外加增數

條如美國設立限禁章程亦許中國照樣設立美國

行註冊例亦許中國仿行以示抵制約文如有疑義

禁法如有不合均交和蘭公斷衙門判斷以杜偏執

並聲明非華工者不在禁限之列禁華工者祇在美

國本境一則實行原禁之意一則預開檀飛之門也

約稿業經擬就日內繕正漢洋兩文即當寄呈

鈞部核奪以上各節統希

代回

邸堂列憲是荷專肅敬請

台安諸惟

朗照

　　　　　　　　　梁誠頓首　光緒三十年五月初四日

　　　　　　　　　　　　　　美字第三十五號

敬再啟者粵漢鐵路近來辦法及美外部復文允認

獨自有權辦理美公司交涉事件各節經於美字第

三十四號函詳陳一切並將往來照會漢洋文一併

鈔達在案祗奉

巧電查詢各節誠適在紐約迓晤美公司總理惠第爾

商將此董二員撤退並將此人帶士迓窩路德二名

所佔八百股收回以符原約再四磋磨幸得照辦經

於哿電肅陳

鈞聽現在尚有提取小票一事美公司堅執合同並無

別項辦法祇須督辦將工程估價批准便可隨時提

取　查孫宮保以為必須先行稟准督辦按次批明

數目始得提取與誠所見亦正相同昨已專函誠公

司迅速遵照議定提票格式每次取票將此格式呈

由督辦簽名交公司會簽然後作為憑單持向受託

公司取票斷不容其推託致滋流弊福士達福開森

亦持是說或可竭力辦到此後情形若何再當續陳誠

日前親往美公司查閱股票名冊經已照錄寄交

查孫宮保查閱茲特另錄一分併譯漢文附呈

台安

代回為荷再請

鈞覽即希

　　　　　梁誠文頓首　光緒三十年五月初四日
　　　　　　　　　　　美字文第三十五號

附漢洋文股票名單各一紙

美國合興公司股票名單

List of Stockholds as of November 9, 1903.

Names.	Addresses.	
C. A. Whittier,	320 Broadway, N. Y.	400
F. W. Whitridge,	59 Wall St., N. Y.	15
Jacob H. Schiff,	52 William St., N. Y.	50
August Belmont,	23 Nassau St., N. Y.	40
Thos. W. Joyce,	23 Wall St., N. Y.	40
A. W. Bash,	Seattle, Washington	20
Wm. A. Read,	16 Nassau St., N. Y.	40
Chauncey M. Depew,	Grand Central Station, N. Y.	50
Frederic P. Olcott,	54 Wall St., N. Y.	40
Jas. N. Jarvie,	Old Slip & Water St., N. Y.	35
John R. Hegeman,	I Madison Ave., N. Y.	40
Antony N. Brady,	54 Wall St., N. Y.	40
Edward J. Berwind,	1 Broadway, N. Y.	40
A. M. Townsend,	C/o Hongkong & Shanghai Banking Corporation, New York	20
Hugh J. Grant,	54 Wall St., N. Y.	40
John P. Branch,	Richmond, Va.	40
Fearon, Daniel & Co.,	90 Wall St., N. Y.	20
Jul. A.Stursberg,	80 Leonard St., N. Y.	40
Levi P. Morton,	C/o Morton Trust Co., N. Y.	50
Thos. F. Ryan,	32 Nassau St., N. Y.	40
Geo. P. Wetmore,	U. S. Senator, Washington, D. C.	100
Wm. Barclay Parsons,	320 Broadway, N. Y.	425
Luther Kountze,	120 Broadway, N. Y.	150
John Crosby Brown,	C/o Brown Bros., Wall Street, N.Y.	40
Clementine Bash,	Seattle, Washington	150
Arthur Coppell,	52 William St., N. Y.	2
J. Pierpont Morgan,	23 Wall St., N. Y.	628
Southern Trust Co.,	59 Wall St., N. Y.	40
Emery Bros.,	5 East 68th St., N. Y.	110
Edw. H. Litchfield,	59 Wall St., N. Y.	10
Thos. H. Hubbard,	25 Broad St., N. Y.	20

List of Stockholds.--Continued.

Names.	Addresses.	
Albert Thys,	48 Rue de Namur, Brussels, Belgium,	400
J. Devolder,	48 Rue de Namur, Brussels, Belgium,	400
Pierre Mali,	83 & 85 Worth St., N. Y...........	401
Shewan,Tomes & Co.,	16 Beaver St., N. Y..............	20
La Banque de Paris et de Pays Bas,	Paris, France....................	206
Societé Asiatique,	Brussels, Belgium...............	1794
Willis E. Gray,	12A Szechuen Road, Shanghai, China.	4
	Total......................	6000

鈔件

照譯美國合興公司股票名單 西一千九百三年十一月九日冊載

西、愛惠弟爾　以下紐約　四百股

愛扶荅必汝輝特立進　十五股

這碻愛進施扶　五十股

滇格斯提俾路芒　四十股

所士荅必汝在士　四十股

愛荅必汝、巴時　華盛頓省鐵路　二十股

威林、愛、立德　以下紐約　四十股

上議紳爽謝唵狄彪、　五十股

扶來德立玊、阿路葛、　四十股

詹士噉、查維　三十五股

專亞赫進門　四十股

安端尼、噉布拉地　四十股

義德華、這伯雲　四十股

匯豐銀行總辦愛唵湯遜、　二十股

好、這、格蘭德　四十股

專玊布蘭進　勿真尼省立進門　四十股

斐倫丹尼路公司　以下紐約　二十股

珠路愛士特堡　四十股

前美國副總統立維玊摩頓　五十股

所士愛扶來安　四十股

佐治玊維摩爾　美京華盛頓　一百股

威林巴克禮柏森士　以下紐約　四百二十五股

盧昔、肯士　一百五十股

名稱	地	股數
專、克羅士北布朗		四十股
克列門泰巴時	華盛頓省舍路	一百五十股
亞昔、哥蒲路	以下紐約	二股
遠、壬爾磐、摩根		六百二十八股
南托辣斯公司		四十股
奮黙利兄弟		一百十股
義德華、愛進李次飛路		十股
所士愛進赫伯		二十股
巴收回 阿路伯、帶士、	比利時都城	四百股
巴收回 遠、狄窩路德	比利時都城	四百股
正愛爾馬利	紐約	四百一股
施萬通士公司	紐約	二十股

名稱	地	股數
法蘭西及和蘭銀行	法蘭西都城	二百六股
亞細亞會社	比利時都城	一千七百九十四股
威利士、衣、葛利	中國上海	四股

統共六千股

逕啟者適接本國外部來函內稱西本年九月初八日即中七

月二十九日在華盛頓設立第八次萬國綜核地理會寄來

請帖一分囑代該會辦轉送如中國派員赴會該會定

深欣慰等因此會雖非本國政府管理亦甚望中國派往

人員茲將所寄請帖與所印會章附送

貴親王查照想經閱畢該會中情形自必能悉也特此泐

布即頌

爵祺附送洋文並請帖會單各件

名另具　五月初八日

F.C. No.673.

H.

LEGATION OF THE UNITED STATES OF AMERICA,

PEKIN, CHINA.

June 20th 1904.

Your Imperial Highness:

I have the honor to state that I am in receipt of a communication from the Department of State enclosing an invitation to the Minister of Foreign Affairs of China, inviting the Government of China to be represented by one or more delegates at the eighth International Geographic Congress, which is to convene in the city of Washington on September 8, 1904. I am instructed to transmit this invitation on behalf of the Congress, and to state that the management would be greatly pleased if China would send representatives to this convention.

Although this Congress will not be under the auspices or patronage of the Government of the United States, nevertheless I am quite sure that my government would be verymuch gratified if China should find it of advantage to accept the invitation.

I have the honor to enclose, along with the written invitation, a printed announcement explaining the general nature of the Congress, which has also been sent to me for transmission to Your Imperial Highness. I avail myself of the opportunity to renew to Your Imperial Highness the assurance of my highest consideration.

Envoy Extraordinary and
Minister Plenipotentiary
of the United States.

To His Imperial Highness, Prince of Ch'ing,
President of the Board of Foreign Affairs.

Washington, April 30, 1904.

His Excellency
  The Minister for Foreign Affairs of China.

Excellency:

The Committee of Arrangements of the Eighth International Geographic Congress, in behalf of the Congress, has the honor, through Your Excellency, to extend to the Government of China a cordial invitation to be represented by one or more delegates at the Eighth International Geographic Congress which is to convene at the City of Washington on September 8, 1904.

The enclosed preliminary announcement will acquaint Your Excellency with the arrangements which have been made for the entertainment of the gentlemen who may attend the Congress and with the subjects to be discussed by it.

In the sincere hope that some, at least, of these subjects are of such interest to His Majesty's Government as will induce its acceptance of the invitation, we beg to assure Your Excellency of the distinguished consideration with which we are,

Your most obedient servant,

W J McGee
Chairman.

Attest:
J H McCormick
Secretary.

大清國外務部大臣鈞鑒

敬啟者於一千九百零四年九月在華盛頓

設立第八次萬國經緯地理會茲由舉

荷本會事宜之會員代表本會懇求

貴大臣轉請

貴國政府簡派一員或數員前赴本會

為此附呈會章兩冊備載擬待赴會

入員之辦法及會中擬議之兄事甚望

擬議之事或有足以引動

貴政府之靈俾以俯允順請也

　　　　會荷馬箕謹啟 一千九百零四
　　　　　　　　　　年四月廿鄉
　　　　　　　　　　自華盛頓發

PRELIMINARY ANNOUNCEMENT

Eighth International Geographic Congress
Washington, 1904

HUBBARD MEMORIAL HALL
Washington, D. C., U. S. A.
January, 1904

THE Executive Committee of the Seventh International Geographic Congress held in Berlin in 1899 having voted to convoke its next session in Washington, the National Geographic Society, as the organization responsible for the management of the sessions in the United States, will welcome the Eighth Congress and its friends to the National Capital of the United States in September, 1904.

Geographers and promoters of geography throughout the World, especially members of Geographic Societies and cognate institutions of scientific character, are cordially invited to assemble in Washington, D. C., on September 8th, 1904, for the first international meeting of geographers in the Western Hemisphere.

On the invitation of the National Geographic Society, the following Societies join in welcoming the Congress and undertake to co-operate toward its success, especially in so far as sessions to be held in their respective cities are concerned :

The American Geographical Society   The Geographical Society of Philadelphia
The Geographic Society of Baltimore   The Appalachian Mountain Club
The Geographic Society of Chicago   The Geographical Society of the Pacific
The Geographical Society of California   The Sierra Club
The Mazamas   The American Alpine Club
The Peary Arctic Club   The Harvard Travellers Club

Sessions — The Congress will convene in Washington on Thursday, September 8th, in the new home of the National Geographic Society, and will hold sessions on the 9th and 10th, the latter under the auspices of the Geographic Society of Baltimore. Leaving Washington on the 12th, the Members, Associates, and Guests of the Congress will be entertained during that day by the Geographical Society of Philadelphia, and on the 13th, 14th and 15th by the American Geographical Society in New York, where scientific sessions will be held ; on the 16th they will have the opportunity of visiting Niagara Falls (en route westward by special train), and on the 17th will be entertained by the Geographic Society of Chicago ; and on Monday and Tuesday, September 19th and 20th, they will be invited to participate in the International Congress of Arts and Science connected with the World's Fair in St. Louis. Arrangements will be made here for visiting exhibits of geographic interest. In case any considerable number of Members and Associates so desire, a Far-West excursion will be provided from St. Louis to the City of Mexico, thence to Santa-Fe, thence to the Grand Canyon of the Colorado, and on to San Francisco and the Golden Gate, where the western Geographic **Excursions** Societies will extend special hospitality; afterward returning by any preferred route through the Rocky Mountains and the interior plains to the eastern ports.

If the membership and finances warrant, the foreign delegates will be made guests of the Congress from Washington to St. Louis, via Baltimore, Philadelphia, New York, Niagara Falls and Chicago. On the Far-West excursion special terms will be secured, reducing the aggregate cost of transportation with sleeping-car accommodations and meals materially below the customary rates. It may be necessary to limit the number of persons on the Far-West excursion. It is planned also to secure special rates for transportation of foreign Members from one or more European ports to New York, provided requisite information as to the convenience and pleasure of such Members be obtained in time. Final information on these points will be given in the Preliminary Program of June, 1904.

The subjects for treatment and discussion in the Congress may be classified as follows:

1. Physical Geography, including Geomorphology, Meteorology, Hydrology, etc.
2. Mathematical Geography, including Geodesy and Geophysics.
3. Biogeography, including Botany and Zoology in their geographic aspects.
4. Anthropogeography, including Ethnology.
5. Descriptive Geography, including Exploration and Surveys.
6. Geographic Technology, including Cartography, Bibliography, etc.
7. Commercial and Industrial Geography.
8. History of Geography.
9. Geographic Education.

A special opportunity will be afforded for the discussion of methods of surveying and map-making, and for the comparison of these methods as pursued in other countries with the work of the Federal and State Surveys maintained in this country.

Membership Members of the Congress will be entitled to participate in all sessions and excursions, and to attend all social meetings in honor of the Congress; they will also (whether in attendance or not) receive the publications of the Congress, including the daily Program and the final Compte Rendu, or volume of proceedings. Membership may be acquired by members of Geographic and cognate Societies on payment of $5 (25 francs, one pound, or 20 marks) to the Committee of Arrangements. Persons not members of such Societies may acquire membership by a similar payment and election by the Presidency. Ladies and minors accompanying members may be registered as Associates on payment of $2.50 (12½ francs, or 10 shillings, or 10 marks); they shall enjoy all privileges of Members except the rights of voting and of receiving publications.

Geographers and their friends desirous of attending the Congress or receiving its publications are requested to signify their intention at the earliest practicable date in order that subsequent announcements may be sent them without delay, and that requisite arrangements for transportation may be effected. On receipt of subscriptions, Members' and Associates' tickets will be mailed to the subscribers. The privileges of the Congress, including the excursions and the social gatherings, can be extended only to holders of tickets.

Societies and Delegates It is earnestly hoped that the Congress of 1904 may be an assemblage of Geographic and cognate Institutions no less than of individual Geographers; and to this end a special invitation is extended to such organizations to participate in the Congress through Delegates on the basis of one for each one hundred members up to a maximum of ten. No charge will be made for the registration of Institutions, though the Delegates will be expected to subscribe as Members; and in order that the list of affiliated Institutions (to be issued in a later announcement) may be worthy of full confidence, the Committee of Arrangements reserve the right to withhold the name of any Institution pending action by the Presidency. The publications of the Congress will be sent free to all Institutions registered. It is especially desired that the Geographic Societies of the Western Hemisphere may utilize the opportunity afforded by this Congress for establishing closer relations with those of the Old World, and to facilitate this, Spanish will be recognized as one of the languages of the Congress, with French, English, German, and Italian, in accordance with previous usage; and communications before the Congress may be written in any one (or more) of these languages.

Institutions not strictly Geographic in character, Libraries, Universities, Academies of Science, and Scientific Societies are especially invited to subscribe as members in order to receive the publications of the Congress as issued.

Members and Delegates desirous of presenting communications before the Congress, or wishing to propose subjects for discussion, are requested to signify their wishes at the earliest practicable date in order that the titles or subjects may be incorporated in a Preliminary Program to be issued in June, 1904. The time required for presenting communications should be stated, otherwise twelve minutes will be allotted. It is anticipated that not more than twenty minutes can be allotted for any communication unless the Presidency decide to extend the time by reason of the general interest or importance of the subject. The Presidency with the complete Organization of the Congress (including Delegates) will be announced in the Preliminary Program of June, 1904. **Communications**

All papers or abstracts designed for presentation before the Congress, and all **Program** proposals and applications affecting the Congress, will be submitted to a Program Committee who shall decide whether the same are appropriate for incorporation in the announcements, though the decisions of this Committee shall be subject to revision by the Presidency after the Congress convenes.

Any proposal affecting the organization of the Congress or the program for the Washington session must be received in writing not later than May 1, 1904. Communications designed to be printed in connection with the Congress must be received not later than June 1, and any abstracts of communications (not exceeding 300 words in length) designed for printing in the General Program to be published at the beginning of the Congress must be received not later than August 1, 1904. Daily Programs will be issued during the sesions.

All correspondence relating to the Congress and all remittances should be addressed—

THE EIGHTH INTERNATIONAL GEOGRAPHIC CONGRESS,

Hubbard Memorial Hall,

Washington, D. C., U. S. A.

COMMITTEE OF ARRANGEMENTS

W J McGEE, National Geographic Society, *Chairman*.
HENRY G. BRYANT, Geographical Society of Philadelphia.
GEORGE B. SHATTOCK, Geographic Society of Baltimore.
A. LAWRENCE ROTCH, Appalachian Mountain Club, Boston.
ZONIA BABER, Geographical Society of Chicago.
GEORGE DAVIDSON, Geographical Society of the Pacific, San Francisco.
FREDERICK W. D'EVELYN, Geographical Society of California, San Francisco.
JOHN MUIR, Sierra Club, San Francisco.
RODNEY L. GLISAN, Mazamas, Portland.
ANGELO HEILPRIN, American Alpine Club.
HERBERT L. BRIDGMAN, Peary Arctic Club.
WILLIAM MORRIS DAVIS, Harvard Travellers Club.
J. H. McCORMICK,
Secretary.

FINANCE COMMITTEE

JOHN JOY EDSON, *Chairman*.　　DAVID T. DAY,　　CHARLES J. BELL,
President Washington Loan and　United States Geological Survey.　President American Security
Trust Company.　　　　　　　　　　　　　　　　and Trust Company.

第八次萬國綜核地理會章程

本會於二千合九十九年在柏林舉行第七次會議當即議定第八次會應

在華盛頓舉行本國地理有承辦此次會務之責為此恭請本會友於一

千九百零四年九月光臨美都

本會特請天下之地理專家弁各地理會人員於二千九百零四年九月八號

齋集華盛頓以便舉行西半球地理家之首次會議茲已恭請下列各會幣

襄此舉以收眾幫易舉之效

　　　　計開

美國地理會　　　　　　　費拉戴樂斐亞地理會

保樂提卯地理會　　　　　阿帕拉其恩測山會

其略勾地理會　　　　　　太平洋地理會

喀利佛呢亞地理會　　　　山嶺會

馬仔馬斯會　　　　　　　美國高山會

兩極會　　　　　　　　　哈爾瓦爾得游歷會

九月

初八日開會

初九日本會議事

初十日全前

十二日出華盛頓各會員及赴會各員同赴費拉蓋爾斐亞之宴請并會議

十三日赴紐約地理會之宴請并會議

十四日同前

十五日同前

十六日乘專車西行同觀呢阿嘎拉瀑布

十七日赴其喀勾地理會之宴請

十九日同赴散魯伊斯博覽會之萬國工藝各學會

二十日同前

此後在此處公司議定如何往觀會場中有關地理名物如會員中多有樂於

西遊者即行備辦一切由散魯伊斯同赴墨西哥城散費大堪烟舊金

山金門諸處自有西方地理各會格外歉待在此處酌定歸路取道大山并

直達東邊各海己之內地平原各處倘會歉可待所有各國赴會人員

由華盛頓經過保樂提本爾費拉蓋爾斐亞紐約呢阿嘎拉瀑布其喀勾至

散魯伊斯一路費用均本會供給由此西逛應需火車其寢車飯食及一切

應需各件亦必設法照常償核實折減惟西遊人數或須稍有限制其本

會之外國會員由歐洲前來紐約者其船價現亦設法另定數目惟須先

期告知方可其詳細辦法將載入本年六月章程內

本會應行研究及議論各件分列如左

一地文學　附氣象學　水論

二算學地理　附測地術　格致地論

三生植物地理學　附花木學　動物學

四論人性之地理學　附人種學

五圖畫地理學　附探地法　測量法

六地理技術學　附圖解　古書記載

七商務製造地理學

八地理教授法

九地理史記

擬將特定會期會議測量繪圖各法並取各國所用之法與本國國家

所用者互相參改

會中一切會議游歷宴會之利益各會員均得享受會中之冊報

文件刊刻後亦必分送各會員看閱各地理等會員若在本會

交納美金五元合二十五佛郎或二十馬克即可作為本會會員其並

非地理會中之人擬入此會亦必交納以上之款並由會長處公舉凡隨同會

員之婦女若每人交納美金三元五角即可作為副員並享受會中一切利益

惟無議舉之權本會亦不發給各項文件

地理專家及其友人等如擬赴會並得會中文件即請早日示知以使

此後之會章可以隨時寄主本會接到各會員並副員捐納之費後即

將准充會員之票交郵局寄去會中一切利益非有此等票者不得享受

本會甚望此次他會之來入此會者甚多少於地理專家入會者之數

為此特請各會委員前來俾每百名會員之中有他會之委員一人多則十人

凡他會之掛名於此會者均無庸交納掛名之費惟望各委員均繳會費

作為會員無論何會之名統俟本會長之命始行刊入單內凡在本會掛

名之會均可得本會之文件由本會遞送不取分文本會並願西半球之地

理各會乘此機會聯絡天下各會故本會中除用法德英義文外擬並用

西班牙文字俾便於各會凡致本會之文件論說用以上所列不論何國

之文皆可

本會特請相關地理學之會弁書樓大學堂專門學堂專門學會均

各遠員捐資入會以便領取本會刊發各件

凡寄本會之函件及滙款均請送至下列之住址

美國華盛頓和貝彌得麥卯利亞拉好拉第八次萬國綜核地理會查收

外務部

州

六月初六

咨呈

頭品頂戴兵部尚書署理兩廣總督岑　為

咨呈事案照承准

前總理衙門咨行出使美日秘國楊大臣與美國使署

律師科士達詳酌擬定華人往美漢洋文護照程式咨

粤照辦嗣後華人往美一體仿照所擬程式飭由粤海

開發給等因茲有商民黃廷欽鄭貫賢溫刼宏林沛祥

鄭桂廷溫計龍鄭開謙陳獻標蔡坤南黃松泰等請照

前往美國散魯伊斯城賽會票由粤海關驗填護照並

無騙拐假冒情弊且有殷寔鋪保具結存案核與章程

相符准粤海關咨請核咨前來除咨復並照章咨行

出使美秘古墨國大臣駐美金山總領事查照辦理外

相應咨呈為此合咨

貴部謹請察照備案施行須至咨呈者

外　務　部

右　　咨　　呈

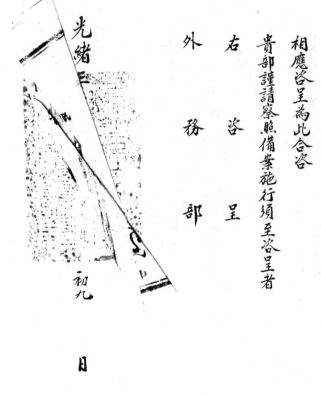

光緒三

初九

日

清代外務部中外關係檔案史料叢編
——中美關係卷 第六冊·國際會議

欽差出使美秘古墨國大臣梁　為

咨呈事竊照光緒三十年五月十五日承准

貴部咨開准美康使函稱接奉本國外部來函美國精製飲食會在散魯伊

斯開會自本年西歷九月二十六號至十月一號為止囑將該會印送之單轉請中國

派員赴會等語除函復外相應咨行查照崔期酌量派員前往藉資考證查有

等因承准此查該精製飲食會係為衞生起見自應派員前往赴會並聲復本部

美署二等參贊官周自齊三等參贊官孫士顏業經派赴萬國律司會應令一併

前往赴會除札飭外理合咨呈

貴部謹請查照施行須至咨呈者

右　咨　呈

外　務　部

光緒三十一年五月　十六　日

欽差出使美秘古墨國大臣梁　為

咨呈事竊照光緒三十年五月十五日承准

貴部咨開准美康使函稱接奉本國外部來函云美國牙醫會在散會伊斯開會

自本年西歷八月二十九號至九月三號為止囑將該會印送之單轉請中國派員赴會等

語除函復外相應咨行查照屆期酌量派員赴會並督復本部等因承准此查該

牙醫會係為衛生起見自應派員前往藉資考證查有美署二等參贊官周自

齊三等參贊官孫士頤業經派赴萬國律司會應令一併前往赴會除札飭外理合

咨呈

貴部謹請查照施行須至咨呈者

右　咨呈

外務部

光緒三十年五月　拾陸　日

咨呈

咨呈印

月

逕啟者接准本國外部來文以中國赴散魯伊斯賽會商人運

貨至舊金山因護照違式駁阻一案查此案本大臣當巳照譯

貴親王來文所云未經起程之華商自當嚴飭照新章定式

領照前往其業經首途或巳到美境者其所持之照即或違式

請寬待勿阻等言於正月二十八日轉達外部辦理兹准復稱

此事應歸商部大臣查辦現接有商部所復之文寄送前來囑

即抄送

貴親王查照又商部大臣云中國發給官商赴會護照如查

係從本日以前繕給者即違定式可不計論嗣必格外盡心按

照會章勸助中國赴會官商登岸前往會場並於游觀各所

擺設貨物一切事務均行幫扶照料云云想

貴親王一經閱畢所送商部之文即深悉本國於中國來

美赴會官商不欲有所阻難甚願隨時相助也特布即頌

爵祺 附送洋文並抄商部文一件

名另具 五月二十五日

權算司

呈為咨行事光緒三十年五月二十六日准美康使函稱

賽會華商運貨至舊金山因護照違式駁阻一事茲

接本國商部大臣文稱中國發給官商赴會護照如查

係在本日以前繕給者即遵定式可不計論嗣後必格

外盡心按照會章襄助中國赴會官商登岸前往會

場並於一切事務均各幫扶照料等語並將商部來文

附送等因前來相應將美使所送商部原文咨行

貴大臣查照傳諭赴會各華商遵照可也須至咨者附件

出使美國大臣梁

光緒三十年六月　日

十 六月十二

欽命前赴散魯伊斯賽會正監督貝勒貝子溥　為

　咨呈事據賽會副監督黃開甲詳稱竊開甲前蒙

外務部奏派前赴散魯伊斯賽會副監督遵奉

劉飭先行赴美布置賽會一切事宜在案開甲即

於上年三月出京五月赴美行抵散魯伊斯會場

業將商定基址建造房屋並華商賽會章程節

經妥為經理先後詳請爵憲查照核辦亦在案

開甲查美國賽會為百年之盛舉中華赴會係萬

國之觀瞻造端宏大旣非一人之耳目所能周頤緒

繁叕更非一人之精神所能繼欲資臂助必賴

羣材查有戶部候補郎中李福恒花翎候選

同知余朝榮監生唐福裴監生歐陽祺等四員

襄辦賽會事宜一年以來均能實力實心不辭勞

瘁合無仰懇爵憲咨明外務部立案一俟會務

告竣准其奏請獎敘以酬勞勩而示鼓勵為此

詳請爵憲垂譽訓示等語　查副監督黃開甲

詳稱各節係屬實在情形該員李福恒等四

員襄同辦理會場事宜補屬奮勉從公不辭

勞瘁至所請咨呈

貴部立案准其獎敘之處 相應咨呈

貴部酌核辦理並希咨覆以憑劄飭該副監

督遵辦可也須至咨呈者

右　咨　呈

外　務　部

光緒叁拾年肆月　　日

清代外務部中外關係檔案史料叢編——中美關係卷 第六冊·國際會議

欽命前往散魯伊斯賽會正監督貝勒行稽田貝子溥　　為

咨呈事本監督現在應遞

安摺二封正摺一封於五月初一日由散魯伊斯

拜發相應鈔錄奏底附送印花咨呈

貴部代為呈遞可也須至咨呈者

右　咨　呈　計抄原奏一件　印花一封

外　務　部

光緒叁拾年伍月　日

　　　　　　日

奏底

奏為陳報奴才起程日期恭摺具陳仰祈

奴才溥倫跪

聖鑒事竊奴才前將行抵散魯伊斯並開會日期業經

恭摺奏報在案目三月中旬開會以來經會務總

辦福蘭西司邀觀會場各處環球名物燦然備陳

通商惠工洵屬法良意美歷觀陳列各所甚布星

羅粗知領要奴才即行前赴各埠游歷該地方官

紳等邀觀學堂等處旋即遄返會場叠接外務部

電咨恭送

皇太后聖容赴美敬謹供奉奴才會同出使美國大臣梁

誠預備恭迎敬謹供奉禮成經奴才會同出使美

國大臣梁誠恭摺奏報在案奴才現擬於五月初

一日由散魯伊斯起程前赴紐約搭坐輪船回華

所有奴才陳報起程日期謹恭摺具陳伏乞

皇太后

皇上聖鑒謹

奏

京博濬　陳報起程日期由

六月二十二日

外務傳僑飭

這知陳指明起程日期某抵某其陳如祉

至墾戸籍地方前帖乃抵敬譽伊斯至兩会日期書

謹差择查報至纂句三月中旬兩会以来経

左掛镶丽福岗西引豁觀会塲各事環璵

物懷此僑陳道寄東工問所法政意美歷觀

陳列紅紬各布星羅班列頗覺可觀以方便應赴

各埠游歷俟地方官紳籌議辦法再當電請旋即

遴派會場迷攜分發新聞電告茶送

皇太后至寬赴業敬謹供幸由方會同出俟美國大臣

梁誠預備茶延敦謹供幸永威經由方會同出

俟美國大臣梁誠原招連揌立案查中國赴會

一應狂已商備粵撫于五月初一日由敦魯伊

輪按招芳赴紐約搭走輪船四義玉美國會

趨須玉十月中旬方能藏事領館幸即監督

新起程芳赴紐約搭走輪船四義玉美國會

黃開甲揚朵寄寰心經理訊示治方陳報譬

日期謹繕摺恭呈伏乞

皇太后

皇上垂鑒謹

奏

光緒三十年六月二十二日奉

硃批知道了欽此

五月二日

奏溥倫

〇京外務部

六月二十二日

奴才溥倫跪

奏為恭謝

皇太后聖容行抵散魯伊斯供奉禮成恭摺具陳仰祈

聖鑒事竊奴才前准外務部咨稱光緒三十年二月

二十一日

由廷口侍玖在恭摺

皇太后聖容告竣交外務部祇領飭總稅務司敬謹齎美

即由實倫正監督奉迎至散魯伊斯會場供

瞻仰俟該監督公事畢后令出使美國大臣梁

達漢阮敬謹選美國國家專司國際監會集美

康侯轉達美國政府外相商咨行欽遵又准電

開恭繕

皇太后聖鑒告成出洋稅務司謹齎會場亦即預備處

前敬謹齎臺之滬電聞

皇太后聖鑒已派沈道餘虎于三月十九日搭輪美國

協隆準行西比利亞輪船由滬起程奉屬赴美

奉旨張如才伏查番海

皇太后聖鑒告成由外務部飭總稅務司敬謹遵進赴

美英法荷五國迤邐直達沈敝電由此奉真一

同赴美迤徑途小出敝美國大臣梁誠遵迤

搭連美國政府照飭金山領中奉條抵準

敬謹迤脚以悅悵重美國出使大臣梁誠振撓

分防部在電容芳約送日才遂迤來四

月十五日懷查山徑前由電字

皇太后聖鑒奉抵本山宵俟分者電容分勒郅立案並

飭前監臂苦剛甲斯尔署電技誅敝公同選備

輪車茶遠此敝魯伊斯亞會會辦俟一幣福

蕭西旬惠心巡料碑讓海涵四月會同出俟美

國大自粱諭議英近于二廿八日于安少抵會場

于三十日韶謹俟左永國際俱我

皇太后聖壽溯洄

寰恫惝嫦

天心春佑

壽考其明此肺文迺另釐慶徐篝

日月恍倘

呼籲平寫東瞻就

雲美伸覿

容光之必照長席禘皇煌刻畫曾重秋金石而裏眉

舜月觀贈未花作瀛懷今当美國百年闹会之

期茶值

聖蓉美星遠頌三月

龍光栽御如闻警躍之声像譯艦巍其栽承平之緒

合親寄四方以觀礼会衣冠尊国而裏仪如才

荌恭逢

盛典慶幸莫名欤

聖德之光明中外咸微夫禔福禰

徽音之巍懷隐逃看頼以蒙庥除俟会稀感乃克由

出使美國大臣梁诚轃遠继洗敬謹斋送美國

国家外部有荣祇遵恭迎供奉礼成缘由谨

会同出使美国大臣梁诚会词具陈伏乞

皇太后

皇上圣鉴谨

奏　光绪三十年六月二十二日奉

朱批　敬悉钦此

四月三十日

欽差出使美秘古墨國大臣梁　為

咨呈事竊照光緒三十年七月初二日承准

貴部咨開光緒三十年五月二十一日准此萬使照稱西歷一千九百零五年在此國黎

業斯地方舉行萬國賽會一事貴國已派駐此大臣楊兆鋆屆時前往觀會查美

國聖路易斯賽會貴國運出各土產并工藝物件請傳示各商人於聖路易斯

賽會之後所剩各物就便運赴本國黎業斯會場一賽等因前來除照復此使

外相應咨行查照傳諭赴美賽會商人等是否情願前往黎業斯赴會各聽

其便併聲復本部可也等因承准此除咨行賽會副監督亞曉諭華商人等

外理合備文咨呈

貴部謹請察照須至咨呈者

右咨呈

外　　務　　部

此

咨呈

　　　月　　　日

光　　　年

　　　月　　　日

權算并司

呈為照復事光緒三十年六月二十九日准

照稱一千八百九十七年六月十五號在華盛頓所定萬國

郵政章程現英國藩政大臣於本年五月二十四號為奧

斯達利亞合國代出允此郵政章程之文憑由駐華盛

頓英國頭等欽差大臣於六月二十號將所出文憑交

美國外部存案應轉知貴國郵政衙門備案等因

前來本部業經剳行總稅務司轉飭郵政總辦查

照備案相應照復

貴大臣查照可也須至照復者

美康使

光緒三十年七月　　　日

敬啟者恭送

聖容赴會一事前於五月初二日據電稱安抵會場無誤云

玉呈

貴部在案現有賽會副監督柯爾樂繕備收據一紙

轉由上海稅務司恭寄到京除將此項收據送呈

查閱外一俟會畢

聖容一座另有何項

飭辦之處應請

酌示以便轉飭柯副監督遵辦可也專此佈泐順頌

升祺附收據壹紙

名另具光緒叁拾年柒月初伍日

赫德

安格聯

Received from the Shanghai Commissioner two cases marked (F.A.C.) and (F.A.C.) containing portrait of H.I.M. the Empress Dowager of China for the St. Louis Purchase Exposition

Francis A. Carl

Assistant Commissioner to the Louisiana Exposition

St. Louis, 13. June, 1904.

咨赴美賽會正監督所有副監
督薪水應比照頭等參贊酌加
每月六百兩由

行　　行

左侍郎聯　六月 廿 日

右侍郎伍　六月 廿 日

榷算司

呈為咨復事光緒三十年六月十一日接准

咨稱據副監督黃開甲詳稱前蒙外務部奏派赴

美賽會副監督業奉劄飭遵照副監督應比照何項

人員支領薪水祈酌核示遵等語本監督查奏定出使

章程內並無明文該副監督應如何支給薪水之處應

請核復以憑飭遵等因前來本部查出使章程內開

頭等參贊官月給俸薪五百兩該副監督赴美幫帶同照

料賽會事宜自應比照酌加俸薪每月六百兩以示優

異相應咨復

貴正監督查照辦理可也須至咨者

賽會正監督

光緒三十年六月

廿
省
月
二
十
日

欽命前赴散齊伊斯賀會正監督員勳衔酉山貝子溥　　　為

咨呈事本監督前赴美國於上年奏調隨員

内務府員外郎誠璋戸部主事彭毅孫分

省補用道程大澂江蘇補用知縣馮國勳又

咨調供事候選知縣周祖彝候選筆帖式錫

瑄等六員隨同前往現在由美回京於七月

十六日恭覆

恩命所有前經奏調咨調各該員內務府員外郎

誠璋戶部主事彭穀孫應即飭令仍回本衙

門當差江蘇補用知縣馮國勳請假省親尚未

回京分省補用道程大徵候選知縣周祖彝候

選筆帖式錫瑄均已回京相應咨呈

貴部查照可也須至咨呈者

右　咨呈

外　務　部

光緒叁拾年柒月貳拾
拾
日

欽命前赴散曾伊斯賽賽正監督員勒衛圖山貝子溥 　為

咨呈事據江蘇補用知縣馮國勳呈稱竊

國勳前蒙爵憲奏調隨同赴美遵即束裝

隨同前往在案現在爵憲由美回華行抵

上海國勳寄居上海擬懇爵憲恩准賞假

一個月回家省親一俟假期屆滿月應迅

即北上不敢稍有眈延併懇咨明外務部

北洋大臣查照實為德便等語　本監督查

該員呈請給假一個月回家省親自應准如

所請除飭該員一俟假滿趕緊回京銷假外

相應咨呈

貴部查照可也須至咨呈者

右　咨　呈

外　務　部

光緒叁拾年柒月貳拾日

逕啟者西曆過年五月間華盛頓設立萬國鐵路會想已由

比國政府函請

貴國派員赴會茲接本國政府文稱已由本國上下議院

議定本國可入此會並允攤捐經費中國如欲派員赴會本國

須頒知其銜名並囑本大臣轉達

貴親王查照屆開會時本國自應行囑各口海關稅務司仍

照常例免稅引領進口也特泐即頌

爵祉附送洋文

名另具八月二十六日

一一八

欽命前赴散魯伊斯賽會正監督貝勒銜固山貝子溥　為

咨呈事本監督奏造銷出洋收支經費繕具清單

一摺單一件於光緒三十年九月二十八日具奏奉

旨依議欽此欽遵由軍機處鈔交前來相應造具清冊一

本咨呈

貴部查照核銷至不敷銀兩業經咨明戶部照數

補發須至咨呈者　計清冊一本奏底一件

右　咨　呈

外　務　部

光緒叄拾　年　　　月　十五　日

三十月十五日

三六四

奏底

奏為造銷出洋收支經費開列四柱清單繕呈

御覽恭摺具陳仰祈

聖鑒事竊查光緒二十九年三間准戶部咨稱本部奏覆

由江海關墊撥賽會經費庫平銀柒拾伍萬兩奉

旨咨行遵照前來當經奴才備文關領在案內除撥給副監

督黃開甲庫平銀肆拾伍萬兩副監督柯爾樂庫平

銀拾伍萬兩計收庫平銀拾伍萬兩開支庫平銀拾伍萬

叁千叁百貳拾捌兩零捌分實在不敷銀叁千叁百貳拾捌

兩零捌分謹繕四柱清單恭呈

御覽相應請

旨飭下外務部戶部准其開銷至不敷銀叁千叁百貳拾捌

兩零捌分一併請

旨飭下戶部補行發給仍由奴才備文關領以昭核實除造

冊咨部核銷外所有造銷出洋收支經費緣由理合

恭摺具陳伏乞

皇太后

皇上聖鑒謹

奏

前赴美國賽會正監督造銷

光緒參拾年收支經費四柱清冊

鑒核

　計開

　舊管

　　　無項

　新收

收戶部由江海關墊撥庫平銀柒拾伍萬兩內除撥付副監督黃

開甲經費庫平銀肆拾伍萬兩副監督柯爾樂庫平銀拾伍萬

兩計實收庫平銀拾伍萬兩

開除

謹將前赴美國散魯伊斯賽會收支經費繕具清單恭候

薪水項下

一開支貝勒銜固山貝子前赴美國賽會正監督溥計薪水五個月零二十七日按照定章每月貳千兩共庫平銀壹萬壹千八百兩

一開支隨員內務府員外郎誠璋計薪水五個月零二十七日按照定章每月貳百兩共庫平銀壹千壹百八十兩

一開支隨員戶部主事彭穀孫計薪水五個月零二十七日按照定章每月貳百兩共庫平銀壹千壹百八十兩

一開支隨員分省補用道程大澂計薪水五個月零二十七日按照定章每月貳百兩共庫平銀壹千壹百八十兩

一開支隨員江蘇知縣馮國勳計薪水五個月零二十七日按照定章每月貳百兩共庫平銀壹千壹百八十兩

一開支隨員候選通判全森計薪水兩個月按照定章每月貳百兩計庫平銀壹百八十兩該員於二月間由橫濱請假回京合併聲明

一開支供事候選知縣周祖彝計薪水五個月零二十七日按照定章每月壹百兩共庫平銀五百九十兩

一開支供事筆帖式錫瑄計薪水五個月零二十七日每月發給壹百兩共庫平銀五百九十兩

一開支護衛長祥計薪水五個月零二十七日每月發給壹百兩共庫平銀五百九十兩

一開支護衛雲祥計薪水五個月零二十七日每月發給壹百兩共庫

平銀五百九十兩

置裝歸裝項下

一開支貝勒銜固山貝子前赴美國賽會正監督溥定章一年以內按照各一個月薪水開支共庫平銀五百九十兩

一開支隨員內務府員外郎誠璋定章一年以內按照各一個月薪水開支共庫平銀肆千兩

一開支隨員戶部主事彭穀孫定章一年以內按照各一個月薪水開支共庫平銀肆百兩

一開支隨員分省補用道程大澂定章一年以內按照各一個月薪水開支共庫平銀肆百兩

一開支隨員江蘇知縣馮國勳定章一年以內按照各一個月薪水開支共庫平銀肆百兩

一開支隨員候選通判全森定章一年以內按照各一個月薪水開支該員於二月間由橫濱請假回京合併聲明

一開支供事候選知縣周祖彝定章一年以內按照各一個月薪水開支共庫平銀貳百兩

一開支供事筆帖式錫瑄定章一年以內按照各一個月薪水發給共庫平銀貳百兩

一開支護衛長祥按照各一個月薪水發給共庫平銀貳百兩

一開支護衛雲祥按照各一個月薪水發給共庫平銀貳百兩

禮物項下

一開支正監督贈送日本皇帝皇后太子太子妃親王大臣美國總統及夫人
會場總辦及夫人並會場各紳董禮物共庫平銀八千七百七十七兩

川貨項下

一開支由橫濱至舊金山正監督一員副監督一員隨員四員俱頭等艙
位供事二員護衛二員俱二等艙位剃匠二名伺役四名俱三等艙
位船價共合庫平銀陸千零二十五兩

一開支由紐約至哈南正監督一員隨員四員俱頭等艙位供事二員
護衛二員俱二等艙位剃匠一名俱三等艙位船價共合
庫平銀貳千肆百捌拾兩

一開支由馬賽至上海正監督超等艙位隨員四員俱頭等艙位
供事二員護衛二員俱二等艙位剃匠二名伺役四名俱三等艙位
船價共合庫平銀陸千零二十五兩

一開支由舊金山至華盛頓包車一輛連買床票共合庫平銀貳千貳百六十兩

一開支由華盛頓至散魯伊斯包車一輛連買床票共合庫平銀壹
千貳百二十八兩

一開支由散魯伊斯至西卡古包車一輛共合庫平銀貳百肆拾兩

一開支由西卡古至印甸那波厘斯包車一輛共合庫平銀壹百八十八兩五錢

一開支由印甸那波厘斯至白福婁包車一輛連買床票共庫平銀百八十兩

一開支由白福婁至紐約克彐車一輛連買床票共庫平銀捌百柒拾兩五錢

一開支由紐約克彐至散魯伊斯包車一輛連買床票共庫平銀壹千伍百壹拾兩

一開支由散魯伊斯至紐約克彐包車一輛連買床票共庫平銀壹千伍百壹拾兩

客寓項下

一開支橫濱客寓庫平銀陸百貳拾捌兩

一開支舊金山客寓庫平銀壹千壹百拾伍兩

一開支華盛頓客寓庫平銀肆千壹百伍拾兩

一開支散魯伊斯客寓前後兩次共庫平銀壹萬玖千陸百肆拾捌兩

一開支印甸那波厘斯客寓庫平銀伍千捌百肆拾陸兩

一開支西卡古客寓庫平銀壹千玖百肆拾柒兩叁錢

一開支紐約客寓庫平銀壹千伍百壹拾兩

一開支哈南客寓庫平銀壹千肆百壹拾柒兩

一開支馬賽客寓庫平銀壹千捌百拾壹兩肆錢

一開支巴黎斯客寓庫平銀捌百壹拾伍兩肆錢

一開支格薐埠客寓庫平銀陸拾柒兩五錢

一開支紐約克彐客寓前後兩次共庫平銀貳百肆拾肆兩

一開支白福婁客寓庫平銀壹百肆拾兩

一開支西貢客寓庫平銀捌拾柒兩五錢捌分

賞耗項下

一開支由京至津火車往返兩次共賞庫平銀捌拾兩

一開支由神戶至東京火車賞庫平銀叁拾兩

清代外務部中外關係檔案史料叢編——中美關係卷 第六冊·國際會議

一開支由東京至橫濱火車賞庫平銀貳拾兩
一開支由舊金山至華盛頓火車賞庫平銀壹百伍拾兩
一開支由華盛頓至散魯伊斯火車賞庫平銀壹百伍拾兩
一開支由散魯伊斯至西卡古火車賞庫平銀伍拾兩
一開支由西卡古至印甸那波厘斯火車賞庫平銀叁拾兩
一開支由印甸那波厘斯至白福婁火車賞庫平銀叁拾兩
一開支由白福婁至紐約克火車賞庫平銀叁拾兩
一開支由紐約克至散魯伊斯火車賞庫平銀叁拾兩
一開支由散魯伊斯至白福婁火車賞庫平銀叁拾兩
一開支由巴黎至馬賽火車賞庫平銀貳拾兩

一開支東京觀見宮內省備馬車賞庫平銀伍拾兩
一開支東京芝離宮備馬車賞庫平銀壹百兩
一開支金山地方備馬車賞庫平銀伍拾兩
一開支會場備馬車賞庫平銀貳百兩
一開支公司備馬車賞庫平銀壹百兩
一開支拉非燕爾汽車賞庫平銀壹百兩
一開支由金山至華盛頓飯車賞庫平銀壹百兩
一開支由神戶至東京火車上晚餐賞庫平銀拾兩
一開支由福婁地方備馬車賞庫平銀拾兩
一開支由華盛頓至散魯伊斯飯車賞庫平銀叁拾兩

一開支由西卡古至印甸那波厘斯飯車賞庫平銀叁拾兩
一開支由印甸那波厘斯至白福婁飯車賞庫平銀叁拾兩
一開支由白福婁至紐約克飯車賞庫平銀叁拾兩
一開支由紐約克至散魯伊斯飯車賞庫平銀叁拾兩
一開支由散魯伊斯至白福婁飯車賞庫平銀貳拾兩
一開支由巴黎至馬賽飯車賞庫平銀貳拾兩
一開支由馬賽至西貢輪船賞庫平銀肆百陸拾兩
一開支由紐約克至哈甫輪船賞庫平銀叁百貳拾兩
一開支由橫濱至舊金山輪船賞庫平銀陸百陸拾兩
一開支由津赴滬又由滬回津安平輪船前後兩次共賞庫平銀伍百陸拾兩
一開支由西貢至上海另換輪船賞庫平銀壹百兩
一開支天津吳楚公所賞庫平銀伍拾兩
一開支上海洋務局前後兩次賞庫平銀叁百兩
一開支格籥埠撥船賞庫平銀拾兩
一開支神戶西常盤迎賓館賞庫平銀貳拾兩
一開支東京芝離宮賞庫平銀壹千貳百兩
一開支橫濱客寓賞庫平銀肆拾兩
一開支金山客寓賞庫平銀捌拾兩
一開支華盛頓客寓前後兩次賞庫平銀貳百兩
一開支散魯伊斯客寓前後兩次賞庫平銀壹千貳百兩

一開支西卡古容寓賞庫平銀壹百陸拾兩

一開支印向那波厘斯容寓賞庫平銀伍百伍拾兩

一開支拉非燕爾容寓賞庫平銀壹百拾兩

一開支白福妻容寓賞庫平銀壹百伍拾兩

一開支紐約克容寓前後兩次共賞庫平銀陸百貳拾兩

一開支哈甫容寓賞庫平銀肆兩

一開支巴黎容寓賞庫平銀壹百兩

一開支馬賽容寓賞庫平銀壹百陸拾兩

一開支格崙埠容寓賞庫平銀貳拾兩

一開支西貢容寓賞庫平銀叁拾兩

一開支芝離宮看影戲把戲賞庫平銀捌拾兩

一開支淺草寺賞庫平銀貳拾兩

一開支紅葉館日本官員公請賞庫平銀捌拾兩

一開支會場跳舞賞庫平銀貳百兩

一開支會場茶會賞庫平銀伍拾兩

一開支中國開會會場送樂一部樂工賞庫平銀貳百兩

一開支上海工部局前後兩次賞庫平銀壹百兩

一開支上海中國巡捕賞庫平銀叁拾兩

一開支印度馬兵巡捕賞庫平銀肆拾兩

一開支舊金山巡捕賞庫平銀壹百兩

一開支會場巡捕賞庫平銀壹百兩

一開支沿途車船上下搬運行李賞庫平銀共肆百肆拾兩

一開支船上水手捐賞庫平銀壹百貳拾兩

一開支會場工匠賞庫平銀叁百兩

捐款項下

一開支日本盲啞學堂捐庫平銀壹百陸拾兩

一開支日本帝國教育會捐庫平銀捌拾兩

一開支留學會館捐庫平銀壹百陸拾兩

一開支清華學校捐庫平銀捌拾兩

一開支神戸學堂捐庫平銀捌拾兩

一開支組約學堂捐庫平銀貳百兩

一開支檀香山醫院捐庫平銀貳百兩

一開支輪船禮拜捐庫平銀貳拾兩

一開支馬賽白十字會捐庫平銀貳百兩

雜費項下

一開支剃匠二名每名每月給薪工五十兩置裝歸裝各照一個月新工支每名應支四百兩二名共支庫平銀捌百兩

一開支二十九年二月至三十年正月文案處筆墨紙張火食共庫平銀伍百柒拾兩

一開支功牌執照庫平銀捌拾壹兩

一開支外務省岩村代錄庫平銀捌拾兩

一開支宮內省朝倉代錄庫平銀捌拾兩

一開支宮內省屬官代儀庫平銀叁拾兩

一開支由橫濱至金山輪船上請茶會一次庫平銀貳百柒拾壹兩

一開支中國會場開會請茶會一次庫平銀叁萬叁千貳百叁拾捌兩

一開支美國火車上飯食庫平銀壹千壹百貳拾兩

一開支由橫濱至金山行李水腳庫平銀壹百貳拾兩

一開支由金山至華盛頓行李水腳庫平銀壹千貳百肆拾兩

一開支由華盛頓至散魯伊斯行李水腳庫平銀貳百叁拾捌兩

一開支由散魯伊斯至紐約行李水腳庫平銀貳百貳拾捌兩

一開支由紐約至哈甫行李水腳庫平銀陸拾捌兩伍錢

一開支由哈甫至馬賽行李水腳庫平銀貳百玖拾兩

一開支由巴黎至馬賽行李水腳庫平銀壹百陸拾柒兩

一開支印甸那波厘斯請茶會庫平銀壹千貳百捌拾兩

一開支由馬賽至上海行李水腳庫平銀伍百壹拾伍兩

一開支電報費庫平銀貳千壹百捌拾兩

一開支由馬賽至上海輪船電氣風扇庫平銀叁拾貳兩伍錢

一開支華洋筆墨紙張庫平銀叁百柒拾肆兩

一開支換買公事板箱二次庫平銀叁拾肆兩

以上共開支庫平銀拾伍萬叁千叁百貳拾捌兩零捌分

實在

計不敷庫平銀叁千叁百貳拾捌兩零捌分

旨依

權算司

呈為咨行事光緒三十年十月十五日准散魯伊斯賽

會正監督貝勒銜固山貝子溥咨稱本監督奏造

銷出洋收支經費繕具清單一摺單一件於光緒三

十年九月二十八日具奏奉

議欽此相應造具清冊咨部查照核銷至不敷銀

兩業經咨明戶部照數補發等因前來本部查散

魯伊斯賽會經費係由

貴部撥用所有正監督收支各款應由

貴部核銷會同本部辦理相應咨行

貴部查照核辦可也須至咨者

戶部

光緒三十年十月　　日

逕啟者茲接散魯伊斯賽會福大臣蘭西電稱請為轉奏中國

大皇帝日昨本總理派同首事人等接請美國

大伯理璽天德駕臨賽會場中國國家建造公所中國黃副監督和

  謁迎接

大伯理璽天德實深褒獎賽會場中受中國前來赴賽之福等因本

  大臣茲甚願為轉達

貴親王查照希代爲轉奏可也特泐順頌

爵祺附送洋文

名另具　十月二十三日

康格

F.O. No.740

H.　　　LEGATION OF THE UNITED STATES OF AMERICA,
PEKIN, CHINA.

November 28 1904.

Your Imperial Highness:-

I have the honor to inform you that I
have today received a telegram from David R.Francis, president
of the Louisiana Purchase Exposition, asking me to inform His Imperial Majesty that President Roosevelt, accompanoed by himself
and the reception committee visited the Chinese pavilion yesterday; that they were gracefully received by vice commissioner
Wang; and that the President expressed great admiration and appreciation of China's participation in the universal exposition.

It gives me pleasure therefore to trans-
mit his message in this letter, as requested, and, trusting that
you will convey the message in proper form to His Imperial Majesty , I takew the occasion to renew to Your Imperial Highness
the assurance of my highest consideration.

American Minister.

To His Imperial Highness, Prin ce Of Ch'ing,

President of the Board of Foreign Affairs.

清代外務部中外關係檔案史料叢編——中美關係卷 第六冊·國際會議

一二一

敬復者奉到本月二十五日

鈞函以准駐此楊大臣來電稱黎業斯賽會總稅司辦

有貨物否乞示復等語為此函詢曾否辦有貨物赴

黎業斯賽會希見復以憑電復楊大臣等因奉此查

二十九年八月初八日本年三月十二日兩奉

鈞劄飭照向章辦理並將籌辦赴會情形隨時知照駐

比楊大臣各等因當按向章通飭各口稅務司將比

國設會一事曉諭商民凡有赴會物件出口一概免

稅俟全貨出境後再將各口所免稅數詳報去訖惟

開會尚未到期此時尚未據各口稅務司將赴會情

形具報到京至如何籌辦一節

貴部原有咨明商部轉行南北洋大臣曉諭商民赴會

之語所有籌辦各事似係商部經理之件各稅務司

只有免稅具報之責再此次若有即應赴會之情勢

不若將散魯伊斯入會物品運赴比會計散城畢會

在即頗有餘暇包裝運比即交駐比

楊大臣陳列會場一轉移間大省周折倘可照辦除

電飭稅務司柯爾樂照送外亦可電飭告假在籍之

稅務司阿理嗣人比國就近接收隨同

楊大人料理一切現奉前因理合備函復呈

鈞鑒可也專是佈復順頌

升祺

名另具光緒叁拾年拾月貳拾陸日

外務部

卄

戶部為知照事北檔房案呈准實會

正監督固山貝子溥　咨本監督奏

銷出洋收支經費一摺單一件光緒三

十年九月二十八日具奏奉

旨依議欽此至不敷庫平銀三千三百二十

八兩零八分應請戶部照數補發等因

前來　除剳　行銀庫司員在於庫存

項下提庫平銀三千三百二十八兩零八

分折合二兩平銀三千五百二十七兩七

錢六分四厘除知照賽會正監督溥　查

照承領外相應知照

貴部查照可也須至知照者

右知照

外務部

郎中斌

一二三

附奏准美康使函稱美總統至散魯伊斯會場由
國公所甚為欣悅請代奏由

奏　奏

左侍郎聯　奏
十月
二十六
日

右侍郎伍　奏
十月二十六日

再臣部准美國駐京使臣康格函稱接散魯伊
斯賽會總理大臣福蘭西電稱本總理派同首
事人等接請本國

大伯理璽天德駕臨賽會場中貴國

國家建造之公所黃副監督開甲和藹迎接

大伯理璽天德實深欣悅此次賽會甚蒙中國前

來赴賽之福請為轉奏貴國

大皇帝陛下等語理合附片具陳伏乞

聖鑒謹

奏光緒三十年十一月初一日具奏奉

硃批知道了欽此

敬啟者美會物品移往比國一事現據柯稅務司復

電稱飭送比國之棹椅器具早經拍賣一空至有無

存銀一節現有些須餘銀尚堪用作赴比入會之費

云云又

楊大臣飭辦之棹椅等器具請開一詳細清單

擲下或用寧波之物抑用福州廣東之物希即一併

示知以便轉飭備辦送往可也專是佈達順頌

日祉

　　名另具光緒叁拾年拾壹月初拾日

清代外務部中外關係檔案史料叢編——中美關係卷　第六冊·國際會議

大亞美理駕會眾國欽命駐劄中華便宜行事全權大臣康　為

照會事茲接本國外部大臣訓條內開按照一千八百九十九年

七月二十九日在荷蘭亥革弭兵會所立萬國和衷之規條第十九

款所有先准畫押之國各留已權互相定調和之約為將彼等

所以能調和一切之事務即照此法辦理此條款之意已有數國按

此立約矣尤以法英兩國所立之約為至要而美國常存之意見

即係此國若與彼國有事應行和衷調理此意天下實所共知

美國政府係數次照辦無庸詳論矣即如囊日一千八百七十四年

六月十七號美國下議院闡發之意亦總應以調和戰息兵事為

保全四海兄弟之仁術所以下議院衆人允准之情列下美國百

姓咸盼天下萬國均和平輯睦今本國各處已得此太平之慶美

國人甚願此情形歷久不渝且无盼天下各國均獲此福所以下議

院各人代美國百姓勸勉天下人將連籌攻擊之深謀變為和衷

調理之良策等語又於一千九百零三年十二月七號美國

總統行文於上下議院即係末次所行之文云若遇兩國有事不可擅

啟兵端理應另籌善法以結此等意見考之現在情形應於文

明之國必格外相信乎不能虛言將屈各國弭兵之地步尤不言

及理應鄭重本國之益處與本國之聲名此等事能常按照與

各國和衷調理之辦法惟以乎之誠意若用堅心智慧見識能除

却肇釁兵端許多情由時免血戰而另設一甚合宜之法能了結

兩國糾纏之事弭兵會在亥革所設立萬國調和之處為至善之

榜樣足可證天下各國能用此法調理國事之地步故我僑須竭

力鼓舞此等辦法等語因以上

總統所云又相信中國與美國同心合意情願鼓勵此調理之法故

飭外部轉囑駐華康使臣請詢中國政府願否同美國訂

立一和衷調理之約如法英兩國於一千九百零三年十月十四號

所立之約相同該約法英兩文附送貴使臣轉達如中國政府允

准立約必須請中國政府行飭駐華盛頓中國欽使同

總統將欲特派全權大臣會商立約簽押等因是以本大臣按照前

文照會

貴親王請問

貴國政府願否與美國訂立此樣和衷調理之約茲將本國外

部寄到之法英所立合塵約文一張轉送

貴親王查閱傳得格外明晰美國所請與中國訂約之式樣允望

貴國政府允准早為見後為此照會須至照會者 附送洋文並 洋約件

右　照　會

大清欽命全權查便宜行事軍機大臣總理外務部事務和碩慶親王

一千九百四拾貳年　貳拾壹
光緒叁拾年拾壹月　拾伍　日

清代外務部中外關係檔案史料叢編——中美關係卷·第六冊·國際會議

F.O. No. 746.

W.   LEGATION OF THE UNITED STATES OF AMERICA,
PEKIN, CHINA.

December 20th. 1904.

Your Imperial Highness:-

I have the honor to inform Your Imperial Highness that I

am just in receipt of instructions from the Secretary of

State at Washington, saying:-

"By Article XIX of the Convention for the Pacific Settlement of International Disputes, concluded at the
Hague on July 29, 1899, the signatory Governments reserved to themselves the right of concluding agreements
with a view to referring to arbitration all questions
which they shall consider possible to submit to such
treatment.
Under this provision certain agreements have already been concluded, notably that between France
and Great Britain.
The long-standing views of the United States concerning the settlement of international disputes by
arbitration, to which it has given practical effect
in numerous instances, are too well known to need
re-statement.
As long ago as June 17, 1874, the House of Representatives by a unanimous vote, gave expression to
its opinion that 'differences between nations should,
in the interest of humanity and fraternity, be adjust-
ed, if possible, by international arbitration'. It
was therefore resolved,
'That the people of the United States, being devoted to the policy of peace with all mankind, enjoy-
ing its blessings and hoping for its permanence and
its universal adoption, hereby through their Representatives in Congress recommend such arbitration as
a rational substitute for war'.
The President, in his last message to the Congress
of the United States, on December 7, 1903, stated:-
'There seems good ground for the belief that there
has been a real growth among the civilized nations
of a sentiment which will permit a gradual substitu-
tion of other methods than that of war in the settlement of disputes. It is not pretended that as yet we
are near a position in which it will be possible wholly to prevent war, or that a just regard for national interest and honor will in all cases permit of the
settlement of international disputes by arbitration;
but by a mixture of prudence and firmness with wisdom we think it is possible to do away with much of
the provocation and excuse for war, and at least in
many cases to substitute some other and more rational
                              method

(F.O. No. 746.)

        method for the settlement of disputes. The Hague
        Court offers so good an example of what can be done
        in the direction of such settlement that it should be
        encouraged in every way'.
           Moved by these views the President has charged me
        to instruct you to ascertain whether the Government
        to which you are accredited, which he has reason to
        believe is equally desirous of advancing the princi-
        ple of international arbitration, is willing to con-
        clude with the Government of the United States an ar-
        bitration treaty of like tenor to the arrangement
        concluded between France and Great Britain on Octo-
        ber 14, 1903.
           I inclose herewith a copy of both the English and
        French texts of that arrangement. Should the response
        to your inquiry be favorable, you will request the
        Government to authorize its Minister at Washington
        to sign the treaty with such plenipotentiary on the
        part of the United States as the President may be
        pleased to empower for the Purpose."

In compliance with these instructions, I have the honor

now to ask Your Imperial Highness whether or not the Gov-

ernment of China is disposed to enter into such a treaty

of arbitration with the United States as is proposed.

    I have the honor to forward inclosed a copy of the

English and French texts of the treaty between France and

Great Britain to which His Excellency the Secretary of

State refers, that Your Highness may the better under-

stand the character of the convention into which Your

Highness' Government is asked to enter with the United

States.

    Hoping to receive an early and a favorable response

to this invitation, I avail myself of the opportunity to

renew to Your Imperial Highness the assurance of my high-

est consideration.

                       Envoy Extraordinary and

                        Minister Plenipotentiary

                          of the United States.

To His Imperial Highness, Prince of Ch'ing,

President of the Board of Foreign Affairs.

Agreement between the United Kingdom and France providing for the settlement by arbitration of certain classes of questions which may arise between the two Governments.

Signed at London, October 14, 1903.

THE Government of His Britannic Majesty and the Government of the French Republic, signatories of the Convention for the pacific settlement of international disputes, concluded at the Hague on the 29th July, 1899;

Taking into consideration that by Article XIX of that Convention the High Contracting Parties have reserved to themselves the right of concluding Agreements, with a view to referring to arbitration all questions which they shall consider possible to submit to such treatment,

Have authorized the Undersigned to conclude the following arrangement:—

ARTICLE I.

Differences which may arise of a legal nature, or relating to the interpretation of Treaties existing between the two Contracting Parties, and which it may not have been possible to settle by diplomacy, shall be referred to the Permanent Court of Arbitration established at the Hague by the Convention of the 29th July, 1899, provided, nevertheless, that they do not affect the vital interests, the independence, or the honour of the two Contracting States, and do not concern the interests of third Parties.

ARTICLE II.

In each individual case the High Contracting Parties, before appealing to the Permanent Court of Arbitration, shall conclude a special Agreement defining clearly the matter in dispute, the scope of the powers of the Arbitrators, and the periods to be fixed for the formation of the Arbitral Tribunal and the several stages of the procedure.

ARTICLE III.

The present Agreement is concluded for a period of five years, dating from the day of signature.

Done in duplicate at London, the 14th day of October, 1903.

LE Gouvernement de Sa Majesté Britannique et le Gouvernement de la République Française, signataires de la Convention pour le règlement pacifique des conflits internationaux conclue à La Haye le 29 Juillet 1899;

Considérant que par l'Article XIX de cette Convention, les Hautes Parties Contractantes se sont réservé de conclure des accords en vue du recours à l'arbitrage, dans tous les cas qu'elles jugeront possible de lui soumettre,

Ont autorisé les Soussignés à arrêter les dispositions suivantes:—

ARTICLE I.

Les différends d'ordre juridique ou relatifs à l'interprétation des Traités existant entre les deux Parties Contractantes qui viendraient à se produire entre elles, et qui n'auraient pu être réglés par la voie diplomatique, seront soumis à la Cour Permanente d'Arbitrage établie par la Convention du 29 Juillet 1899 à La Haye, à la condition toutefois qu'ils ne mettent en cause, ni les intérêts vitaux ni l'indépendance ou l'honneur des deux États Contractants, et qu'ils ne touchent pas aux intérêts de tierces Puissances.

ARTICLE II.

Dans chaque cas particulier, les Hautes Parties Contractantes, avant de s'adresser à la Cour Permanente d'Arbitrage, signeront un compromis spécial, déterminant nettement l'objet du litige, l'étendue des pouvoirs des Arbitres et les délais à observer, en ce qui concerne la constitution du Tribunal Arbitral et la procédure.

ARTICLE III.

Le présent Arrangement est conclu pour une durée de cinq années, à partir du jour de la signature.

Fait à Londres, en double exemplaire, le 14 Octobre 1903.

(L. S.)　　LANSDOWNE.
(L. S.)　　PAUL CAMBON.

法兩國因恐交涉各件將來致啟端特立條約以備呈請公會調處

一千八百九十九年英法兩國曾在哈咕立約遇有兩國爭端約以和平調處因恐
　（七月二十九日）
後遇第十九款兩國盟堂應如立約將一切爭端求民和平調處無庸於此外別行照辦等

　特派以下書押處員立此條約

　　第一款

凡有爭端　律例　或兩國係約辦妥有意見不同或那公使所餘應請公會調處
　　　　　　　（例）

該會異于一千八百九十八年七月二十九日所立條約內設在哈咕之調處公會之盛等

必須與兩國存之榮辱及自繫之權之關天與地國利害各涉方可照辦

　　第二款

凡遇一案須由盟堂先立寺約辯爭論之由譯出敘準舉本佩調妥兩之權限與及宰期

集本調查人員令委于次游法之期限週一詳呢聲敘

　　　第一款

此千二百初自畫押之日起　以五年為海期

一千四百九十年七月十四日立於哈咕敬署

照會

大亞美理駕合眾國欽命駐劄中華便宜行事全權大臣康

照會事茲奉本國外部大臣寄到訓條囑本大臣轉達

貴親王本年在散魯伊斯萬國議院會聚集時會中

人請美國

大伯理璽天德轉請

各國政府派員設第二次弭兵會其在何時與何處地

方聚會應候商定會中所欲商者約有三端一所有

亥革弭兵會上次聚集明言望將來有二次聚商之數事

二所有此次派官前來聚商之

各國政府須彼此相商調停之約、三聚商可否設一萬

國議院有一定年數、將萬國之交涉聚商一次、云在

一千九百零四年九月二十四號、萬國議院會特派

官員

覲見美國

總統、將以上所言奏達經本國

總統允准並

降諭必早為約同在亥革弭兵會所訂約章已簽約之各大
國、再派官員聚商將弭兵會所尚未達之目的得有成功
之進步本國外部並囑請詢

貴親王、

貴政府願否照此辦理本國

總統如是約請

各國政府未曾預備所商各事之單緣為時尚早應先

由各政府相商方可知各國均願商何事兹將外部所

寄訓條法英全文二紙照會附送、即希

貴親王詳閱自必格外明晰本國

總統論此要事有何意見也須至照會者、附洋文並法英文訓條

右　　照　　會

大清欽命全權大臣便宜行事軍機大臣總理外務部事務和碩慶親王

一千九百四十年拾貳月貳拾肆
先緒叁拾年拾壹月拾捌

日

清代外務部中外關係檔案史料叢編——中美關係卷　第六冊·國際會議

敬肅者前寄二十一號函計達

鈞座美國總統重開弭兵會請各國公議弭兵條例事宜查弭兵

會自西曆一千八百九十九年前俄皇尼古拉斯在和蘭國哈

克地方開議創辦此會所議係禁用行軍毒烟利器妥定陸

戰章程並推廣紅十字會海戰則例以及商辦各國公審事

件誠以兵端一開生靈塗炭故設會以弭之法至善也美廷

業已詢之各國何時何地可以開會議事奧國現已允赴此

會德國當必允從俄國亦允派定赴會議事之員刻下和蘭

政府正與美政府彼此函商立會之事並將所議章程定妥

請由美總統閱定畫押然後宣布現聞提議三事係美外務

部大臣所擬定一兩軍交戰守中立者以何為本二海戰不

得損壞私家貨產三戰船攻擊海口以及他處地方應如何布

置均須切實商議至各國水陸各軍武備預算表亦宜減省

籌備無論何國有無在外駐紮公使皆可派員會議大約明

年夏秋間仍在哈克開會情形與前次相仿彿但與目今俄

日戰事不相干涉日本派員赴會已經日政府宣言美廷既

有請帖赴會屆時自應派員前往但會議之際不得提及

此次戰務等語而美國海部大臣復於前項三欵作為論

說畧謂守中立國與袖手旁觀者情形微有不同凡中立
國所有舉動雖與戰事無碍究不能免與兩戰國有彼此糾
轕之事惟中立國必須按照兩戰國所定章程辦事等語又
聞有人請美總統於會議時轉請沿海各國商一妥善中
立規則以便保護海面以及私家財産免被戰國扣拿等
情其餘應行考訂中立條規如待遇戰國以及不得損害
公私信件之事細目當復不少現值日俄戰事固結不解
我國不獲已而守中立此次美廷舉行此會所注意於中
立條規如此其審慎詳切則與我國極有關繋今由

大部派員赴會正可乘此機會將此次俄日開釁所損害於我

東三省者與夫西藏將來善後事宜凡利害所關統籌規畫

預訂條欵指授機宜俾使臣切實與商實於大局裨益匪淺

況日俄之釁開將來如果日勝則俄人尋仇報復當未有艾

後事關繫於我者正多似應及早綢繆時會所至機不可失

凡此諒己

燭照先機有以善處之也耑此肅泐敬請

鈞安　楊晟　謹肅　十一月二十一日川字第二十二號

清代外務部中外關係檔案史料叢編——中美關係卷 第六冊·國際會議

花翎 左參議 涯

花翎侍郎銜 左丞紹

二品銜 右丞陳

庶務司

呈為照會事光緒三十年十一月十八日接准

照稱本年在散魯伊斯萬國議院會聚集時會

中人請美國

大伯

理疆天德轉請

各國政府派員設第二次弭兵會經本國

總統

兄准並

降諭

必早為約同在亥革弭兵會所訂約章已簽約

之各大國再派官員聚商將弭兵會所未達之

目的得有成功進步本國外部並囑請詢

貴親王貴政府願否照此辦理茲將所寄訓條

法英全文附送即希詳閱自必格外明晰本國

總統意見等因本部查此次萬國議院會擬設第二

次弭兵會詳閱

貴大臣來照並所送

外部大臣訓條具見

貴國

大伯理璽天德力主和平維持大局本爵大臣等同

深欽佩現在中國政府深願照此辦理俟將來

開會時再將應商各事派員公同會議相應照復

貴大臣轉達

貴國外部查照可也須至照復者

美康使

先緒三十年十二月　日

敬啟者上月二十五日肅布美字第五十四號函言

粵漢廢約事計日可邀

堂鑒前於十一月二十二日奉

馬電敬悉美國擬按照荷蘭弭兵會公斷條款訂立和

衷調理之約請飭駐使與總統所派全權會商立約

簽押經

大部奏奉

諭旨著梁誠會商辦理欽此飭即欽遵餘事咨達誠當將奉

電欽遵緣由先行電復

冰案旋於次日晤海外部面傳一切海云前奉總統傳

諭旨飭行商辦日間擬定約稿即行送上候貴大臣定期開

商催詢令既欽奉

諭通知各國英法荷比等國均已妥訂簽行正擬奉

議識告以約稿可先送來核度仍須候我國訓條到

後始能開議康使照會有英法相同之語此次約稿

想係一律海謂各國皆屬一律此利時曾欲稍易數

字本國迄未允許此等公斷條約未便畸輕畸重現

在專候約稿送來查取英法各本核對有無歧異再

當電請

列憲詧核定期開議查英法條約載有各約文義解釋不

同應交公斷一款正與誠原擬工約所列第十一款

相同前次送稿律部大臣頗以不符成案為嫌壁欲

刪去正費躊躇今能與英法一律於公斷約中明載

此款則工約之內自應除出以免參差或貽口實是

否有當另候

指示遵行所有奉飭商辦公斷條約緣由先此馳復即希

代回

邸堂列憲詧核為荷肅此祗請

均安

梁誠頓首 光緒三十年十二月初一日

美字第五十五號

敬再啟者民人何采言在廣州被美國兵船水手擲

溺一案前奉

電飭告美外部按照原議秉公妥結經向海約翰面陳

一切茲計康使公牘全案供證當已到美復於上月

二十九日繕具照會將港滬各報摘錄送去業據照

復前來先行錄呈

省覽統希

冰案以備

代回是荷再請

均安

　　　　梁誠再頓首

附呈漢洋文鈔件

光緒三十年十二月初五日

美字文第五十六號

堀
L
正月廿日

照譯致美外部海約翰文 光緒三十年十一月二十九日 西一千九百五年正月初四日

為照會事案照西上年十一月面談華人何采言在廣州被

美國兵船水手拋擲落水溺斃一案本大臣前准我

外務部電咨情形並言

貴國駐京公使業已具報想經

貴部查照兹特鈔錄原電並將上海刊刻議及此事之

英文報章兩件摘要一併附送以便

貴大臣參閱想

貴部現在當已詳悉此案底蘊是以再為瀆陳惟望

貴大臣早日將此案妥酌秉公辦理務期平允想應照會

貴大臣請煩查照須至照會者

照譯署理美外部盧米斯復文 光緒三十年十二月初五日
西一千九百五年正月九日

為照復事本部接准

貴大臣西本月四日文開華人何采言於西九月二十六日在廣

州被美國兵船水手溺斃一案請本國政府妥酌辦理務

期公允等因本部自當即行查核辦理相應照復

貴大臣請煩查照須至照會者

逕啟者接准散魯伊斯賽會總理福大臣蘭西来電請轉達

中國政府令副監督黃開甲照其所奉中國剳飭將賽會地方

既有中國建造之亭舍均行交付本大臣特即電謝等因本署

大臣相應據電函達

貴親王查照是荷此頌

爵祺附送洋文

名另具十二月初九日

固立之

F.O. No.760

H.   LEGATION OF THE UNITED STATES OF AMERICA,
                    PEKIN, CHINA.

                              January 14 1905.

Your Imperial Highness:-

          I have the honor to inform your Imperial
Highness that I have this day received a telegram from Hon. David
R. Francis, President of the Louisiana Purchase Exposition, as
follows:- "Please express to Chinese Government my sincere appre-
ciation Chinese Pavilion on Exposition grounds which Commissioner
Wang has presented to me under Government instructions".

          I have the honor, therefore, to transmit
the above telegram to Your Imperial Highness as requested, and at
the same time I seize the opportunity to renew to Your Imperial
Highness the assurance of my highest consideration.

                         John Gardner Coolidge
                              Chargé d'Affaires.

To His Imperial Highness, Prince of Ch'ing,

President of the Board of Foreign Affairs.

敬稟者光緒三十年十一月十三日奉

憲台文電內開公所或贈會長或贈博物院均可總期永久作為記

念希酌辦電復等因奉此查會場所借公地一俟會完須將屋宇

一律拆盡地仍歸還原主乃美國賽會之章程也此次會場美國

自建房屋並鐵軌車輛傢具等項統計用洋三千七百萬金元今

已全行售出僅得價洋四十五萬金元其拆卸之費係歸受主給

發各國所建公所大牢賤售以省拆費今中國建造賽會公所遵

諭贈於會長該會長不勝欣感願將原房另行擇地移置作為永久

記念除先行電復外理合稟報以副

崖系再奉

電諭適值西節停工辦理稍遲數日合併陳明肅稟恭叩

鈞安伏乞

垂鑒 二品銜四品卿銜前赴散魯伊斯賽會副監督黃開甲謹稟

卅 二月十三日

咨呈

欽差出使美秘古墨國大臣梁　為

咨呈事竊照光緒三十一年正月初四日承准

貴部咨開美國願與中國訂立弭兵會和衷調理之約一事經本部於

光緒三十年十一月二十一日具奏奉

硃批著梁誠會商辦理欽此等因除由本部摘要電達外相應抄錄原奏並往

來照會及法英原約咨行查照欽遵辦理並鈔件等因承准此本大臣先於

光緒三十年十一月二十一日承准

貴部馬電開美使照稱美外部奉總統命願與中國訂立和衷調理之約按

照和蘭弭兵會公斷條約第十九款辦法與法英所立之約相同請飭駐使

與總統所派全權大臣會商立約簽押等因本日經本部奏奉

諭旨著梁誠會商辦理欽此希欽遵餘咨達等因當經電復在案茲承前因

除照會美外部欽遵並俟訂期會議再行咨報外理合將奉文緣由先行

聲復為此咨呈

貴部謹請詧照須至咨呈者

右　咨　呈

外　務　部

光緒叁拾壹年正月　初伍　日

（鈐用空白）

以

正月初七日

大美國欽命駐劄中華便宜行事全權大臣　田

照會事查西曆去歲十二月二十四號曾經

康大臣將本國

大伯理璽天德諭意以中國亦當匡襄第二次在亥革

設立弭兵會照會

貴親王當據照復情願入會等情在案兹復准本

國外部大臣寄來通行公牘仍係論及第二次弭

兵會之事囑本署大臣將該公牘送請查核其公

牘內提及之意是以本署大臣深望

貴親王將此通行公牘提及之意詳為討論照復

是荷須至照會者　附送洋文及通行文件

右　　照　　會

大清欽命全權大臣便宜行事軍機大臣總理外務部事務和碩慶親王

光緒叁拾壹年正月　　初柒

一千九百伍年貳月　　拾　　拾　　號　　日

F.O. No. 771.

H.　　LEGATION OF THE UNITED STATES OF AMERICA,
PEKIN, CHINA.

February 10th 1905.

Your Imperial Highness:-

　　　　I have the honor to inform Your Imperial
Highness that I have received from the Secretary of State a circu-
lar regarding the assembling of a second Peace Conference at the
Hague, which circular I am instructed to send to Your Imperial
Highness, inviting consideration of the suggestions made therein.

　　　　I have the honor to remind Your Imperial
Highness that upon the 24th of December last, Mr. Conger communicated to you the President's invitation to take part in a second
Peace Conference, and that a reply was subsequently received from
Your Highness accepting the invitation.　I trust therefore, that
Your Highness will give due consideration to the suggestions made
in the above-mentioned circular, which I have the honor to enclose
h erein.　Awaiting your reply, I seize the opportunity to renew to Your Imperial Highness the assurance of my highest consideration.

　　　　　　　　　　Chargé d'Affaires.

To His Imperial Highness, Prince of Ch'ing,

President of the Board of Foreign Affairs.

DEPARTMENT OF STATE,

Washington, December 16, 1904.

[To the Representatives of the United States Accredited to

the Governments Signatories to the Acts of The Hague

Conference, 1899.]

Sir:

By the circular instruction dated October 21, 1904,

the representatives of the United States accredited to the

several Governments which took part in the Peace Conference

held at The Hague in 1899, and which joined in signing the

Acts thereof, were instructed to bring to the notice of those

Governments certain resolutions adopted by the Interparlia-

mentary Union at its annual conference held at St. Louis in

September last, advocating the assembling of a Second Peace

Conference to continue the work of the first, and were di-

rected to ascertain to what extent those Governments were

disposed to act in the matter.

The replies so far received indicate that the proposi-

tion has been received with general favor. No dissent has

found expression. The Governments of Austria-Hungary, Den-

mark, France, Germany, Great Britain, Italy, Luxemburg,
Mexico, the Netherlands, Portugal, Roumania, Spain, Sweden
and Norway, and Switzerland exhibit sympathy with the purposes of the proposal, and generally accept it in principle,
with a reservation in most cases of future consideration of
the date of the conference and the programme of subjects for
discussion. The replies of Japan and Russia conveyed in
like terms a friendly recognition of the spirit and purposes
of the invitation, but on the part of Russia the reply was
accompanied by the statement that, in the existing condition of things in the Far East, it would not be practicable
for the Imperial Government, at this moment, to take part in
such a conference. While this reply, tending as it does to
cause some postponement of the proposed Second Conference, is
deeply regretted, the weight of the motive which induces it
is recognized by this Government and, probably, by others.
Japan made the reservation only that no action should be
taken by the conference relative to the present war.

Although the prospect of an early convocation of an
august assembly of representatives of the nations in the in-

terests of peace and harmony among them is deferred for the

time being, it may be regarded as assured so soon as the in-

terested powers are in a position to agree upon a date and

place of meeting and to join in the formulation of a general

plan for discussion. The President is much gratified at the

cordial reception of his overtures. He feels that in

eliciting the common sentiment of the various Governments in

favor of the principle involved and of the objects sought to

be attained a notable step has been taken toward eventual

success.

Pending a definite agreement for meeting when circum-

stances shall permit, it seems desirable that a comparison

of views should be had among the participants as to the scope

and matter of the subjects to be brought before the Second

Conference. The invitation put forth by the Government of

the United States did not attempt to do more than indicate

the general topics which the Final Act of the First Confer-

ence of The Hague relegated, as unfinished matters, to con-

sideration by a future conference--adverting, in connection

with the important subject of the inviolability of private

property in naval warfare, to the like views expressed by

the Congress of the United States in its resolution adopted

April 28, 1904, with the added suggestion that it may be

desirable to consider and adopt a procedure by which States

nonsignatory to the original Acts of The Hague Conference

may become adhering parties. In the present state of the

project, this Government is still indisposed to formulate a

programme. In view of the virtual certainty that the Presi-

dent's suggestion of The Hague as the place of meeting of

a Second Peace Conference will be accepted by all the

interested powers, and in view also of the fact that an

organized representation of the Signatories of the Acts of

1899 now exists at that Capital, this Government feels that

it should not assume the initiative in drawing up a pro-

gramme, nor preside over the deliberations of the Signatories

in that regard. It seems to the President that the high

task he undertook in seeking to bring about an agreement of

the powers to meet in a Second Peace Conference is virtually

accomplished so far as it is appropriate for him to act,

and that, with the general acceptance of his invitation in

principle, the future conduct of the affair may fitly follow

its normal channels. To this end it is suggested that the

further and necessary interchange of views between the

Signatories of the Acts of 1899 be effected through the

International Bureau under the control of the Permanent

Administrative Council of The Hague. It is believed that in

this way, by utilizing the central representative agency

established and maintained by the powers themselves, an

orderly treatment of the preliminary consultations may be

insured and the way left clear for the eventual action of

the Government of the Netherlands in calling a renewed con-

ference to assemble at The Hague, should that course be

adopted.

  You will bring this communication to the knowledge of

the Minister for Foreign Affairs and invite consideration

of the suggestions herein made.

    I am, Sir,

      Your obedient servant

        JOHN HAY.

一千九百零四年十月二十一號傳諭內開萬國公議會

於前九月間在聖魯義舉行週年之會業經議定

懇請斜與會二次集議以續首次之功並詢各國欲於

此事辦到如何地位等因本此當即轉諭美國駐劄各

國之代表人員將此知照二十八百九十九年在亥革會議

並經簽名之各國一體查照在案茲接各處覆文均

蒙嘉許並無異言其與丹法德英意魯仙白墨西哥

荷蘭葡萄牙羅蠻你亞西班牙瑞典耶威及瑞士

等國均表同恩概行遵照惟集議之期及所議之件

尚待再酌等語日俄覆文亦認立意之善惟在俄

國則日規因遠東情形末便入會將使二次集議

展緩日期良深婉惜然其為勢所逼本國鑒之

諒各國亦同鑒之也日本僅云集議時不得提及現

時戰務再觀此情形凡願共享和平之國其代表人

欲早集議不得不暫展緩矣雖然一俟入會諸國

定有準期準地及會議各法諒我國總統必欣然

樂觀厥成也此會設法立意既經感動各國嘉許總

統之意以為業經著有成效矣何時集議現難不

能遽定然第二次擬議之宗旨事件似宜各抒己見

以備互相考核也美國政府前發請帖不過將亥革

第一會末條之大概宗旨表明尚未完結須俟下會

再議並及水戰之時不得損傷私產一千九百零四

年四月三十八號美國之會亦經定有此議又擬設

法使亥革之會未簽名者亦得補行入會當此

時勢本國尚不欲將各條開列清單也一因總統

擬以亥革為第二會集議之地必為各國許可

一因一千八百九十九年簽名代表之人現今尚在

亥革是以本國不應倡繕清單亦不應先各簽

名之人而有思議也總統以為其與此大舉以求

各國再會凡所應為者已告放矣各國既先其

所請將來行事當可遵從止道也其意在此因

將陳說擬由亥革選任議員所管之萬國公署

使一千八百九十九年簽名之人須再交換意見

如此善用各國所自創守之中興代辦處則前

此所商議者諒可保其就緒也且此法若立則

荷國請在亥革重會之理亦自昭然若揭矣

將此照會外部大臣請煩思之

一千九百零四年十二月十六號即華盛頓國部致

書於美國派駐於一千八百九十九年亥革會議

簽名之各國代表人員

海約翰謹上

一千九百零四年十月二十一號傳諭內開蒙國公議會北通九月間在聖魯義舉

行週年之會業經議定懇請貴兵會三次聚議以續首次之功詢悉貴國欲於此

多詔即為何地位等因奉此應即特諭美國駐劄為國之代表人員悉此類照一千

八百九十年玍亥舉會議之為國一體查照在案荼樣各愛露文均蒙嘉許幷行簽名

所威及瑞士等國均表同心俠行速。惟集議之旨及所議之件為待再酌考理

日低盧文亦退立玄之善惟在俄國別項現因遠東情形暫耐未便入會妙候二次

車議將可屐期良洋微情怒贊為勢所逼本國舉之諒兜國亦同舉之也本

僅云集謙時不仍提及現衛弦年覗此性形此顯其事和平之國史代表人情

早集謙不仍不智屐優美離述一俟以意殯在立意臨文第二次擦譯之宗旨栈多佝宜各持己見

我國傾统必破起世菜聰顉威之此會餧茌立意臨文第二次擦譯之宗旨栈多佝宜各持己見

以備酌機巴美國招爾昔發諸怡不過昭亥革第一會謙締玄大概崇高表呢尚未完結

陛議下會通譯莊及此辦之時某將接傷私處一千九百零四年四月二十八號美國之會
亦經定者此議又辦頭成俟亥革之會奉各省此亦得補預之第高此時預必參預
若不別將各條開到華也一周興於摺以亥革之所以舉之會軍乃至之事亦當行之
一國一千八百九十一至本華等省領我民歐等必行亥革省乃本國不應以之各國語事
等必六　先多營喬之人而官民益於此其興大幸以求各國再會及所
應兩者已著成素各國院先先所諸此其此及其所雨特陳
説某田亥革實任譯員所管之各國公署使一千八百九十九年簽各名之人須再延錄意見
功此等用各國所自創守之中央代辦委辦而此所商諸共諸于保共就統也此
法子立別各原有國諸查亥革重會之限之自開先美韓美邸此照會外訂次函諸項
異之

一千九百零四年十二月十六號華盛梗國部政務作十八號九十九年接於一千各
九十五年亥革會議答各之各國代表人見

海約翰譯五

欽命頭品頂戴督辦山海關內外鐵路大臣刑部右堂胡　為

咨會事案據山海關內外鐵路總局詳以第七囘萬國鐵路公會

將屆舉行之期前本路酌派工程司詹道天佑廊守孫謀卹須前

往惟現以京張鐵路正在商辦籌造之際此路工程亦甚關緊要

詹道似難遠離職道等公同酌擬卽派委廊守孫謀一員前往美

國倭生湯地方入會會議亦足以資得力如蒙允准該守起行時

應持之赴會文憑應否由職局先行發給或由憲轅填發交該員

祇頎抑或由憲台轉咨

外務部發給之處乞核奪施行並請在京就近知會比公使以便

接洽查廊守原名景陽現改名孫謀合併聲明等情前來本大臣

正在核辦間旋准

貴部咨准比葛使照稱該員准於下月開辦貴國所派四員於到

美之際可領得專員赴會文憑等語請轉飭該員等遵照等因當
即將原咨隨批抄發行令該總局轉飭遵辦在案茲復據該總局
詳稱職局遵即飭知廓守查照預備前往去後茲據該守稟稱為
時已促現在漢沽橋工正在下橋之際關繫緊要未便遽離如來
搭十一日所開赴美之船實來不及等語職局查倭生湯會場開
議係華四月初一日起即西五月四號至初十日止即西十三號
如不能搭十一日赴美之船前往遲則至時必已收會且該守現
辦漢沽橋梁要工正在下橋必須親同照料其勢亦有未便遽離
復按此次鐵路公會會議雖係考究利益然會中所議大要將來
必刊之報章如其果有改良善法職局亦可隨時考核仿行以上
均係實在情形職道等公同商酌此次即不派廓守赴會似亦無
關緊要除詳請

督辦大臣袁　鑒核外理合具文詳請鑒核俯賜咨明

外務部查照實為公便等情到本大臣據此相應備文咨會

貴部請煩查照並希照會比公使知照施行須至咨者

右

咨

外　務　部

洛呈事光緒三十一年四月十九日擬農工商務局司道

詳稱竊照美國跦崙地方現開漁業賽會東省地環

黃海亟亟振興寔業以關利源茲查一有指分縣丞夏

建勲曾充余道台隨員回國熟悉情形堪以委派

且該員情殷遊學極願自備資斧前往考察除逕

行札委外所有本局委派夏縣丞建勲赴美賽會場

考察漁業商務緣由理合詳請鑒核俯賜咨會

出使美國大臣梁　查照保護寔為公便等情到

本署院拟此除分咨外相應咨呈　為此咨呈

貴部謹請　查照施行須至咨呈者

右　呈

外　務　部

日

外務部

楊兆鋆片

舟查向來中國遇有賽會皆由總理衙門飭令

總稅務司派員辦理而商情未甚踴躍工藝未

聞改觀者推原其故蓋由稅司領如以西人置

華貨所擇已未必精且未必躬自採購日後則

一紙飭銷遂以塞責同有書據汜述未嘗曉

守華商於工藝無從考證尤可惜者陳所不

應陳之物徒供西人驕視非笑之資至膜視華商

輒加抑制更無論已竊傷之伏念近年設立

商部提倡商業漸與規模而賽會一事於商

務極有關係臣愚以為此後赴賽宜由商部盡

派熟悉商情丞參一員充當監督會同駐紮

該國便臣和衷共濟並酌帶幹練譯員書記

大使署未有商務隨員飭令相助分所當為

似此亦法有三善商前此貨物之良糟銷場

之通塞僅亦會之稅司知之今則一物一名監督

執加考察藉以改良上藝卑華商知所折

衷一也商人未洞言語不通運貨報關下揚

交易動須照料若遇關折遇巨或免徵地租或

略予欤助酌盈劑虚留心體恤二員與賽

各國主持會務閒其本國官前此次日本即派

商務部參事官為監督今以華官以華官以導

國使三也全散會伊赴賽之物移在藝業斯應於

藏事時由總稅務司護具清單呈請外務部

轉咨商部存案一面就正點交使署封存以備也

国設會陳賽可省往返運資俟以後赴賽商

人源源而来則基礎粗立藉備觀摩萬一應

者寬寬宜用高部貴成名直省海関道由

籌數千金置些精美土庫派商人會循例出

售以資倡率而颣銷塲縱脫售无多而原

物仍在所耗者派人用費耳无事

国家弟辦賽物為此區大查名国賽會局面

不同夷考近年以美之散會但為大日本反

比国次三尚有小於此者但於設會以前視其

會章地段三大小規模之廣狹可得大概乱得

會章寺差定用費之多宜

国家既不增置一物祇此租地建屋傭薪欷費

川資運腳保險存棧等費亦可示限制兩節

虛糜要兩論之備官物以起賽乃一時之行權

今商務漸興自以鼓舞工藝為要義用若仍

以領會非因之通例今商部既立自以專委

逐參為得宜至管見所及擬請

飭下外務部商部核議施行似於商務大有裨益

是否有當謹附片密陳伏乞

聖鑒訓示謹

奏

　光緒三十一年六月三十日奉

硃批外務部商部知道欽此

清代外務部中外關係檔案史料叢編——中美關係卷 第六册·國際會議

庶務司

呈為照復事昨准

照稱上海會審章程一事領衘大臣於西

九月二十七號代各國大臣照會請急速辦

理准復稱江南地方官尚未聲復迄今又滿

二箇月仍未辦此要件本大臣須代本國

政府切請速為設法不准地方官再行延

宕以阻礙整頓上海會審章程最要之事

等因查此項章程迭經本部咨催南洋大臣

妥籌聲復在案茲准該大臣電稱上海會

審章程與滬道往返熟商酌擬定稿昨已

備文咨復等語是該大臣復文業經交驛

遞送不日即可到部除俟咨到酌核照復外相

應先行照會

貴大臣查照須至照會者

美柔使

光緒三十一年十月

逕啟者　茲接本國外部大臣來函奉

總統諭云於一千九百零七年設立萬國海陸軍賽會於滬爾

金屯飛那屬之漢屯路水面一帶地方此會為記念美國之

生日益來英人初抵西半球之記念故請全球各國政府流

人赴會等語本大臣擬照所轄把此諭附送

貴親王查閱並提及本國

總統頎聽

　貴國政府派往兵輪及相當陸軍赴會復有宅米思屯於

此次賽會之際如設一商務賽會於內本本臣甚悅將此

達知

　貴親王查照是荷此泐順頌

爵祺　　附洋文及論單
　　　　並外附冊一本

名另具　十二月初吾

柔克義

To F.O. No.

H.   LEGATION OF THE UNITED STATES OF AMERICA,
PEKIN, CHINA.

December 30 1905.

Your Imperial Highness:

          I have the honor to transmit herewith
1/ a printed copy of a Proclamation issued by the President of the
United States, inviting , in the name of the Government and
people of the United States, the Governments of the world to
take part in an international naval, marine, and military celebration in 1907; to be held at and near the waters of Hampton
Roads in the State of Virginia, in commemoration of the birth
of the American nation, the first permanent settlement of English-speaking people on the Western Hemisphere.

        I am instructed by the Secretary of State to communicate
this invitation to Your Highness' Government, and to state that
the President will learn with great pleasure the intention of
the Chinese Government to participate in the celebration by
the sending of its naval vessels and such representation of its
military organizations as it may deem proper.

        Contemporaneously with this celebration there will be held
an international exposition under the auspices of the Jamestown
Exposition Company, notice of which I take pleasure in bringing
to Your Imperial Highness.

        I seize the opportunity to renew to Your Imperial Highness
the assurance of my highest consideration.

                 Envoy Extraordinary and
                     Minister Plenipotentiary
                       of the United States.

To His Imperial Highness, Prince of Ch'ing,
    President of the Board of Foreign Affairs.

Enclosure: 1/ Printed copy of President's proclamation.

[JAMESTOWN CELEBRATION.]

By the President of the United States of America.

A Proclamation.

WHEREAS the Congress of the United States has passed an Act approved March 3, 1905, and entitled, "An Act To provide for celebrating the birth of the American nation, the first permanent settlement of English-speaking people on the Western Hemisphere, by the holding of an international naval, marine, and military celebration in the vicinity of Jamestown, on the waters of Hampton Roads, in the State of Virginia; to provide for a suitable and permanent commemoration of said event, and to authorize an appropriation in aid thereof, and for other purposes.";

And Whereas Section 3 of the said Act reads as follows:

"SEC. 3. The President of the United States is hereby authorized to make proclamation of said celebration, setting forth the event to be commemorated, inviting foreign nations to participate by the sending of their naval vessels and such representation of their military organizations as may be practicable, ... ":

Now, therefore, I THEODORE ROOSEVELT, President of the United States, by virtue of the authority vested in me by the said Act, do hereby declare and proclaim that there shall be inaugurated, in the year nineteen hundred and seven, on and near the waters of Hampton Roads, in the State of Virginia, an international naval, marine and military celebration, beginning May 13, and ending not later than November 1, 1907, for the purpose of commemorating, in a fitting and appropriate manner, the birth of the American nation, the first permanent settlement of English-speaking people on the American Continent, made at Jamestown, Virginia, on the thirteenth day of May, sixteen hundred and seven, and in order that the great events of American history which have resulted therefrom, may be accentuated to the present and future generations of American citizens. And in the name of the Government and of the people of the United States, I do hereby invite all the nations of the earth to take part in the commemoration of an event which has had a far reaching effect upon the course of human history, by sending their naval vessels to the said celebration and by making such representations of their military organizations as may be practicable.

In Testimony Whereof, I have hereunto set my hand and caused the seal of the United States to be affixed.

DONE at the City of Washington, this 29th day of March, one thousand nine hundred and five, and of the Independence of the United States, the one hundred and twenty-ninth.

[SEAL.]

THEODORE ROOSEVELT

By the President:
ALVEY A. ADEE
Acting Secretary of State.

譜蘐桐
子紫陳陶大東

仁兄大人閣下敬啟者本月初十日接准

貴部文開准美柔使函稱接本國外部大臣來函美總統

云於一千九百零七年設立萬國軍賽會於渥爾金尼亞所

屬之漢屯路水面一帶地方請全球各國政府派人赴會

等語將原送附冊一本咨行查照辦理聲覆等因到部當

即飭司將附冊洋文譯漢查原文設會宗旨重在關於水

陸軍之工藝科學教育學等項應否咨行練兵處之處即

希查照酌辦至柔大臣來照所稱於此次賽會之際加設

一商務賽會於內一節所送原冊並未敘及應俟該國另

有辦法章程送到再行酌核辦理可也專此奉佈敬請

勛安　附譯件

愚弟　紹　英

熙　彥　頓首　十二月十七日

附收

照錄譯美總統舉列宅未思屯賽會布告

美政府將於一千九百七年至滙爾金尼亞省之宅

未思屯及漢屯路開記念會美總統魯士佛乃

布告於美眾曰本總統於一千九百五年三月三號

因本國上議院公議准於滙爾金尼亞省所屬

之宅未思屯及漢屯政一第水面地方開一會

場知此地球美國之派兵籛水師並相當之

陸軍前來賽會此賽場係慶賀我人於三

百年前五此地方發現以豐有目前最輩圖

最綿長之詐並公請本總統預籌報項以着此

會經費本繼統以此原因布告大眾自子九百七年

五月十三號自是年十二月一號止開大會於滙

以金尼省之漢屯踏一帶水面以追記我操莢

國語言之人於一万六千七年五月十三歸始保

有於土以葬現於世界之上並涉我閩於水陸軍

之工藝科學教育學等及三万年歷史之

學院三万年中我美國之奇賢往指嘉言遠

引及其他可励可懲之事皆於是會作大記念

心地球之國可於是會文派兵練水師及他航

船並相為之陸軍務於期內尚赴漢屯路一帶

水面以方賽會以期與我美國之學名相稱

幸總統敢肉我全國人民表同情寫子九万万

年三月廿九歸

敬密肅者前奉五十六號函計邀

鈞鑒近来西報轟傳華民仇洋言論危悚甚至捏造枝節

語涉

宮闈駭人聞聽竊揣此種謠言所由起定有奸人從中播弄經晟詳

密採訪細為查察實是美人因我國民抵制禁約不買美

貨以致虧損甚鉅遂造此種謠言惑亂人心時復勾引不

逞之華人偽造電報以為證據蓋冀藉此恫嚇以解散拒約

公會此等作用即外交家所謂藉報館勢力搖動衆情以施

其刁猾技倆者也　晟既訪聞確切祇以中美政府彼此敦

萬睦誼碍難顯為揭破熟籌抵制此種舉動方策惟有

暗為運動亦藉報館之力駁正宣告則不露痕迹不傷

邦交四面靈空解釋似易晟在奧既久所有奧京官報

總辦暨名大報主筆以及英法德義各大報之駐奧訪

事人苓平時聯絡交歡均為我用業經迭次囑其或假託

西人之詞或逕作晟之言論婉切駁正並由奧官報電傳全

歐各國大報采登之後謠言漸息即倫敦露透等電亦經

先後認明傳言失實日来羣情已安堪慰

蓋念西報之風潮既銷則我國造言生事之人亦必拑口矣

南昌教案歐報亦言曲在教士然為今之計還宜速為了

結免致外人藉口牽動大局是否有當伏乞

裁奪考察政治

端

戴大臣不日可到德京此間一切業已由晟預為考察

督飭館員將所有奧國政治大旨詳訪博諮編繕成

册並預囑各部大臣屆時導示一切俾

兩大臣到來易於措手知在

塵注附此奉陳肅請

鈞安　楊晟　謹肅　二月初九日川字第五十七號

○○奏 外務部再奏美國賽會由正副監督帶領員襄理會
務臣等
命赴會曹電商外務部即派使署人員襄理以節廉
費其赴往來公牘飭令譯員徐家庠辦理開
會之初事務尚簡即派三等參贊官沈瑞麟四
等繙譯官劉錫昌往駐會所保護商人比閱於
華員洵有當難五興辦論得免例外需索之
月初舉行評獎臣帶同隨員顧賜書陳洋楊
駐粵省復派留學生監督吳宗濂駐法員
水鈞駐廣東復商人盧焕文暨四員之人充評
獎員此事洵係較重一時疏略即為他國捷占沈
國諡三大宗評較贊美與國一時言固獲超
假絲印茶日本瓷器充作泰西日餂諸員於中
懇推獎餘賞亦不遺餘力詎西員梓光核辦外
所有文該員自抬玄終勤慎將事並不多支薪
佳於會費多所靡省可否將沈瑞麟吳宗濂徐
家庠劉錫昌水鈞銀廣東復顧賜書陳洋八
員諸

聖鑒詞示謹
與嘉獎商人盧焕文
賞給六品頂戴以示鼓厲之意出有
逾格鴻施謹附片陳請伏乞
聖鑒詞示謹
奏
光緒三十二年二月十八日奉
硃批著照所請該部知道欽此

清代外務部中外關係檔案史料叢編——中美關係卷　第六冊·國際會議

清廿

謹將中國赴散魯伊斯城賽會免稅各物開列於後

計開

金陵新關所辦各件

緞機壹架佸關平銀壹拾捌兩壹錢壹分 免出口正稅銀壹兩玖錢柒釐

扣帶套付佸關平銀陸兩 免出口正稅銀叁錢

官帽壹件佸關平銀玖兩捌錢柒分 免出口正稅銀肆錢玖分肆釐

朝帽壹件佸關平銀拾壹兩壹錢叁分 免出口正稅銀伍錢陸分柒釐

朝帽壹件估關平銀拾壹兩叄錢叄分 免出口正稅銀伍錢陸分柒釐

庫金估關平銀肆拾陸兩 免出口正稅銀貳兩叄錢

緞估關平銀貳兩陸錢柒分 免出口正稅銀壹錢叄分肆釐

絨估關平銀陸兩陸錢柒分 免出口正稅銀叄錢叄分肆釐

絨估關平銀伍兩貳錢柒分 免出口正稅銀貳錢陸分肆釐

緞重壹斤拾叄兩 免出口正稅銀壹分捌釐

絨重叄拾玖斤 免出口正稅銀肆兩陸錢捌分

摹本緞重拾柒斤 免出口正稅銀貳兩肆分

綢重貳斤玖兩 免出口正稅銀叄錢捌釐

貢緞重肆斤捌兩 免出口正稅銀伍錢肆分

欄杆重壹斤玖兩 免出口正稅銀壹錢伍分陸釐

南洋大臣自辦各件

庫金估關平銀陸拾兩陸錢 免出口正稅銀叄兩叄分

庫金估關平銀陸拾兩陸錢 免出口正稅銀叄兩叄分

庫金估關平銀捌拾兩陸錢壹分 免出口正稅銀肆兩叄分壹釐

庫銀估關平銀貳拾陸兩捌錢玖分 免出口正稅銀壹兩叄錢肆分伍釐

庫金估關平銀肆拾貳兩陸錢柒分 免出口正稅銀貳兩壹錢叄分肆釐

金羅緞估關平銀伍拾柒兩柒錢肆分 免出口正稅銀貳兩捌錢捌分柒釐

庫緞重拾肆斤肆兩 免出口正稅銀壹兩柒錢壹分

緞重貳斤陸兩 免出口正稅銀貳錢捌分伍釐

摹本緞重伍斤玖兩 免出口正稅銀陸錢分捌釐

絨重拾肆斤伍兩 免出口正稅銀壹兩柒錢壹分捌釐

椑帛估關平銀肆拾伍兩叄錢貳分 免出口正稅銀貳兩貳錢陸分陸釐

手帕估關平銀貳兩柒錢 免出口正稅銀壹錢叄分伍釐

繡貨估關平銀拾捌兩捌錢伍分 免出口正稅銀玖錢肆分叄釐

緞聯估關平銀捌兩玖錢捌分 免出口正稅銀肆錢肆分玖釐

緞聯估關平銀捌兩玖錢捌分　免出口正稅銀肆錢肆分玖釐

錦緞估關平銀拾貳兩伍錢叁分　免出口正稅銀陸錢貳分玖釐

繡屏捌幅估關平銀壹百肆拾叁兩陸錢叁分　免出口正稅銀柒兩壹錢捌分貳釐

牙雕櫃子壹個估關平銀壹百柒拾柒兩柒錢貳分　免出口正稅銀捌兩捌分陸釐

全漆茶盆壹個估關平銀肆拾肆兩捌錢捌分　免出口正稅銀貳兩貳錢肆分肆釐

全漆掛架壹對估關平銀貳拾陸兩玖錢叁分　免出口正稅銀壹兩叁錢肆分柒釐

銀煙盆壹個重陸兩柒錢貳分　免出口正稅銀肆分貳釐

銀叉拾貳把重拾肆兩貳錢　免出口正稅銀捌分玖釐

銀盅盒壹個重壹兩肆錢壹分　免出口正稅銀玖釐

銀咖啡壺壹對重貳拾捌兩　免出口正稅銀壹錢柒分伍釐

銀花瓶壹對重伍兩陸錢　免出口正稅銀叁分伍釐

銀胡椒盅壹對重壹兩伍錢　免出口正稅銀玖釐

銀糖夾壹對重叁兩貳分　免出口正稅銀壹分玖釐

銀糖夾壹對重叁兩貳分 免出口正稅銀壹分玖釐

銀煙灰盆拾個重叁兩伍錢伍分 免出口正稅銀肆分柒釐

銀鹽盅連挑陸付重肆兩肆分 免出口正稅銀貳分伍釐

銀調羹貳拾肆把重陸兩柒錢叄分 免出口正稅銀肆分貳釐

銀五味架壹個重肆兩貳錢叄分 免出口正稅銀貳分柒釐

銀調羹貳拾貳把重叄兩捌錢陸分 免出口正稅銀貳分肆釐

銀扣帶陸付重拾兩肆錢貳分 免出口正稅銀陸分叄釐

銀茶瓶壹個重叄兩陸錢捌分 免出口正稅銀貳分叄釐

銀酒盅壹對重陸拾兩 免出口正稅銀肆錢貳分伍釐

銀相片架壹個重貳拾捌兩肆錢伍分 免出口正稅銀壹錢柒分捌釐

銀糖盅壹個重伍兩叄錢叄分 免出口正稅銀叄分肆釐

銀牛奶壺壹個重肆兩叄錢 免出口正稅銀貳分玖釐

銀大酒盅壹個重柒拾伍兩 免出口正稅銀肆錢陸分玖釐

銀牛奶壺壹個重肆兩柒錢　免出口正稅銀貳分玖釐

銀大酒盅壹個重柒拾伍兩　免出口正稅銀肆錢陸分玖釐

雕雲毋壳壹對佔關平銀貳拾陸兩玖錢叄分　免出口正稅銀壹分叁錢肆分柒釐

雕牙扇貳柄佔關平銀貳百拾伍兩壹肆分　免出口正稅銀拾兩柒錢柒分貳釐

金漆工夫箱壹個佔關平銀壹百拾陸兩柒錢　免出口正稅銀伍兩叁錢柒分貳釐

金漆蓮花壹座佔關平銀壹百柒拾兩柒錢貳分　免出口正稅銀伍兩叁錢捌分陸釐

古瓶壹個佔關平銀捌拾玖兩柒錢叄分　免出口正稅銀肆兩肆錢捌分玖釐

繡花屏肆幅佔關平銀肆拾叄兩玖分　免出口正稅銀貳兩壹錢伍分伍釐

爐屏貳幅佔關平銀壹百貳拾伍兩陸錢叄分　免出口正稅銀陸兩貳錢捌分肆釐

以上共免稅關平銀玖拾陸兩陸錢陸分伍釐

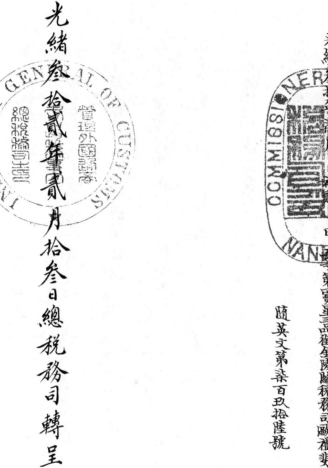

光緒參拾貳年貳月拾參日總稅務司轉呈

光緒參拾年柒月初貳日等因第寶呈三品銜金陵關稅務司歐禮斐呈報

隨英文第柒百玖拾陸號

逕啟者、本大臣茲代達美國

大總統綸言、因中政府及華商人等、於一千九百四年、在散魯伊斯賽

會事、故于一千九百五年三月三號、美國上下議院議定、美政府

與民人等、同深感謝中國政府華商於此賽會實像非常無以加

尚之襄助、並協同我國記念前壹百年購定魯伊斯亞那之地、

其購地事、為美國最注重交涉之史記、相應函達

貴親王查照是荷尚此順頌

爵祺 附送洋文

名另具 四月十九日

柔克義

LEGATION OF THE UNITED STATES OF AMERICA,
PEKIN, CHINA.

To F.O. No. *126.*   May 12 1906.

H.

Your Imperial Highness:

      In pursuance of the Joint Resolution
of Congress, approved March 3, 1905, I take great pleasure
in conveying in the President's name the expression of the
grateful appreciation of the Government and people of the
United States for the invaluable aid contributed by the Government and people of China to the success of the Louisiana
Purchase Exposition at St. Louis in 1904, and for their friendly participation in the commemoration of the one hundredth
anniversary of the purchase of the territory of Louisiana,
one of the most important international events in the history
of the United States.

                           Envoy Extraordinary and
                           Minister Plenipotentiary
                           of the United States.

To His Imperial Highness, Prince of Ch'ing,
    President of the Board of Foreign Affairs.

逕啟者接准本國外部函囑代請中國派員赴美國第十五次軍醫

會該會定於西本年九月十一至十四號在鈕約屬之伯福洛地方

開設查上年第十四次會係於米西干省第得羅得地方舉行美

政府及該會甚喜款接中國所派往醫生三員茲深望此次中國

仍行派員與會是荷此布即頌

時祉附洋文

名另具閏四月初四日

桑克義

LEGATION OF THE UNITED STATES OF AMERICA,
PEKIN, CHINA.

To F.O. No. *133.*

H.   May 25, 1906.

Your Imperial Highness:

I Have the honor to inform Your Imperial Highness that I am in recipt of instructions from the Department of State directing me to extend on behalf of the Association of Military Surgeons of the United States, an invitation to the Government of China to be represented at the fifteenth Annual Meeting of that Association, which will be held at Buffalo, New York, on September 11th to 14th 1906 inclusive.

In forwarding this invitation to Your Highness I may say that both the Department and the Association were very much pleased to receive three delegates sent by your Government to the Fourteenth Annual Meeting of this society held in Detroit in 1905, and would, I am sure, be glad to learn of the acceptance by the Chinese Government of this second invitation.

I avail myself of the opportunity to renew to Your Imperial Highness the assurance of my highest consideration.

Envoy Extraordinary and
Minister Plenipotentiary
of the United States.

To His Imperial Highness, Prince of Ch'ing,
President of the Board of Foreign Affairs.

二

咨明事據署金陵關道羅章呈稱案奉憲札准

外務部咨凡欲運物赴某處賽會者須由本商先期赴就近海

關監督處呈請發給運物執照俟所運貨物報關出口時將此

執照一併呈驗方准免稅仍隨案報明本部存查又准江海

關移送抄稟內開各關給照經過滬關轉運入會者應由各關另

行移會滬關一面諭令原商到滬後將所領執照並搭定船名

呈明關道以便核明函致稅務司一體驗免放行各等因奉經

遵辦在案茲准江南商務局函稱奉辦漁業賽會刻已購齊

魚具各項計木箱四箇又照相圖說兩套魚叉魚簍五捆共

十一件伍本洋五百三十一元六角開送逐件佰本清單請發色

稅執照前來除遵章繕發免稅執照函關驗放並移江海關
道核辦外理合呈祈鑒核咨明

外務部查考實為公便等情到本大臣據此相應咨明為此

咨呈

貴部謹請查照施行須至咨呈者

右咨呈

外務部

光緒　　　　年　　伍　　月　　　　日

和會司

呈為照復事前准

照稱准外部函囑代請中國派員赴美國第十五

次軍醫會該會定於西曆本年九月十一至十四號

在紐約屬之福伯洛地方開設等因當經本部咨

行練兵處核辦去後茲准復稱准北洋大臣電稱

美國十五次軍醫會擬派正醫官陳世華周貴生

二員屆時前往與會等因前來相應照復

貴大臣查照即希轉達

貴國外部可也須至照復者

美柔使

光緒三十二年五月　　　日

欽差全權大臣太子少保會辦練兵大臣直隸總督部堂袁　為

咨呈事案查前准

貴部咨開接准美柔使函稱准外部函囑代請中國派員

赴美國第十五次軍醫會該會定於西歷本年九月十一

至十四號在紐約屬之伯福洛地方開設查上年第十四

次會係於米西干省第得羅地方舉行美政府及該會甚

喜款接中國所派往醫生三員茲深望此次中國仍行派

員與會等語除行知練兵處外咨行酌核辦理并望見復

可也等因到本大臣准此當經分行查照辦理具覆核咨

去後據軍醫局稟派正軍醫官陳世華正醫官周貴生堪

以赴會業經咨呈在案現又准南北洋海軍薩提督鎮冰

呈稱查上年派赴美國第十四次軍醫會之海軍醫院總

醫官何根源參考新法學業頗有心得此次擬請仍派該

員前往與會籍資考查等情除札委該員料理行裝趕緊

前往並咨明

出使美國大臣妥為照料外相應咨呈

大部謹請查照須至咨呈者

右　咨　呈

外　務　部

光緒

日

和會司

呈為照會事前准

照稱本年西歷九月在紐約屬福伯洛地方開

設第十五次軍醫會請派員赴會一事業經

本部轉行練兵處派員前往照會在案茲復

准北洋大臣咨稱准南北洋海軍薩提督呈稱

上年派赴美國第十四次軍醫會之海軍醫

院總醫官何根源參考新法學業頗有心得此次仍

擬派該員前往與會藉資考證等因前來相

應照會

貴大臣查照轉達

貴國外部可也須至照會者

美柔使

光緒三十二年六月　　　　日

欽命總理練兵處王大臣 為

咨行事案查美國第十五次軍醫會業由北洋派定

陳世華周貴生二員前往前經咨復在案茲准會辦

練兵大臣直隸總督袁 咨稱擬飭該員等留美三

月分赴各製藥廠悉心考究俟回國後集資仿辦又

准咨稱據南北洋海軍薩提督鎮冰呈稱查上年派

赴美國第十四次軍醫會之海軍醫院總醫官何根

源參考新法學業頗有心得此次擬請仍派該員前

往與會藉資考查除札委該員等料理行裝趕緊前

往並咨明出使美國大臣妥為照料外咨呈查照各

等因到處相應咨行

貴部查照可也須至咨者

右　咨

外　務　部

逕啟者、非利濱羣島醫學會於西歷一千九百七年二月二十八、

三月初一二等日、在滿呢拉城開會、已請日本印度新加坡呸哇

新金山東京暹羅各國等處特行派委醫官同深明理化之

人及醫生等與會、該會中之意、中國亦應委派醫官前來、

是以非利濱總督即請轉達

貴國政府亦可派員赴會、等因本大臣甚望

貴親王按照所請、允准派員前往、並希將所派定之員、早日

見復是荷此頌

爵祺、附洋文

名另具 十月十一日

LEGATION OF THE UNITED STATES OF AMERICA,
PEKIN, CHINA.

To F.O. No. 196.

W.   December 26, 1906.

Your Imperial Highness:-

　　I have the honor to inform Your Imperial Highness that the annual meeting of the Philippine Islands Medical Association will be held at the city of Manila on February 27, 28, and March 1, and 2, 1907, and will be attended both by official delegates and by unofficial professional and scientific men from Japan, India, the Straits Settlements, Java, Australia, Indo-China, and Siam, so it is expected.

　　The members of the Society desire that an official representative be sent by China, if possible, and I am requested by the Governor General of the Philippines to ask Your Imperial Highness' Government to kindly appoint an official representative to attend this meeting.

　　Trusting that Your Highness may be able to comply with this request, and that I may be notified of the appointment, I avail myself of the occasion to renew to Your Imperial Highness the assurance of my highest consideration.

　　　　　　　　　　　Envoy Extraordinary and
　　　　　　　　　　　　Minister Plenipotentiary
　　　　　　　　　　　　　of the United States.

To His Imperial Highness, Prince of Ch'ing,
President of the Board of Foreign Affairs.

清代外務部中外關係檔案史料叢編——中美關係卷 第六冊·國際會議

陸　軍　部　為

咨呈事練兵處移交卷內前准

貴部咨開光緒三十一年十二月初五日准美柔使函稱接本

國外部大臣來函奉總統諭云於一千九百零七年設立萬國

海陸軍賽會於涅爾金尼亞所屬之漢屯路水面一帶地方此

會為記念美國之生日並為英人初抵西半球之記念故請各

國政府派人赴會等語本大臣按照所囑將此諭附送查閱並

提及本國統領願聽貴國政府派往兵輪及相當陸軍赴會復

有宅来思屯於此次賽會之際加設一審於賽會於内本大臣

甚悅將此達知查照等因前來相應將原送附冊一本洛行查

照酌核辦理等因當經轉商北洋大臣在案兹准北洋大臣洛

開准總理南北洋海軍事務薩提督文稱美國設立海陸軍賽

會中國應派員赴會一案查有海軍兵船總稽查副將衞參將

沈壽堃又北洋陸軍軍械官千總榮志海坼船駕駛大副千總

林頌莊等員均堪派赴美國赴會應請察核分別加札飭遵等

國到本大臣准此查海軍兵船總稽查參將沈壽堃已委代統

北洋海軍責任重要不能前去北洋陸軍軍械官千總榮志事

繁責重亦不能派往其海圻船駕駛大副千總林頌莊堪飭令

赴會並委北洋海防營務處副將李鼎新一併前往以資考究

各國海軍事宜除札委該員等遵照並令前赴貴部聽候選定

暨咨明

外務部外其陸軍人員相應咨請貴部酌量委派等因到部查

海軍人員既據北洋大臣派定所有陸軍應派人員亦應即行

遴委俾得計時起程以免貽誤查有陸軍第一鎮管帶官蕭良

臣第二鎮執事官王燕賓堪以派往美國赴會並考查陸軍一

應事宜除札飭該員等遵照並咨明北洋大臣外相應咨呈

貴部希即查照施行須至咨呈者

右　咨　呈

外　務　部

光緒三十二年十一月　廿四日

　署用兵部舊印

監督官照鑑

逕啟者日前學部已派醫科進士謝天保為赴醫學

會與會人員、經本大臣電達飛利濱總督查照等因.

去後、茲接回電云此次中政府敦誼派員赴會本督實

深謝、並請本大臣將此意代為轉致、相應備函達知

貴親王查照是荷此泐、即頌

爵祺、附送洋文

名另具　十二月十三日

柔克義

AMERICAN LEGATION,
PEKING, CHINA.

To F.O. No. 205.
LW.   January 26, 1907.

Your Imperial Highness:-

I have the honor to state that I acquainted
the Governor General of the Philippine Islands by telegraph with the appointment of Tsai Tien-pao, M.D., by
the Imperial Chinese Board of Education to attend the
meeting of the Philippine Islands Medical Association,
as a delegate.

I am now in receipt of a telegraphic reply from
him saying that he, the Governor General, greatly appreciates the action of the Imperial Chinese Government in appointing a delegate to attend this convention, and requesting me to express this sentiment to
Your Imperial Highness.

As in duty bound, therefore, I am communicating
this fact to Your Imperial Highness for your information.

I avail myself of this opportunity to renew to
Your Imperial Highness the assurances of my highest
consideration.

Envoy Extraordinary and
Minister Plenipotentiary
of the United States.

To His Imperial Highness, Prince of Ch'ing,
President of the Board of Foreign Affairs.

逕啟者茲接散路易斯賽會來函附送金質記念賽會圓牌及

特製文憑請轉送

貴親王恭呈

大皇帝

御覽此項金牌係由美國鑄幣局監造該牌並與賽會呈送美國

總統之記念牌相同所有前特派大臣赴會之各國

皇帝

國君

總統今賽會首事亦係照此金牌一律呈遞是以本大臣即請

貴親王按照該會所請將金牌文憑一併代為呈

進見復以便轉達賽會可巴特泗順頌

爵祺附洋文並附送記念牌一座憑照一卷　名另具　十二月十七日

柔克義

LEGATION OF THE UNITED STATES OF AMERICA,
PEKIN, CHINA.

To F.O. No. 207

W.   January 30 1907.

Your Imperial Highness:-

    I have the honor to send Your Imperial Highness
under separate cover two parcels, one containing a gold
medal, the other a special diploma, both of which I am
requested by the Management of the Universal Exposition
of St Louis to forward to Your Imperial Highness to be
presented to His Imperial Majesty, the Emperor of China.

    The medal was struck at the United States Mint
in Philadelphia, and is exactly like the one presented to
the President of the United States, and like those presented to the heads of other, foreign, governments which
participated in the Exposition.

    I have the honor to ask that Your Imperial High-
ness will do the Exposition Management the favor of presenting the medal and diploma to His Imperial Majesty and
that I may be informed of its acceptance.

    I avail myself of the occasion to renew to Your
Imperial Highness the assurance of my highest consideration.

                       American Minister.

To His Imperial Highness, Prince of Ch'ing,
President of the Wai Wu Pu.

清代外務部中外關係檔案史料叢編——中美關係卷　第六冊·國際會議

復美柔使信

逕復者光緒三十二年十二月十七日准

采柄接散路易斯賽會來函附送金質記念

賽會圓牌及特製文憑轉送恭呈

大皇

帝御覽請按照該會所請將金牌文憑一併代為呈

進見

復以便轉達賽會等因並附送記念牌一座文憑一

上意

叄前來本部已於本月二十日將金牌文憑照一併呈

甚為欣悅相應函復

貴大臣查照轉達該會為荷此復順頌

日祉

　　　全堂銜

光緒三十二年十二月　　　日

照會

照會

卅三年十二月廿四日帝字山百六十三号

大比欽差便宜行事全權大臣世襲男爵柯　　為

照會事茲由本國外部寄來西歷一千九百

五年美京華盛頓萬國鐵路會第七期之

會議錄四本自應送請

貴部以一本存案其餘三本即希轉交曾

經赴會之人查前者山海關內外鐵路局

函請本館發給會議錄一本本大臣茲已

照辦逕送該局查收矣相應照會

貴親王查照可也須至照會者

右　　照　　會

大清國全權大臣總理外務部事務慶親王

光緒叁拾貳年拾貳月貳拾肆

日

清代外務部中外關係檔案史料叢編——中美關係卷 第六冊·國際會議

竊鼎新等此次奉委赴美國海陸軍賽

會一差擬明年二月初旬由津起行到

滬改乘公司船赴舊金山乘火車到美

京華盛頓謁

駐美欽使求其領見美政府各大臣即行

赴會冀到會之時俾得其優待以便詳細

考察一切事宜查此會由西曆一千九百

零七年五月十三日即華歷四月初二日

開會以六個月為期如各國能製造軍裝

可將其海軍之新式船匹機械礮械以及

應配船上必需之要件并其陸軍新式之

槍礮器械藥彈以及行軍屯營必需之要

械陳列比較以何國為最優以何國為最

新以何國滿最靈便鼎新等到會後自當

分別悉心考究至會塲如何情形亦應逐

日登記以精詳為主俟各國所派赴會考

察之員何時散去鼎新等亦應同時離會

儘可乘此機緣就近赴各處考察美國海

軍之機器廠礮廠以及船隖軍港等項如

何布置情形并陸軍之軍械廠以及礮台

聯隊等項如何製造操練詳細考究回華

後統行分別彙報以備采擇是否有

當恭候

鈞裁

先緒三十二年十二月　　日委員　李鼎新 林頌莊 蕭良臣 王燕賓 謹呈

謹將奉委赴美海軍賽會應行籌備各節繕

摺恭呈

鈞鑒伏乞

察奪施行

計開

一由津赴滬由滬搭公司船赴美舊金山乘火

車赴華盛頓船費并車費每員約需美金三

百五十員　美金每員合洋銀式元式角

員　以兩個月計每員需美金九百員

一在美住宿伙食每員每日至少需美金十五

一置辦上等禮服并常服靴帽雨衣外套以及

佩刀等項每員需銀式百五十兩

車費住宿伙食等項擬

俟明年正月支領惟船

費據稱公司船須預定

艙位擬請先行

批給

此項應令該員等先行

具領以便備辦

此項津貼據稱所有一切動
用雜費在內應令該員等
開具原差薪水若干再請

鈞定

一由華盛頓赴賽會場并往各處考察海陸軍
各事宜車費每員需美金弍百員
一每員派赴外洋除按月仍支原差薪水外應
請另行酌給津貼以示體恤
一查各國如賽會各項典禮事畢必有宴會
酬應此次美國賽會宴會之後各國如有
設宴酬答中國亦應照辦以崇國體
一在美擱日久所帶之款如有不敷并宴
會應用之費亦不能預計敬請

鈞部預電

駐美欽使先行墊付應用

此項宴會應用之費及
不敷之款擬請
交軍政司糧餉科立案
并預電駐美大臣以
便臨時墊付由本部
撥還

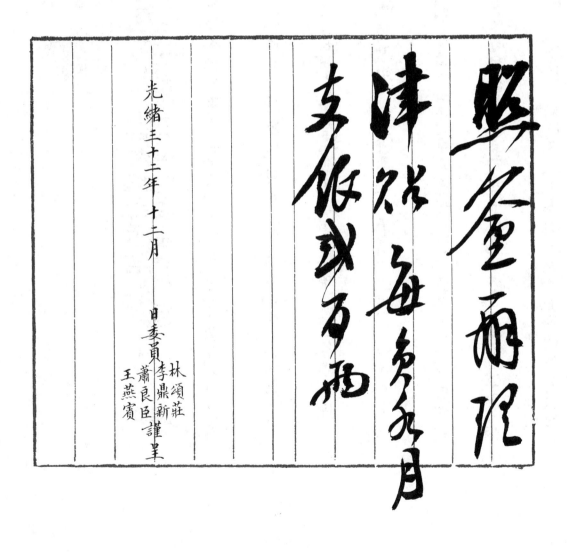

照金兩隻

津貼每多开月

支銀式万兩

光緒三十二年十二月 日委員李鼎新謹呈

林頌莊
蕭良臣
王燕賓

大亞美理駕合眾國欽差大臣為照會事照得本年三月三十一日本署大臣曾行照會貴部大臣案

　　照會事適接本國外部大臣電稱議政國會已將渥爾金尼亞之

漢屯路所定萬國海陸軍賽會日期改定於西本年四月二十六

號開會至西十一月三十號會畢擬請駐華盛頓各國欽使於

是日往觀開會所行之禮並於西五月十三號六月十號七月四號、

觀行特別之禮與海陸軍大操擬除已定數日外復另定行禮

及大操之期由開會日起至會畢日止所有各國來會軍艦及海

陸軍官兵并人員無論何日至美本國政府必派海陸軍大員迎迓

照會

民四月十六

云

　云茲按所奉訓條特將此電達知即請

貴親王查照可也須至照會者　附送洋文

右　　照　　會

大清欽命全權大臣便宜行事軍機大臣總理外務部事務和碩慶親王

　　　　　日

一千九百零五年
光緒叁拾叁年正月
　　　　　和壹
　　　　　拾柒

AMERICAN LEGATION,
PEKING, CHINA.

To F. O. No. 218.
W.   March 1, 1907.

Your Imperial Highness:-

     I am just in receipt of a telegram from the
Secretary of State at Washington, directing me to inform Your Imperial Highness that the Congress of the
United States has changed the date of the opening of
the Military and Naval Celebrations near Jamestown,
and the Jamestown Exposition, to April 26th, and the
date of the closing to November 30th. The foreign representatives at Washington will be invited to attend
the formal opening ceremonies on April 26th, and on
May 13th, June 10th, and July 4th, there will be special ceremonies and military and naval celebrations.
Other celebrations of a similar character will be arranged for later dates most probably. The American
Government will be prepared to welcome through its Army and Navy, at any time from the beginning until the
close of the Celebration and Exposition, all foreign
vessels, officers, and military or naval contingents
that may attend.

     In compliance with my instructions, I have the
honor to communicate to Your Imperial Highness the
foregoing statement for Your Imperial Highness' information.

To His Imperial Highness, Prince of Ch'ing,
President of the Board of Foreign Affairs,
     etc. etc. etc.

I avail myself of the occasion to renew to Your
Imperial Highness the assurances of my highest consideration.

Envoy Extraordinary and

Minister Plenipotentiary

of the United States.

陸軍部為

咨復事准

貴部咨現准駐美梁大臣電稱美國海陸軍賽會各國均派著

名將領帶艦隊來會如欲得平等待遇兼收考察之益宜派海陸

提督各一員巡洋艦一號否則請作罷論

國体邦交均有關係亟請電復等語茲貴部改派之陸軍管帶玉鈺

錦亞前派之海軍副將李鼎新等均非海陸軍提督又未派有巡

洋艦其美國海陸軍賽會應否往赴之處咨行查照酌核聲復

等因准此查此案前於上年經練兵處函商北洋大臣嗣准復稱

中國軍隊年限尚淺不特弁目未語西語即高級指揮官亦頗鮮

精通各國語言深慮臨時不能體會命令諸多不便不如酌派海

陸軍官四五人屆時赴美自開會以迄會政詳細考查備載日記

庶臣華有所依據藉資考校此後與會即有準備較諸驟派軍隊

稍有把握業經派員與美領事略商以為照復經轉達柔公使

據該使函復內称貴國只派水陸將弁代表赴會不派兵船兵隊

合操甚為妥善足見誼篤邦交即請查照辦理等語擬定辦法函

復前來是此項人員既經與美國公使商定妥協自應仍行派往

俾資考查相應咨復

貴部布即轉復該大臣查照可也須至咨者

右咨呈

外務部

光緒三十三年二月 初一 日

監印官聯銜

大美理德合眾國欽命駐劄中華便宜行事全權大臣 柔

公文費

大清欽命全權大臣便宜行事軍機大臣總理外務部事務和碩慶親王

當面開拆

光緒 參拾參年 貳 月 拾肆 日

一千九百柒年 參月 貳拾柒日

大亞美理駕合眾國欽命駐劄中華便宜行事全權大臣柔  為

照會事本大臣奉本國政府文囑、將非利濱醫學會

所議一事、照

中國政府至該會所議、係特行設法祛除傳染瘟疫以

衛民生、緣有日本東京醫士祁他薩托、在會論說、謂瘟

疫一事、豈獨有害一方、凡天下萬邦均視疫如仇敵、

各文明國、理宜併力拒絕、以余管見、應設萬國會、

該會宗旨係為集款備設一萬國驅疫軍、無論是

疫行於何地、必當運籌操有必勝之權云云、嗣後

有人將此論說進達於美國

總統、即奉

諭意、以此事足為至要、現應即擇出、提及在東方亞洲

各國政府、及各在亞東有管轄地之國酌議此舉等語，

故本國外部大臣囑本大臣請將所論設萬國會事

令再添設一分會，俾其便於考查瘟疫原始傳染

之因及各國應如何攻除此等瘟疫、照會

貴親王查照等因查此事果能照辦不惟有益各

國、而中國必更獲益良多本大臣甚望

貴親王、詳細核奪請將

雅意見復是荷為此照會須至照會者 附送洋文

大清欽命全權大臣便宜行事軍機大臣總理外務部事務和碩慶親王

右　照　會

一千九百柒百叁年貳拾柒月拾肆日

光緒叁拾叁年貳月拾肆日

AMERICAN LEGATION,
PEKING, CHINA.

To F.O. No. 232

　　　H.　　　　　　　　　　　　March 25, 1907.

Your Imperial Highness:

　　　　　　　I have the honor to inform Your
Imperial Highness that I have been instructed by the
Department of State to call your attention to a matter
which was brought up at the last meeting of the Philippine Islands Medical Association, and to which the attention of the President of the United States was subsequently called.

　　　　　　　During a discussion on the sub-
ject of the bubonic plague, Prof. Kitasato, of Tokyo,
made an address in the course of which he said:-"Plague
is not only objectionable to the people of one locality
but it is an enemy to mankind in general. All civilized
nations must fight this common enemy. I believe there
should be an international conference to discuss a plan
to collect money and to organize an international army
to combat and vanquish this disease wherever it appears."

　　　　　　　The President of the United States
deems this matter of sufficient importance to justify
its being brought to the notice of the Far Eastern Powers and those others having possessions or interests
in that part of the world.　I am instructed to bring
this matter to Your Highness' attention, therefore, and
to request an expression of your views on the desirability of convoking an international conference to consider the establishment of an international commission to
study the propogation of the bubonic plague, and to con-

　　　　　　　　　　　　　　　　cert.

certain measures for combating it.

As this is a plan which if carried out would be of inestimable benefit to China and of great value to the world at large, I hope Your Imperial Highness will take the matter into consideration, and will send me an expression of your views thereon that I may transmit it to the Secretary of State.

I avail myself of the opportunity to renew to Your Imperial Highness the assurance of my highest consideration.

Envoy Extraordinary and
Minister Plenipotentiary
of the United States.

To His Imperial Highness, Prince of Ch'ing,
President of the Board of Foreign Affairs.
etc.   etc.   etc.

欽差大臣辦理南洋通商事務頭品頂戴陸軍部尚書兩江總督

為

咨復事竊於光緒三十二年十一月二十九日准

貴部咨美兼使函請將中國水師兵艦各等旗幟繪成圖式註明顏

色大小尺寸附送本國海軍衙門咨行轉飭繪送以憑轉送美使等因

當經 本大臣咨會

南北洋海軍總理薩軍門查照轉飭水師各兵艦迅將各等旗幟繪

圖註明顏色大小尺寸備送三分見復核咨在案昨於本年二月十二日復准

貴部咨准美兼使函催咨行轉飭從速繪送等因正在核辦間准

薩軍門將頒行海軍各所式樣繪三分註明顏色尺寸呈請核送

前來除咨復並將所繪圖留存一分備咨外相應將所繪圖咨送為此咨呈

貴部謹請查照核辦施行須至咨呈者

計呈　拼圖二分

右　咨　呈

外　務　部

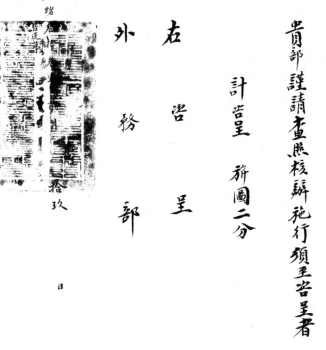

AMERICAN LEGATION,
PEKING, CHINA.

To F.O. No. 243

H.   April 25, 1907.

Your Imperial Highness:

           I have the honor to inform Your Im-
perial Highness that I have just been instructed by the Department of State to extend to Your Highness' Government on
behalf of the Executive Committee of the Seventh International Zoological Congress, an invitation to be represented at
the said Congress by official delegates.

           This Congress will be held at Boston,
in the State of Massachusetts, from August 19th to 23rd 1907,
and it gives me pleasure to enclose herewith a written invitation thereto addressed to the Government of China. I enclose also two copies, in French, of a circular containing
an outline of the program proposed.

           I avail myself of the opportunity to
renew to Your Imperial Highness the assurance of my highest
consideration.

                        Envoy Extraordinary and
                            Minister Plenipotentiary
                               of the United States.

Enclosures:

        1/ Invitation to the Seventh International Zoolo-
           gical Congress.
        2/ Two copies of circular.

To His Imperial Highness, Prince of Ch'ing,
    President of the Board of Foreign Affairs,
        etc.   etc.   etc.

The Seventh
International Zoölogical Congress
has the honor to invite
the
Government of China
to be represented by delegates
at its meeting to be held at
Boston, Massachusetts, U.S.A.
on August nineteenth to twenty-third
nineteen hundred and seven

The favor of a reply is requested
addressed to
Seventh International Zoölogical Congress
Cambridge, Massachusetts, U.S.A.

逕啟者接准本國外部函囑本大臣代美國軍醫會請

貴國政府派員赴第十六次軍醫大會此次該會設在宅米思

屯賽會地方於西本年十月十五號至十八號訂為開會日期並

囑轉達

貴親王知照如

貴國果肯派員與會本國政府甚為欣悅也特泐順頌

爵祺、

附洋文及軍醫會廣告一冊

名另具　三月十五日

**AMERICAN LEGATION,
PEKING, CHINA.**

To F.O. No. 244.

H.   April 25, 1907.

Your Imperial Highness:

      I have the honor to inform Your Im-
perial Highness that I am in receipt of instructions from the
Department of State directing me to extend on behalf of the
Association of Military Surgeons of the United States, an
invitation to Your Highness' Government to be represented
at the sixteenth annual meeting of that Association.

      This meeting will be held from October
15th to 18th 1907, on the grounds of the Jamestown Exposition at Norfolk, Virginia, and in extending this invitation to
Your Highness' Government I am instructed to state that my
Government would be much pleased to learn of its acceptance.

      I avail myself of the opportunity to
renew to Your Imperial Highness the assurance of my highest
consideration.

                        Envoy Extraordinary and

                          Minister Plenipotentiary

                              of the United States.

Enclosure:

      Journal of the Association of Military Surgeons of
the United States.

To His Imperial Highness, Prince of Ch'ing,

      President of the Board of Foreign Affairs,

           etc.   etc.   etc.

敬啟者散魯伊斯賽會獎給中國政府暨官商等獎
牌執照一事茲特將此項獎牌執照並清單一併送呈
貴部查收即希
分別致送為荷專此佈泐順頌
升祺附清單並獎牌執照等件

赫德

稅字第壹佰壹拾號

名号具　光緒叁拾叁年叁月拾玖日

總稅務司函送前美國散魯伊斯賽會獎給

中國政府暨官商等獎牌執照等件原單

計開

中國政府

頭等賞牌十二箇附執照十二張

金牌十六箇附執照十六張

銅牌九箇附執照九張

銀牌十九箇附執照十九張

清代外務部中外關係檔案史料叢編——中美關係卷·第六冊·國際會議

茲將散魯伊斯賽會中國政府並官員所得獎牌等暨

執照數目列後

計開

頭等賞牌

中國政府十二簡執照十二張

茶葉磁器公司一簡隨附執照一張

工藝商局三簡隨附執照三張

金牌

中國政府十六簡隨附執照十六張

工藝商局二簡隨附執照二張

茶葉磁器公司一簡隨附執照一張

蘇芝第一簡隨附執照一張

銀牌

中國政府十九箇 隨附執照 十九張

工藝商局一箇 隨附執照 一張

工藝商局總董黃思永一箇 隨附執照 一張

工藝商局黃中慧
黃中懿 各一箇 隨附執照 各一張

銅牌

中國政府 九箇執照、九張

監督及派赴賽會之人員等一箇執照 一張

工藝商局董事王姓二位各一箇 執照 各一張

記念牌

工藝商局總董黃思永一箇 隨附執照 一張

工藝商局黃中懿
黃中慧
王姓 各一箇 隨附執照 各一張

蘇芝第一箇 隨附執照 一張

農工商部為咨呈事光緒三十三

年四月初四日接准

咨稱准總稅務司函稱散魯伊

斯賽會獎給中國政府暨官商

等獎牌執照其應由部轉贈

等因相應抄錄原單並牌照等

件一併咨送查照轉發等因前

来查獎牌執照各柒拾陸件當

即照單如數驗收除分別轉給

赴賽官商外相應洛呈

貴部查照並希轉行總稅務

司知照可也須至洛者

右洛

外務部

光緒三十　年　月　拾叁日

逕啟者接本國農部大臣函稱中政府擬於本年秋間在

都中開一農務賽會駐美中國公使請本部攢積各植物

籽粒齎置會內會畢即培植於中國公家園中現有本部所特

派在華選擇各色植物之農學師麥爾想其能助中政府於

會內安置籽粒及植物一切故將梁大臣所荐麥爾於農工

商部大堂之書送請本大臣轉投收閱美政府於此事甚

為欣悅並願麥爾在中國賽會場內襄幫等因相應將

梁大臣所致

振貝子蔣麥爾之函送由

貴親王轉致惟查

振貝子現經告退望將此蔣函即交新任農工商部

大堂查收麥爾農學師現在北京若使彼襄助所寄籽粒

安置一切必甚樂為惟彼擬越數禮拜赴內地各處採辦

植物

貴國農工商部如願請其襄辦須預函知照俾其得

於臨近時日前來襄助一切即希

貴親王早為轉致見復可也此泐即頌

爵祺 附函一件 並附洋文

名另具 四月十九日

柔克義

LEGATION OF THE UNITED STATES OF AMERICA,
PEKING, CHINA.

To F.O. No. ? 8?
      W.   May 29 1907.

Your Imperial Highness:-

         I am in receipt of a communication from the
United States Department of Agriculture, saying that, "in
connection with the agricultural exposition to be held this
fall in Peking, the Chinese Minister had asked assistance of
the Department in getting up for him a collection of seeds
and plants for exhibition purposes and later for planting out
in the Imperial Park; ------that it was thought possible
perhaps for Mr.Meyer, an explorer of the Department now in
Peking to render assistance to the Chinese Government upon
the arrival of these seeds and plants, and that therefore a
letter introducing Mr.Meyer to the President of the Board of
Agriculture Industries and Commerce was enclosed."

         I have the honor therefore to forward to Your Imperial
Highness this letter from H.E. Sir Liang Ch'eng, introducing
Mr.Meyer to His Highness, Prince Tsai-chen, and, although
His Highness has resigned the post of President of the Board
of Agriculture Industries and Commerce, I trust it may serve
to introduce Mr. Meyer to the present President of the Board
H.E.P'u-t'ing.   I have the further honor to state that Mr.
Meyer is at present in Peking, and that he will be very hap-
                                         py

To His Imperial Highness, Prince of Ch'ing,
President of the Board of Foreign Affairs.

py to render any assistance that may be needed in arranging
and caring for the plants and seeds sent.

He is planning, however, to make a trip of some weeks'
duration to secure specimens of Chinese plants, and would
like to know beforehand about what time his assistance is
likely to be required.

Trusting that Your Imperial Highness will communicate
these facts to the President of the Board of Agriculture Industries and Commerce, I avail myself of the occasion to renew to Your Imperial Highness the assurance of my highest
consideration.

Envoy Extraordinary and
Minister Plenipotentiary
of the United States.

致美桑使函

逕復者接准

來函接本國農部大臣函開中政府擬於本年

秋間在都中開一農務賽會駐美中國公使

請本部攢積各植物籽粒寄置會內會畢

即培植於中國公家園中現有本部所派在華

選擇各色植物之農學師麥爾想其能助中

政府於會內安置籽粒及植物故將梁大臣所薦

麥爾於農工商部 大堂之書送請轉投並願

麥爾在中國賽會場內襄幫等因相應將梁

大臣所薦麥爾農學師現在北京若使彼襄助

大堂查收麥爾之函送請轉交新任農工商部

所寄籽粒要置一切必甚樂為惟彼擬越數禮

拜赴內地各處採辦植物貴國農工商部如願

請其襄辦須預函知俾得前來襄助希早見

復等語當經本部將原信一函咨送農工商部

查照聲復去後茲准復稱查閱

美國桑大臣函稱各節係由農務賽會安置一切種植而言盛意

實深欣感惟本部現辦農事試驗場與農務

賽會性質迥不相同所有應行試種各品刻已陸續

佈置並無秋間開辦農務賽會之事該農學師擬

為襄助之處一時尚難議及咨請轉復等因前來相

應函達

貴大臣查照可也此佈順頌

日祉

全堂銜

光緒三十三年四月

清代外務部中外關係檔案史料叢編——中美關係卷　第六冊·國際會議

陸　軍　部　為

咨復事案查本年三月十九日准

貴部咨開接准美柔使函稱准本國外部南囑俟美國軍醫會

請中國派員赴第十六次軍醫會此次該會設陸米恩此賽起

政府如派員赴會本國政府甚為歡迎等因相應咨行貴部酌

方於西本年十月廿五號至十八號為開會日期請轉達中國

核辦理並望見復等因到部茲查有候選知府何守仁堪以派

令赴會除札飭遵照即速起程並咨明出使美國大臣查照外相

應咨復

貴部查照轉行知照美使可也須至咨者

右

咨

外務部

光緒三十三年五月　　日

復美柔使

逕復者前准

來函以

貴國博斯屯地方於西本年八月十九號開研究動物

會請派員赴會等因查動物學會於研求物理之舉洵

有裨益現已飭派駐劄

貴國使館參贊官容揆屆期前往與會特此函復

貴大臣查照轉達

貴國外部可也順頌

日祉

全堂衜

光緒三十三年六月　　　日

和會司

呈為咨行事前准

咨稱美國請派員赴動物學會一事電商駐

美大臣就近酌派學生一人赴會茲據復稱

查無研究動物學生惟有二等參贊官容揆

堪以派赴該會除劄行外該參贊赴會車票旅

用請咨明外務部准其作正開銷查該大臣

劄派容參贊赴會車費旅用作正開銷之處

應請酌定迺覆該使并知照本部等因查美

國動物學會既由出使大臣派定參贊容揆

屆期前往所有赴會費用自應准銷除電知

駐美代辦查照外相應咨復

貴部查照可也須至咨者

學部

光緒三十三年六月　　　日

逕啟者、非利濱羣島醫學復擬在滿呢拉城開會、已請日本、

錫蘭島、新加坡、欣哇、新金山、東京、安南、暹羅、澳斯達利亞各

國等處派委醫官及素諳理化人員、與會、因前中國所派

醫員在該會名譽最著、似非枉費曠時、是以再請中國

派委醫官來會、惟會期在一千九百八年內、不開於二月二

十六至二十九號、即定於三月四號至七號開會、仍俟酌定時

再行達知是以非利濱總督即請轉達

貴國政府、可派員赴會等因、相應轉達

貴親王查照、本署大臣甚望按照所請、允准派員前往、盍希

將所派定之員、早日

見復、是荷、特泐順頌

　爵祺　附送洋文

　　　　　　名另具　九月智

AMERICAN LEGATION,
PEKING, CHINA.

To F. O. No. 316

H.   October 10, 1907.

Your Imperial Highness:

          At the instance of the Governor General of
the Philippine Islands I have the honor to extend an
invitation to Your Imperial Highness' Government to
be represented by an official delegate at the next annual meeting of the Philippine Islands Medical Association, which will be held in Manila on February 26-
29 or March 4-7, 1908.   The date will be definitely
fixed later and when so fixed I shall have the honor
to communicate it to Your Imperial Highness.   Official delegates as well as private professional and
scientific men from Japan, India, Hongkong, Straits
Settlements, Ceylon, Java, Australia, Indo-China and
Siam are expected to attend, and it is the desire of
the officers and members of the Association that an
official representative be sent from China.

          The representative from China who attended
the last meeting of the Association took a distinguished part in the scientific program and it is hoped
that the proceedings were of such value and interest
as to justify the sending by Your Imperial Highness'
                                        Government

To His Imperial Highness, Prince of Ch'ing,
President of the Board of Foreign Affairs,
          etc.   etc.   etc.

Government of a representative to the next meeting.

Trusting that I may have the pleasure of informing the Governor General of the Philippine Islands of the acceptance of this invitation, I avail myself of the opportunity to renew to Your Imperial Highness the assurance of my highest consideration.

Charge d' Affaires.

清代外務部中外關係檔案史料叢編——中美關係卷 第六冊·國際會議

咨

學部為咨覆事准外務部咨開

准美國費署使孟稱非利濱群島

醫學復擬在滿呢拉城開會已請

日本等國派委醫官與會前因

中國所派醫員在該會名譽最

著是以再請中國派委醫官來

會惟會期在一千九百八年內不開

於二月二十六至二十九號即定於三月

四號至七號俟酌定再行達知是以

非利濱總督請轉達貴國政府派

員赴會本署大臣甚望按照所請

允准派員前往並希早日見覆等

因相應咨行貴部酌核辦理並希將

派定員名見覆本部以便轉覆等因

前來本部現派醫科舉人鄭豪前往

入會相應咨覆

貴部查照轉覆美使並希將咨

文護照咨送過部以便轉給該員親

賫與會可也須至咨者

右咨呈

外務部

光緒叁拾叁年拾月初四日

逕啟者美國華盛頓省於一千九百零八年由三月初十至

三月十七號特開萬國研究衛護幼稚保姆會函囑本館轉

達等因相應將該會寄來會單附送即請

貴親王查照轉致甚望屆時

貴政府亦派有與會之人是荷祇此順頌

爵祺 附送洋文及會單

名另具 十月十七日

費勒器

AMERICAN LEGATION,
PEKING, CHINA.

To F. O. No.

　　P.　　　　　　　　　　　　November 22, 1907.

Your Imperial Highness:

　　　　On behalf of the National Congress of Mothers
I have the honor to extend to Your Imperial Highness'
Government an invitation to be represented by an official
delegate at the first American International Congress
on the Welfare of the Child, to be held in Washington
from March 10th to March 17th, 1908.　　I enclose, also,
a printed invitation which will inform Your Highness of
the aims of the Congress and the subjects which are to
be discussed.

　　　　I avail myself of this opportunity to renew to
Your Imperial Highness the assurance of my highest consideration.

　　　　　　　　　　　　　　　　Charge d'Affaires.

To His Imperial Highness, Prince of Ch'ing,
President of the Board of Foreign Affairs,
　　　　etc.　　　　　etc.　　　　　etc.

大美理藩會某國欽命㚑節㝎義駐劄中華便宜行事大臣費

照會事准本國外部大臣文囑本署大臣達知

貴親王美國漁業公所與美國漁業會擬於一千九

百零八年九月二十二號起至二十六號在華盛頓京

城開設第四次萬國漁業會想此所開之會確與㝎

業係關最要本署大臣兹按所囑將所送該會印就

章程及所擬提議各事送請

貴親王查照即請

貴政府屆時派員前往赴會可也須至照會者　附洋文
並印單

右

照

會

大清欽命全權大臣便宜行事軍機大臣總理外務部事務和碩慶親王

一千九百柒年拾壹月　貳拾玖

光緒叄拾叄年拾月　貳拾肆　日

AMERICAN LEGATION,
PEKING, CHINA.

To F.O. No.

H.   November 28, 1907.

Your Imperial Highness:

        I have the honor to inform Your Imperial
Highness that the Fourth International Fishery Congress
will meet in the city of Washington from the 22nd to the
26th of September 1908, under the auspices of the United
States Bureau of Fisheries and the American Fisheries Society. It is expected that this will be one of the most
important gatherings ever held concerning matters affecting the fisheries.

        I have the honor to extend an invitation
to Your Imperial Highness' Government to be represented
at this Congress by such delegates as it may nominate, and
to enclose herewith a preliminary circular containing
the rules of the Congress and the provisional program of
the subjects likely to be discussed

        I avail myself of this opportunity to
renew to Your Imperial Highness the assurance of my highest consideration.

                                Charge d'Affaires.

Enclosure:

        Preliminary notice regarding the Fourth Inter-
national Fishery Congress.

To His Imperial Highness, Prince of Ch'ing,
        President of the Board of Foreign Affairs.

INTERNATIONAL FISHERY CONGRESS.

Organized at Parish 1900.

First Congress, Paris, September 1 to 19, 1900.

Invitation of the French Government.

President, Professor EDMOND PERRIER,   Secretary-General, Mr. J. PÉRARD,

     Member of the Institute; Director   Archivist of the Permanent International

     of the Natural History Museum,   Fishery Commission.

     Paris; President of the Permanent

     International Fishery Commission.

SECOND CONGRESS, ST. PETERSBURG, FEBRUARY 24 to MARCH , 1902.

     Invitation of the Imperial Russian Society of Pisciculture and Fishing.

President, Hon. VLADIMIR VESSELAGON,   Secretary-General, Mr. NICHOLAS BORODINE,

     Member of the Council of the Empire   Chief Specialist in Pisciculture of the

     Secretary of State; President of the   Russian Department of Agriculture.

     Imperial Russian Society of Piscicul

     -ture and Fishing.

THIRD CONGRESS, VIENNA, JUNE 4 to 9, 1905.

     Invitation of the Austrian Fisheries Society.

President, Dr. FRANZ STEINDACHNER   Secretary-General, Dr. HEINRICH von KADICH,

     Court Counsellor; Director of the   Administration Counsellor of the Imperi-

     Imperial Natural History Museum,   al Ministry of Agriculture.

     Vienna.

FOURTH CONGRESS, WASHINGTON, SEPTEMBER 22 to 26, 1908.

     Invitation of the United States Bureau of Fisheries.

INTERNATIONAL FISHERY CONGRESS, 1908.

The Fourth International Fishery Congress will convene in the City of Washington, United States of America, in accordance with the decision of the Third International Fishery Congress held in Vienna in 1905. The Meeting, which will be under the auspices of the United States Bureau of Fisheries and the American Fisheries Society, will extend from the 22nd to the 26th of September, 1908.

All persons interested in the fisheries, fish culture, fishery administration, or other matters within the scope of the Congress are invited to attend the meeting and participate in the proceedings. National, State, and provincial governments, societies, associations, clubs, and other bodies are requested to nominate and to send delegates.

Persons who expect to attend the Congress or to submit papers are asked to communicate with the secretary-general as soon as practicable; and the secretaries of institutions and organizations interested in the work of the Congress are requested to register their official designation and address so that they may receive futher announcements, programs, invitation, etc.

REGULATIONS OF THE CONGRESS.

1 Object of the Congress.

The Congress will deliberate on all important affaires concerning fishing and fish culture, and will submit propositions and memorials to governments and to provincial and local authorities.

2 Members of the Congress.

The membership of the Congress will consist of government, state, and provincial representatives; delegates from home and foreign societies; corporations and personages invited by the management of the Congress; and persons at home and abroad who are deemed to have an interest in the purpose of the

Congress and express a wish to take part in it.

3 Rights to Members.

All the members of the Congress have the right to vote, to participate in the discussions, and to make independent propositions. In case a corporation should be represented by several delegates, the members of this delegation have the right to only one vote, which shall be cast by the delegate designated to the presiding officer. The delivery of the card of admission gives to members the right to take part in all the enterprise and excursions projected by the Congress, to receive all the publications, and to wear the insignia of the Congress.The members of the Congress are required to conform to regulations and decisions.

4 Organization of the Congress.

The Congresswill follow officially the preceding international fishery congresses, and will conform to the decisions for the regulation of the international fishery congresses decreed at Paris in 1900. The president and the secretary-general of the Congress are nominated by the United States Bureau of Fisheries; the vice-president are elected by the Congress from among its members

5 Elections and Resolutions of the Congress.

All the resolutions of the Congress are adopted by an absolute majority of the members present having the right to vote(see Sec. 3). In case of division the president's vote will decide. Elections take place by ballot. Formal propositions and resolutions intended for the consideration of the Congress should be in the hands of the local committee by August 1, 1908. The committee will decide on the admission of such propositions; but in case of rejection it is required to make known to the Congress the reasons therefor.

6 Resources of the Congress

The resources of the Congress consist of a special appropriation by the Congress of the United States of voluntary contributions from interested persons, and of membership fees fixed at two dollars for each person. In the case of official representatives of governments the membership fee is remitted

7 Method of Debate.

All the debates of the Congress take place in full assembly. The official language is English, but in presenting papers and in debates members have the right to use also the French, German, or Italian language.

The meetings will be presided over by the president or vice-president, who will conduct the debates according to the established order. The president on yielding the chair, may himself take part in the debates. The duration of the discussion of a subject will be regulated by the extent of the program and will be communicated to the assembly before the commencement of the debate. Members desiring to speak will inscribe their names and subjects during or after the reading of papers, and the president will call on them to speak in the order of their inscription.

A member may speak only twice on the same subject in the same meeting, personal remarks and corrections excepted. The motion for the close of a debate must immediately be put to a vote; this motion once accepted, only the members who have previously asked recognition can speak. The author of a proposition or paper shall at the end of the debate be recognized for a final resume.

8 Minutes and Publications.

Minutes will be prepared on all the proceedings of the Congress which will contain the reports and debates in brief and in extenso. The full transactions of the Congress will be published as soon as practicable After the final adjournment.

9 Additional Regulations.

The local committee of organization will make such futher regulations as may be necessary for the proper conduct of the work of the Congress.

PROVISIONAL PROGRAM.

Among the subjects that are likely to come before the Congress are the following:

1 Commercial Fisheries:

    (a) Apparatus and methods of fishing.

    (b) Vessels and boats.

    (c) Handing preparing and preserving the catch.

    (d) Utilization of neglected and waste products.

2 Matters Affecting the Fishermen and the Fishing Population:

    (a) Hygiene of vessels and houses of fishermen.

    (b) Diseases of fishermen and their families.

    (c) Means for preventing loss of life at sea.

    (d) Technical education in fishing, fish handling, and fish culture.

    (e) Fishery schools.

3 Legislation and Regulation Relative to :

    (a) Fishing.

    (b) Fish culture.

    (c) Pollution of waters.

    (d) Obstruction of waters.

4 International Matters Affecting the Fisheries:

    (a) Regulation and legislation.

    (b) Research.

    (c) Statistics.

5 Aquiculture:

    (a) Fresh-water fishes.

    (b) Salt-water fishes.

    (c) Frogs, turtles and terrapins.

    (d) Oysters and other mollusks.

    (e) Lobsters, crabs, crayfish and other crustaceans.

    (f) Sponges.

    (g) Algae and other plants.

    (h) New appliances and methods.

    (i) Utility of fish culture in the ocean and in large inland waters.

6 Acclimatization:

    (a) American fishes abroad.

    (b) Foreign fishes in America.

    (c) Introduction of other foreign species.

7 Fish-Ways and Fish-Ladders.

8 Biological Investigation of the Waters and Their Inhabitants:

    (a) Methods and appliances.

    (b) Results.

9 Diseases and Parasites of Fishes, Crustaceans, Mollusks, and Other Water Animals.

10 Angling and Sport Fishing.

COMPETITIVE AWARDS.

In connection with the Congress there have been arranged the following competitive awards for the best or most important investigations, discoveries, inventions, etc., relative to fisheries, aquiculture, ichthyology, fish pathology, and related subjects during the years 1906, 1907, and 1908. The awards will be in the form of money, and aggregate $2,200; and, although the individual amounts are not large, it is hoped that the conferring of the awards by so representative a body as the International Fishery Congress will induce many persons to compete and will result in much benefit to the fisheries and fish culture.

1 By the American Fisheries Society:

For a paper embodying the most important original observation and investigations regarding the cause, treatment, and prevention of a disease affecting a species of fish under cultivation . . . . $100 in gold.

2 By the American Museum of Natural History, New York City:

For an original paper describing and illustrating by specimens the best method of preparing fishes for museum and exhibition purposes $100 in gold.

3 By the Forest and Stream, New York City; Mr. George Bird Grinnell, editor:

For the best paper giving description, history and methods of administration of a water, or waters, stocked and preserved as a commercial enterprise, in which angling is open to the public on payment of a fee. . $50 in gold.

4 By the Museum of the Brooklyn Institute of Arts and Sciences, Brooklyn, New

York; Mr. F. A. Lucas, curator-in-chief:

For the best paper setting forth a plan for an educational exhibit of fishes the species and specimens that should be shown the method of arrangement and suggestions for making such an exhibit instructive and attractive . . . .
. . . . $100 in gold.

5 By the New York Aquarium (under the management of the New York Zoological

Society, New York City; Mr. Charles H. Townsend)

Society), New York City; Mr. Charles H. Townsend, Director:

For an exposition of the best methods of combating fungus disease in fish
es in captivity . . . . $150 in gold.

6 By the New York Botanical Garden, New York City; Dr. N. L. Britton, Director

For the best essay on any interrelation between marine plants and an-
mals . . . . $100 in gold.

7 By the Smithsonian Institution, Washington, D. C.:

For the best essay or treatise on "International regulations of the fisheries on the high seas, their history, objects, and results." $200 in gold.

8 By The Fisheries Company, Philadelphia, Pennsylvania; Mr. Joseph Wharton,
president:

For the best essay treating of the effects of fishing on the abundance
and movements of surface-swimming fishing which go in schools, particularly
the menhaden and similar species, and the influence of such fishing on the
fishes which may prey on such species . . . . $250 in gold.

9 By the United States Bureau of Fisheries, Washington, D. C.

For a report describing the most useful new and original principle, method, or apparatus to be employed in fish culture or in transporting live
fishes (competition not open to employees of the Bureau) . . $300 in gold

10 By the Wolverine Fish Company, Detroit, Michigan:

For the best plan to promote the whitefish production of the Great Lakes
$100 in gold.

11 By Mr. Hayes Bigelow, Brattleboro, Vermont, member of the American Fisheries
Society:

For the best demonstration, based on original investigation and experi-
ments, of the commercial possibilities of growing sponges from eggs or
cuttings . . . . $100 in gold.

12 By Hon. George M. Bowers, United States Commissioner of Fisheries, Washington, D. C.

For the best demonstration of the efficacy of artificial of propagation as applied to marine fishes . . . . $100 in gold.

13 By Dr H. C. Bumous, director of the American Museum of Natural History, New York City:

For an original and practical method of lobster culture . $100 in gold.

14 By Mr John K. Cheyney, Tarpon Springs, Florida, member of the American Fisheries Society:

For the best presentation treating of the methods of the world's sponge fisheries, the influence of such methods on the supply of sponges and the most effective means of conserving the sponge grounds . . . $100 in gold.

15 By Prof. Theodore Gill honorary associate in zoology, Smithsonian Institution, Washington, D. C.:

For the best methods of observing the habits and recording the life histories of fishes with an illustrative example . . . . . $100 in gold.

16 By Dr. F. M. Johnson, Boston Massachusetts, member of the American Fisheries Society:

For the best demonstration of the comparative value of different kinds of foods for use in rearing young salmonoids, taking into consideration cheapness, availability, and potentiality . . . . $150 in gold.

17 By the New York Academy of Sciences, New York City; Dr. N. L. Britten, President:

For the contribution, not entered in competition for any other award, which shall be judged to have the greatest practical value to the fisheries or fish culture . . . . $100 in gold.

18 By Messrs. Henry Holt & Company, publishers, New York City:

For the best series of photographs, with brief description, illustrating the capture of food or game fishes . . . . $100 in gold.

CONDITIONS GOVERNING COMPETITION.

(1) Any person, association, or company may compete for any of the awards.

(2) Each competitor shall, before July 15, 1908, notify the general secretary of the Congress as to the particular award for which he competes; and he shall duly qualify himself as a member of the Congress.

(3) Each paper or exhibit offered in competition shall be in the custody of the secretary-general on the day of opening of the Congress.

(4) Papers may be written in English, French, German, or Italian.

(5) Each device, apparatus, process, or method for which an award is asked shall be represented by a sample, a model, or an illustrated description; and each shall be accompanied by a complete statement of the points for which an award is asked.

(6) The Congress reserves the right to publish, prior to their publication elsewhere, any papers or photographs submitted in competition, whether or not such papers or photographs receive awards; provided, however, that in the event of the Congress having failed to publish within six months after the session, an author will be at liberty to publish when and where he may elect.

MAKING OF THE AWARDS.

(1) The papers, appliances, exhibits, etc., submitted in competition for awards will be examined by an international board to be designated by the president of the International Fishery Congress.

(2) The board will determine the competitors who are entitled to awards, and the decision of the board will be final.

(3) The board may call before it, in order to obtain additional information when desirable, persons who may have entered the competition and also other persons.

(4) The board may, at its discretion, withhold the award in any case if in its judgment no sufficiently worthy competition is presented; and it may divide an award if there are two competitions that it deems of equal merit.

(5) The board will make its report to the Congress not later than the day preceding final adjournment.

(6) The awards will be announced at a session of the Congress, and each award will be accompanied by a special certificate or diploma suitably inscribed and bearing the signatures of the officers of the Congress.

CORRESPONDENCE.

Communications regarding the Congress should be addressed to

Secretary-General,

International Fishery Congress,

Washington, D. C., U. S. A.

For the United States Bureau of Fisheries:

GEORGE M. BOWERS,

United States Commissioner of Fisheries.

For the Comittee Committee of the Organization of the Fourth

International Fishery Congress:

HERMON C. BUMPUS,

Director of the American Museum of Natural

History; President of the Congress.

For the American Fisheries Society:

HUGH M. SMITH,

President of the Society;

Secretary General of the Congress.

逕啟者西來年二月·初間在斐利濱島滿呢拉地方擬舉行

運動歡迎賽會此會係開辦只三四日並擬大排筵宴備有游

行旗仗陳列百貨等事此會舉行大意係欲鼓動眾人心嚮滿

呢拉越數日斐督自必備帖奉請屆時再為轉達

貴親王查照茲特將此事樂於先行丰知

貴部俾悉該會甚望中國官商前往赴會並聞此次該會擬

於中國所願赴會之人設法使其赴會得有隨便旅行之益特

此奉布即望

貴部有以贊成為荷順頌

爵祺 附洋文

名另具十一月初三日

AMERICAN LEGATION,
PEKING, CHINA.

To F. O. No. 335

H.

December 6, 1907.

Your Highness:

　　　　I have the honor to inform Your Highness that
it is proposed to hold in the city of Manila, Philippine
Islands, during the week commencing Monday, February third
next a Carnival.　This Carnival is a series of fetes,
street parades, displays, etc., lasting three or four days
and it is given in the hope of attracting visitors to Manila.　A formal invitation will later on be extended by
the Governor General, but in the meantime I beg to inform
Your Highness' Board of the holding of this Carnival and
to express the hope of the Carnival Association that a
large representation of Chinese visitors, merchants and
officials, may attend.

　　　　It is proposed to arrange every facility for
the reception and accomodation of such visitors as may
come from China to attend the Carnival.

　　　　I trust that this project will receive the sym-
pathetic interest and support of Your Highness' Board.

To His Highness, Prince of Ch'ing,
President of the Board of Foreign Affairs.

I avail myself of this opportunity to renew to
Your Highness the assurance of my highest consideration.

Charge d'Affaires.

和會司

呈為咨行事准美貴署使函稱美國華盛頓

省於一千九百零八年由三月初十日至三月十七號

特開萬國研究衛護幼稚保姆會坩送寄來會

單請派與會之人等因前來相應將原送洋文

會單咨送

貴部查核可否派員與會迅即聲復本部

以憑轉復該使可也須至咨者　附洋文會單

學部

光緒三十三年十月　　　　日

廿

大亞美理駕合眾國欽命駐紮中華便宜行事大臣柔 為

照復事昨准

來照以飛利濱於來年西二月間在滿呢啦舉行運

動歡迎賽會一事本署夫臣甚樂聞農工商部擬達

知南洋商會及各省商務總會接待華人旅行該處

辦法茲復接准飛利濱總督電稱此次華人赴滿呢

啦觀運動賽會之執照現已印就分佈駐香港及廣

州廈門福州上海漢口各等處美國領事官收存以

備赴會華人請領西本月十三號本署大臣曾在

貴部與梁大臣面談時並提及該督擬印就此項執

照特與赴會華人收執當時梁大臣以中國官員向

有權發赴美執照者亦可飭其繕發此項專照亦不收費云

云相應照會

貴親王查照聲明此項專照已經印出請即電知有

貴親王查照聲明此項專照已經印出請即電知有
權發照之官接照巳上所擬辦法通諭華民知照如

欲前往赴會可來領照無須照費等情想

貴親王自必樂於贊成本署大臣茲特頒為鳴謝須

至照會者 附送洋文

右　　　　照

會

大清欽命全權大臣便宜行事軍機大臣總理外務部事務和碩慶親王

一千九百〇六年拾貳月貳拾陸

光緒叁拾叁年拾壹月拾陸日

**AMERICAN LEGATION,
PEKING, CHINA.**

To F. O. No.**337**

H.

December 19, 1907.

Your Highness:

  I have the honor to acknowledge the receipt of your note of yesterday's date with regard to the Carnival to be held in Manila in February next, and I learn with pleasure of the promise of the Board of Agriculture, Industry, and Commerce to notify the Chambers of Commerce in the South and the Commercial Bureaus in the provinces, of the contemplated arrangements for the reception of Chinese visitors.

  In this connection I now have the honor to inform Your Highness that I have received a telegram from the Governor General of the Philippine Islands saying that special Section VI. Certificates for the benefit of Chinese wishing to visit Manila at the time of the Carnival, have been printed and forwarded to the American Consuls at Hongkong, Canton, Amoy, Foochow, Shanghai, and Hankow.

  On the thirteenth instant in a personal interview with His Excellency Liang Tun-yen at the Foreign Office I brought up the subject of this Carnival and men-

            tioned

To His Highness, Prince of Ch'ing,
President of the Board of Foreign Affairs.

tioned the fact that such special certificates would
probably be printed, and I was assured that if such arrangements were made the Chinese authorities who are
authorized to issue the regular Section VI. Certificates
would be directed to issue these Special Carnival certificates to applicants free of charge.

It becomes my duty, therefore, to send Your
Highness this notification of the printing of these
special Carnival Certificates, and I have the honor to
request that you will telegraph to the local officials
concerned informing them of the arrangement and directing them to make it generally known that these certificates can be procured from them without charge.

Thanking Your Highness for the friendly interest and support which I am sure you will give this
enterprise I avail myself of the opportunity to renew
to Your Highness the assurance of my highest consideration.

Charge d'Affaires.

榷算司

呈為照復事前准

照稱華人赴滿呢拉觀運動賽會之執照現已印

就分佈駐香港及廣州廈門福州上海漢口各等

囑美國領事官收存以備赴會華人請領請即電

知有權發照之官通諭華民知照如前往赴會可

來領照無須照費等因前來除由本部電知南洋

大臣轉飭各關道按照向章發給前項專照勿取

照費一面通諭商民知悉外相應照復

貴署大臣查照可也須至照會者

美費署使

光緒三十三年十一月

逕啟者西上年十一月二十二號本署大臣曾代美國保姆會

轉請中政府於美國初設之萬國研究幼稚保姆會亦派

有與會之人等因茲復據該會備有請帖寄送前來相應將

其所具請帖附函轉送

貴親王查照是荷即頌

時祉　附洋文並請帖

名另具十二月十四日

費勒器

AMERICAN LEGATION,
PEKING, CHINA.

To F. O. No.344

H.

January 17, 1908.

Your Highness:

On November 22, 1907, I had the honor to extend
on behalf of the National Congress of Mothers, an infor-
mal invitation to Your Highness' Government to be represented by an official delegate at the First American International Congress of Mothers, where the subject of discussion would be the "Welfare of the China".

In this connection I now have the honor to enclose herewith the formal invitation to be represented
at the Congress mentioned, extended to the Chinese Government by the American National Congress of Mothers.

I avail myself of this opportunity to renew to
Your Highness the assurance of my highest consideration.

Charge d'Affaires.

To His Imperial Highness,
    Prince of Ch'ing,
    President of the Board of Foreign Affairs,
            etc.   etc.   etc.

咨呈

學部為咨呈事准外務部咨准

美費署使函稱華盛頓省特

開萬國研究衛護幼稚保姆

會可否派員與會迅即聲覆

等因正在核覆間旋准咨送

請帖前來本部查教養童

稚最為緊要查有顏進士

惠慶現在奉差在美本

部已電駐美公使轉飭該

員就近與會以襄盛舉相

應咨呈

貴部轉復該署使可也須

至咨者

右咨呈

外務部

函復美費署使保姆會事由

行　　行

左侍郎聯　　廿三日

右

署　右侍郎梁

汪　正月廿一日

復美費署使

逕復者前准

來函以華盛頓省特開萬國研究衛護幼稚

保姆會可否派員與會等因當經本部咨行

學部去後茲准覆稱本部查教養童稚最

為緊要現有顏進士惠慶奉差在美本部

已電駐美公使轉飭該員就近與會以襄盛

舉請轉復等因前來相應函復

貴署大臣查照可也順頌

日祉

堂銜

光緒三十四年正月　　日

逕啟者，接准本國外部函囑，代美國軍醫會請

貴國政府派員赴第十七次軍醫大會，此次該會設在

卓爾支省愛得蘭地地方，於西本年十月六號至九號

定為開會日期，並囑轉達

貴親王知照，如

貴國果肯派員與會，本國政府甚為欣悅也，特泐順頌

爵祺 附送洋文

柔克義啟 光緒三十四年三月二九日

AMERICAN LEGATION,
PEKING, CHINA.

To F.O. No. 388.

P.

April 29, 1908.

Your Highness:

I have the honor to inform Your Highness that I am in receipt of instructions from the Department of State directing me to extend on behalf of the Association of Military Surgeons of the United States, an invitation to Your Highness' Government to be represented at the seventeenth annual meeting of that Association.

This meeting will be held from October 6th to October 9th, 1908, at Atlanta, Georgia, and in extending this invitation to Your Highness' Government I am instructed to state that my Government would be much pleased to learn of its acceptance.

I avail myself of the occasion to renew to Your Highness the assurance of my highest consideration.

American Minister.

To His Highness
    Prince of Ch'ing,
        President of the
            Board of Foreign Affairs.

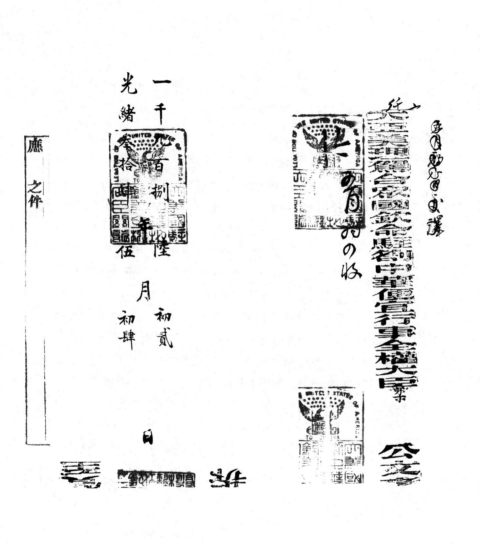

應之件

一千八百捌年陸月初貳
光緒叁拾肆年伍月初肆日

伍廷芳 的收

大亞美理駕合眾國欽命駐紮中華便宜行事全權大臣柔　為

照會事、茲奉本國外部文囑於西本年九月二十一號

起至十月十二號止、在華盛頓開設萬國研究醫治

勞症會、寄送會章一册、欽明會意旨、因美政府

視此醫會為重要、如中政府甚願派員與會、美政

府甚為欣悦等因、相應照會

貴親王查照、希屆時派員赴會可也、須至照會者　附漢文及會章

右

照　會

大清欽命全權大臣便宜行事軍機大臣總理外裕部事務和碩慶親王

先緒卷拾肆　年　陸　月　初貳

一千九百捌　年　陸　月　初肆　日

**AMERICAN LEGATION,
PEKING, CHINA.**

To F. O. No. 402.

P.

June 2, 1908.

Your Highness:

Acting under instructions from the Department
of State I have the honor to extend to Your Highness'
Government an invitation to send representatives to the
International Congress on Tuberculosis which is to be
held in Washington from September 21st to October 12th
of this year.   I enclose herewith a pamphlet fully explaining the character and purposes of the Congress.

I am directed in extending this invitation
to express the hope of my Government that the Congress
will be deemed of such importance as to warrant the acceptance of the invitation and to state the pleasure
with which they would learn of such action.

I avail myself of this occasion to renew to
Your Highness the assurance of my highest consideration.

Enclosure as above.

To His Highness

Prince of Ch'ing,

President of the

Board of Foreign Affairs.

清代外務部中外關係檔案史料叢編——中美關係卷 第六冊·國際會議

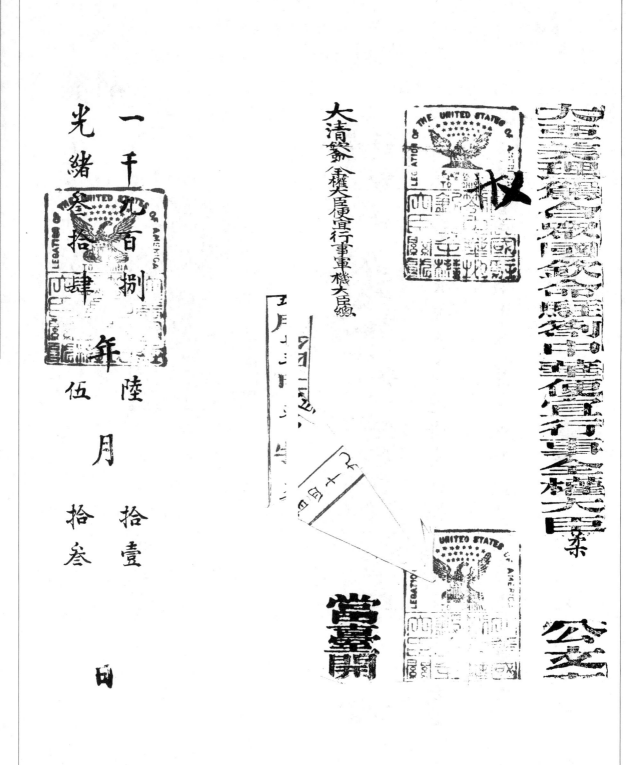

大清欽差全權大臣便宜行事軍機大臣鈐

光緒叁拾肆年

一千九百捌年陸月拾壹

伍月拾叁日

抄

五月十三日收

大美曾總會家國欽命駐劄中華便宜行事全權大臣柔 為

照會事接准飛立濱總督文稱擬在該處立一東亞

醫會已於本年二月二十七號商議考查熱帶一切

之症並應如何治理該醫會立意係欲東亞醫士可

以長相往來並可研究預防熱帶諸症及施治之法、

俾各國居住東亞之人及該本地居民脫離一切危

險茲將其所立會之底稿及會章附送

貴親王查閱所有在東亞陸軍水師各醫官及曾經

與醫會之各國醫士均可入為該會之友前在飛境

地方每年開有醫會於該處甚是有益中國亦曾派

醫官前往頗為重視飛督現定此大會每二年聚集

一次第一次開會係西曆一千九百十年三月以內

該督請中政府屆時選派醫員赴此第一次大會飛

境政府不勝跂盼等因相應照會

貴親王查照可也須至照會者附送洋文

右

　　照

　　　會

大清欽命全權大臣便宜行事軍機大臣總理外務部事務和碩慶親王

一千九百捌陸年拾壹月拾叁

光緒叁拾肆年伍月拾叁日

AMERICAN LEGATION,
PEKING, CHINA.

To F. O. No. 404.

    T.

June 9, 1908.

Your Highness:

     I have the honor to inform Your Highness that
a meeting of delegates accredited to the Philippine
Islands Medical Association for the purpose of forming
a Far Eastern Association of Tropical Medicine was held
in Manila on February 27, 1908, This body, after due
deliberation, deemed it expedient to unite the medical
fraternity of the Far East in an Association, the object of which should be to promote intercourse among
the members of the profession, to advance the knowledge
of tropical diseases, and their prophylaxis, and to extend the application of hygienic measures among the
various peoples in Oriental countries.

     I have the honor to enclose herewith a copy
of the constitution and by-laws of the association.
All associates of regularly constituted medical societies and of the Army, Naval, or Civil Service of each of
the several countries can bcome members of the new

                        association.

To His Highness

     Prince of Ch'ing,

        President of the

           Board of Foreign Affairs.

association.

        The annual reunion of the medical profession at the Philippine Islands Medical Association has been productive of much practical good, and the representatives appointed by Your Highness' Government have invariably taken a leading and valuable part in all its discussions.

        I have the honor, therefore, to extend to Your Highness' Government on behalf of the Philippine Government an invitation to send representatives to the first biennial meeting of the Far Eastern Association of Tropical Medicine which is to be held in Manila in the month of March in the year nineteen hundred and ten. In extending this invitation I am requested also to state that the Philippine Government is particularly desirous that Your Highness' Government may lend its aid toward the success of the new Association and may recognize the importance of its aims by sending, if possible, official delegates to its first meeting.

        I avail myself of this occasion to renew to Your Highness the assurance of my highest consideration.

W. W. Rockhill

Enclosure:

    One pamphlet, as above.

咨學部咨送美國勞症會會章希核復由

左侍郎聯 六月 初三日 行

右侍郎梁 六月 中浣 行

和會司

呈為咨行事接准美柔使照稱奉本國外部

文稱於西本年九月二十一號起至十月十二號

止在華盛頓開設萬國研究醫治勞症會寄

送會章一冊甚願中政府派員與會等語照會

前來相應將原送會章一冊咨行

貴部查核見復可也須至咨者 附洋文會章

學部

光緒三十四年六月　　日

欽差大臣孫李李陸軍部尚書農工商部左

咨逓事據蘇松太道蔡乃煌詳稱本年五月十七日奉憲台批發

江浙漁業公司業經舉代表赴美漁業會並舉員請派會員緣由

奉批此案前唯

張總理來函本屆赴美漁業會請籌撥公費二萬四千兩應用當經電催

為

咨呈

農工商部電復由部提倡撥助銀三千兩暨分電奉天直隸山東廣東

福建浙江沿海各省籌撥銀三千兩除直隸福建兩省尚未准復

現又電催外餘均先後電復惟蘇省應籌之三千兩並經會同

撫部院札飭甯蘇兩藩司照案各半分認統儘六月底匯滬各在案矣

推牌美使署顏參贊代表入會並請派陳貢生臣綱郭訓道于鳳鳴

張教習元廷等為會員以及採取關係漁業各項成法分著論説入會

研究自係為崇事求是起見惟事關重要欲核不厭求詳仰漁業等

監督蘇松太蔡道會商

張總理詳細查明復核由道列日叙具委詳呈候核惟期限已迫切勿稍

延是為至要仍俟咨明

部

撫部院查照此批稟抄發等因到道奉此遵經錄批移商

張總理碨核嗣奉憲台電飭文經函催速復查後慈准

張總理將赴會應行研究各件分別八大綱會議定妥開具清摺並附

送會員名單請電詳前來職道復核無異業已轉電憲台鑒核

在案合將送到員名履歷各議清摺詳送仰祈核洽

外務

農工商部迅電

出使美國伍大臣查一照寔為公便等情並清摺到本大臣據此除批撥詳

已卷查漁業賽會用欵除由

農工商部准撥三千兩提倡外餘由沿海七省各分攤銀二千兩已電

商各省暨札行寗蘇兩藩司均經照數課解至公司派員赴會前

部

據該道來電業經分電

外務

農工商部並准

外務部電復已轉電

伍大臣飭顧參贊知照茲核所送

張總理將赴會應行研究各件分擬八大綱尚屬詳明應俟連同會

員履歷請摺各二分咨送

外務部以一分存部一分轉洽

出使美國伍大臣查核並候咨送

農工商部查照備案仲即轉致

張總理一體知照仍候

作

撫部院批示繳印發英分咨外相片一件清摺咨送為此咨呈

貴部謹請查照核辦施行須至咨呈者

計咨送　清摺肆扣

右　咨　呈

外　務　部

光緒叁拾肆年柒月初貳日

函復美柔使軍醫會擬不派員由

外務部左侍郎聯　　　月　　　日

外務部右侍郎梁　　月　　日

行　行

復美柔使

逕復者案查

貴國軍醫會請派員赴第十七次軍醫大會一事

業經咨行陸軍部去後茲准復稱查美國軍

醫大會自第十四次起本部及北洋歷屆均曾

派員與會頗資獲益惟今年秋操伊邇各醫

員皆任重要職守礙難分遣有辜盛意甚為
抱歉等因相應函復
貴大臣查照轉達為荷順頌
日祉

　　　　　堂銜

光緒三十四年八月

榷算司

呈為照會事美國開設第四次漁業會派員赴會一事

前准農工商部來咨業經本部於二月十二日照復

貴大臣在案兹復准咨稱准直督稱據署提學盧

靖稱查有前北洋水師畢業生現充天津私立第一中

學堂監督張壽春嫻習英國語言文字素明理化博

物諸科堪以派充會員並令參考各種實業及水產美

術各學堂以資觀法並添派學務公所總務課副長

李金藻隨同與議訂於七月下旬起程咨請查照等

因前來相應照復

貴大臣查照可也湏至照會者

美柔使

光緒三十四年八月　　日

事　片行學部片催美國醫學會派員

行　行

外務部左侍郎聯　　月初卒日

外務部右侍郎梁　　月初卒日

和會司

呈為片行事案查美國研究萬國醫學會請派

員一事前准美柔使照會業經本部於六月初五日

咨行在案茲准出使美國伍大臣函稱昨據萬國

研究內傷醫學會函稱本會專為研究內傷病證

邀請各國政府特派深通醫學之員來美集議訂期

西九月二十一號起至十月十二號止前經呈請外部函

致駐京美使照會貴政府派員前來現屆開會之

期未諗貴國所派何人請煩代達迅賜派員赴會等

語查此事未接大部明文用特轉陳乞復等因前來

查該會為期太近是否由

貴部電達伍大臣就近酌量派員入會之處相應片行

貴部查照立即見復可也須至片者

　　　學部

光緒三十四年八月　　　日

咨呈

學部為咨呈事准外務部咨稱准

美柔使照稱奉本國外部文稱於

西本年九月二十一號起至十月十二

號止在華盛頓開設萬國研究醫

治勞症會寄送會章壹冊甚願中

政府派員與會等語照會前來相

應將原送會章一冊咨行貴部查

核見復等因又准咨稱美柔使照

稱准飛立濱總督文稱擬在該處

立一東亞醫會茲將所立會之底稿

及會章附送查閱所有在東亞陸軍

水師各醫官及曾經與醫會之各

國醫士均可入為該會之友中國亦

曾派醫官前往現定此大會每二

年聚集一次第一次開會係西曆一千

九百十年三月以內請中國政府屆時

選派醫員赴此第一次大會等因照

會前來相應將原送會章咨行貴

部查核辦理見復等因並各附會

章前來查醫學關繫甚重除電致

駐美伍大臣派員就近前往與會外

相應咨復

貴部照復美使可也須至咨呈者

外務部

光緒叁拾肆年捌月　　初拾日

清代外務部中外關係檔案史料叢編——中美關係卷 第六冊·國際會議

大亞美理駕合眾國欽差駐紥中華便宣行事全權大臣柔　為

照會事接准本國外部來文云本國欲閱悉近年

各國所派赴各與國人員由一千八百九十三年

施嘎戈大會起回國報告各事囑請中國將所派

赴會委員及監督所呈報或在各與國會內所商

辦各事備抄送部此外如中政府因赴各會曾降

有何

諭旨及中政府印有何評論會中與中國有關情形

書籍並請彙齊一併送部等因本大臣茲按所囑

照會

貴親王查照希即分心飭將近年

貴國所派赴各與國會人員回國報告各事件或

已即就會中於中國有關書籍設便易之法檢送

本館以便轉送本國外部可也須至照會者 附洋文

右

　　照　　會

大清欽命全權大臣便宜行事軍機大臣總理外務部事務和碩慶親王

一千九百捌拾肆年　　月　　日
　　　　　　拾壹　　拾陸

光緒叁拾肆年柒月　拾陸　日

**AMERICAN LEGATION,
PEKING, CHINA.**

To F.O. No. 444.

    T.

September 11, 1908.

Your Imperial Highness:

    I have the honor to inform Your Highness
that I have received a despatch from the Department
of State containing the following request:

    " The Department will be pleased to have
you forward as soon as possible copies of the reports
made by the Commissions of the Governments to which
you are accredited to each of the international
expositions at which it may have been represented
since and including the World's Fair at Chicago in
1893.   Also any other information on the subject of
international expositions which has been published
by that Government."

    If such publications have been issued by
the Chinese Government I shall esteem it a favor if
Your Highness will forward copies to be used by the
American Government in the work on International
Expositions which the Government is compiling.

    I avail myself of this opportunity to renew
to Your Imperial Highness the assurance of my highest
consideration.

To His Imperial Highness

    Prince of Ch'ing,

       President of the

          Board of Foreign Affairs.

公斷約案

駐美伍大臣電 八月十六 公斷專條事本部本日具奏請授駐美大臣為全權大臣將該約畫押硃批依議由

中美公斷專約事本部本日具奏請授駐美使

臣伍廷芳為全權大臣將該約畫押硃批依議欽

此除抄咨外希欽遵辦理外銳

清代外務部中外關係檔案史料叢編——中美關係卷 第六冊·國際會議

覆美柔使

逕復者前准

函稱准貴部照稱以美國開設第四次漁業會經

貴政府派有北洋畢業生天津中學堂監督張

壽春課長李金藻與會訂於七月下旬起程等情

本大臣茲特函請將張監督等此次赴美與會搭坐

何船及由何口入美請轉詢函知本館以便轉電美國

關員等語當經本部咨行農工商部查明聲復去

後茲准復稱張會員由滬乘天洋九向太平洋係由

加利福呢阿省改趁大車赴美等因前來相應函復

貴大臣查照轉電

貴國關員於該會員抵美時妥為照料可也此佈

順頌

日祉

全堂銜

逕復者·

來函以美國開設漁業會·

貴政府所派與會之張壽春李全藻會員係由滬乘天洋九放

洋赴美加利福呢阿省請轉電關員照料等因、本大臣巳轉該

電

憲關員照料矣、據想張會員原扗七月下旬乘船赴美此時

料巳登岸、惟恐該電反行落後此復、順頌

日祉　附洋文

柔克義啟　九月初七日

AMERICAN LEGATION,
PEKING, CHINA.

To FO No. 451.

October 1, 1908.

Your Imperial Highness:

I have the honor to acknowledge the receipt
of your letter of September 29, 1908, informing me that
the two Commissioners to the Fisheries Congress had
sailed for California by the S. S. "T'ien Yang".

I have sent the information to the American
Government, though as the Commissioners left in the
7th Moon it is possible that they may have already
arrived.

I avail myself of this occasion to renew to
Your Imperial Highness the assurance of my highest consideration.

To His Imperial Highness
        Prince of Ch'ing,
                President of the
                        Board of Foreign Affairs.

清代外務部中外關係檔案史料叢編——中美關係卷　第六冊·國際會議

收駐美伍大臣電 九月十五

中美公斷專約十四日遵旨畫押乞先代奏約本

另咨呈並具摺奏聞 廷芳叩鹽

以

外務部收

咨

欽差出使美墨秘古國大臣伍　為

咨呈事竊光緒三十四年六月初十函卷公斷專約事光緒三十年美康使曾

大部電開四月初十函卷公斷專約事光緒三十年美康使曾

奉其總統之命向我提議與英法一律訂約經本部奏准梁使

會商辦理旋於次年正月接梁使電稱英法約作廢因而罷議

將來再訂仍邀我國等語查此項專約誠如尊論關係和平大局美國

向我提議在先現與英法日本等國均已訂約則我國仿立自不容緩

應先向美廷續申前議再由本部照案奏明請

旨辦理希查照電復等因承准此當即與美外部妥商經將約稿譯就漢

文寄呈

大部察核旋於八月十六日承准

銑電內開中美公斷專約事本部本日具奏請

授駐美使臣伍廷芳為全權大臣將該約畫押奉

硃批依議欽此除鈔咨外希欽遵辦理等因遵即與美廷簡派議約全

權大臣現任外部大臣路特訂期於九月十四日互將約本畫押蓋印訖

當於十四日電達

大部並請代奏在案除將遵

旨畫押情形恭摺具

奏外謹將約本封固另由郵局妥慎寄呈

大部核定請

旨批准互換爲此咨呈

大部謹請察照施行須至咨呈者

計呈正副約本各壹分

右　咨　呈

外　務　部

光緒

日

清代外務部中外關係檔案史料叢編——中美關係卷 第六册·國際會議

外務部

公函第拾肆號

承

參

　　　　　堂　大　人　勛

美館械寄

　　　　　　　　　啟

敬再啟者頃據美京藏書樓總理普門函稱本書樓珍

藏富有各國書籍罔不搜羅貴國圖籍送經採訪並由

駐京柔使陸續購寄回國庋藏不少惟圖書集成一書

最為中國著名巨帙獨闕焉未備良用歉然查前數年

本國紐約省哥林比亞大校藏書樓落成時曾蒙中國

大吏寄贈是書至今膾炙人口本書樓為一國之冠可

否代請貴國政府惠贈一帙俾儲之庫藏籍資參攷則

舉國上下同深紉感等語　廷芳查是樓建設之宏搜藏之

富不特甲於全國抑且冠絕環球似宜俯允所求以示

睦誼統祈

代回

堂憲是禱專此再敬

勛安

廷芳再頓首

收十七月駐美伍大臣電十一月廿一

頃美外部照稱中美公斷專約經上議院議准隨時

可互換諸速照覆等語謹電陳廷號

清代外務部中外關係檔案史料叢編——中美關係卷 第六冊·國際會議

大亞美理駕合衆國欽差駐劄中華便宜行事全權大臣

照會事西歷明年二月由二號至九號本國於飛

利濱滿呢拉地方開一與本年二月間所開一律

之賽會即係與

貴親王於去歲十二月十九日來照所提及之賽

會相同茲奉本國外部大臣文囑謂該處仍印就

禁外人赴會之護照特為華人可以聽便前往請

轉達

貴部按照西上年所請赴會成案通行各省有權

發照官員曉諭華人如欲前往請領此項護照可

以無須照費等因相應照會

貴親王查照轉行可也須至照會者 附送洋文

右 照 會

大清欽命全權大臣便宜行事軍機大臣總理外務部事務和碩慶親王

光緒叁拾肆年拾壹月貳拾玖日

一千九百捌年拾貳月貳拾貳日

AMERICAN LEGATION,
PEKING, CHINA.

To FO No. 480.

December 21, 1908.

Your Imperial Highness:

      I have the honor to inform Your Imperial Highness that a Carnival will be held at Manila from the second to the ninth of next February, inclusive, similar to the one held there last February of which I had the honor to inform Your Highness in my note of December 19, 1907.

      In this connection I have the honor to state that I am instructed by the Department of State that Special Section Six Certificates for the benefit of Chinese wishing to visit Manila at the time of the Carnival will be issued by the authorities at Manila and I am directed by the State Department to request that Your Highness' Board will, in accordance with the precedent established last year, instruct those officials empowered to visa Section Six Certificates to visa these Special Certificates free of charge to the applicants.

      I avail myself of this opportunity to renew to Your Imperial Highness the assurance of my highest consideration.

W. W. Rockhill

To His Imperial Highness
    Prince of Ch'ing,
      President of the Board of
        Foreign Affairs.

敬啟者
陳伯悕
子

仁兄先生大人閣下都門判袂諸荷

青垂回思半載同舟深以獲

益良多為幸

燕雲在望感佩交縈敬承

政祉綏康

蓋籌密懋引詹

喬采莫名頌私　玉麟等由京起程取道秦島航海而

南於前月廿七日午刻抵滬暫寓旅館翌日謁滬

道暨各當道旋即拜晤美總領事田夏禮君接
談良久知美國會員約於西曆正月十五後可以到滬
又訪江海關稅務司好博遜君據稱海關有房屋
十一間可作會場但少傢具玉麟等察看一週覺辦
事房尚屬可用獨無會議廳將来各國會員到
後恐不適於用嗣經美領事介紹租定滙中旅館
房屋寬敞樓高五層大可選擇現正籌畫布置一
面先發儉冬兩電禀告

堂憲諒邀

鑒及昨閱報章知　午帥已將禁烟公會一事通電各省
有派代表來滬之說並聞滬道為南洋代表未知得
能邀准否倘各省均派代表事權能否統一辦法如
何擬議均乞

尊處轉稟

堂憲候示遵行是所盼禱摺件係何日呈遞敬念〻

如已遞呈請將原摺草稿寄示一讀尤所感盼耑

肅奉布容再續陳敬請

　勛安諸維

　垂詧不備

徵

　霭翁霱均此　恕不另函

霱

　　　　　　　　　唐國安

　　　　　　　　　劉玉麟制　謹肅 十二月初三日滬字壹號

　　　　　　　　　吳葆誠

乙和四百七十六

卅

陸軍部為咨覆事前准

貴部咨開美國約請各國派員赴滬

會議禁烟事宜查有北洋軍醫學堂

總辦徐道華清堪以派為會議禁烟專

員屆時赴滬與議除劄飭該道遵照外

相應咨行查照等因准此除劄知該總辦

束裝前往並咨行北洋大臣查照外相應咨覆

貴部查照可也須至咨者

右　咨

外　務　部

光緒二十四年十二月　初柒　日

軍機司監印　桕熙　邊齡

具奏美國約請各國在滬會議禁煙事宜派員與議並請派大員蒞會由

奏

外務部左侍郎聯　十二月初九日

奏

外務部右侍郎梁　十二月初八日　奏

謹

奏

為美國約請各國在滬會議禁煙事宜臣部派員前

往與議並請

聖鑒

欽派

大員屆時赴滬督率恭摺具陳仰祈

事竊臣部於上年五月間接准駐京美國使臣柔克

義照會以美國政府約請東方有屬地之法德英和

日本等國政府各派專員考查鴉片情形詢請中國

願否派員會查經臣部答以此項章程辦法均未詳

悉無憑核復嗣美使又來照聲明此次考查鴉片

不惟欲考究販運與吸食者表面之結果且有專

門用格致之法詳細調查與鴉片有關之一切其已

允派員協查之各國均係於亞洲向有屬地各該

屬地之鴉片或由自種或由他國運售均以禁止為

最要機關並非派員會商即為已經允從亦非

照會員所擬之法抑勒導行各員僅將查出實情

詳報各本國政府核辦等語臣因允其所請並

調前南斐洲總領事候補道劉玉麟為會議此
　派本部丞參上行走直隸

事專員嗣因各國所派議員不止一人因添派此

洋軍醫學堂總辦直隸補用道徐華清〔歷部儲〕〔為清辦留學英國畢業醫學博士五建歷〕

才館學員試用州同唐國安並商由南洋大臣端方

派江蘇布政使瑞澂江海關道蔡乃煌均為會議

專員又派臣部司員候補主事吳葆誠會同辦

理查中國禁煙之舉各國均甚注意亦無不贊成

此次美政府約請各國派員會查意在使凡各

國在亞洲境內之屬地與中國同時一律禁絕鴉片

之害用意固堪嘉尚所擬會議調查辦法亦聽各

本國政府自為主持在我正可藉資協助現定於

西曆明年二月一號即華曆明年正月十一日為

會議之期以上海為會議之地徐由臣部飭令

該員等屆期前赴上海與各國所派之員悉心

考查隨時報告並由臣部詳核妥辦外應請

大員屆時赴滬督率開會以昭鄭重而資聯絡所有

派員赴滬會議禁煙並請派大員蒞會緣由

理合恭摺具陳伏乞

簡派

皇上

聖鑒謹

奏

光緒三十四年十二月初八日具奏奉

旨著

派端方屆時赴滬督率開會欽此

照會美柔使添派瑞藩司滬道
為會議禁烟專員並奏請派大
員屆時赴滬督率開會由

行 行

外務部左侍郎聯 十二月 初 日

外務部右侍郎梁 十二月 初十日

榷算司

呈為照會事派員赴滬會議禁烟辦法一事

前派劉道玉麟徐道華清唐司員國安業

經照會

貴大臣在案現本部商由南洋大臣添派江

蘇布政使瑞澂江海關道蔡乃煌同為會

議專員並奏請

欽派

大員於開會時赴滬督率奉

旨著派端方屆時赴滬督率開會欽此欽遵相

應照會

貴大臣查照可也須至照會者

　　　　　美柔使

光緒三十四年十二月　　日

照會美柔使會議禁烟事添派稅務司
柯爾樂幫辦甘福履會同辦理由

署外務部右侍郎鄒

外務部右侍郎梁 十二月 十六 日

行 外務部左侍郎聯 十二月 十六 日

行

權算司

呈為照會事派員赴滬會議禁烟一事前經本部函

商稅務處轉飭總稅務司在海關造冊處選擇人員

屆期赴滬會同辦理以資襄助去後茲准復稱據總稅

務司呈稱查得現任山海關稅務司柯爾樂堪以派赴上海

會同辦理又署中署總理文案副稅務司頣等幫辦甘

福履堪以派往隨同辦理等情咨請查照等因前來相

應照會

貴大臣查照可也湏至照會者

美柔使

光緒三十四年十二月

丹

函復美柔使飛利濱醫學會已電伍
大臣派員與會由

署外務部右侍郎鄒

外務部左侍郎聯

行 行

十二月

十二月三十日

日

復美柔使

逕復者接准

函稱准飛利濱總督來文稱於西本年二月十號至十

三號在滿呢拉舉行醫學會請中政府派員與會等因

函達前來除電出使

貴國伍大臣就近派員與會外相應函復

貴大臣查照轉達飛利濱總督可也順頌

日祉

全堂銜

光緒三十四年十二月　　　　　日

子怡
慰伯清
潤田瀾

仁兄先生大人閣下敬蕭者十六日曾上滬字第四號

燕函諒邀

台覽 前日奉到

尊處沁電敬悉壹是仰見

蓋籌周密欽佩莫名惟是玉麟等弟以斷斷於提

議各條件者亦自有說謹將下懷敬為

諸公一陳之查此次禁菸會議提倡於美而必在我國

設會者良以鴉片之出產行銷與夫國民受其毒

害均以我國為最將來開議為各國所注目倘我

國無一提議外人必謂我視禁煙為無足重輕之事

不特辜負美國提倡苦心抑且為環球所輕視英

國駐京參贊李智報告藍皮書謂我國禁煙

除專賣外實難辦到倫敦勸禁洋煙會宣布

公函謂參贊既有是説中國欲行禁煙善法有限

於保約者英國應聲明通融勿責令遵守等語

此次復派駐滬代表畢登擬具禀各國議員照公

函附説提議該會費數十年之心血唇舌鼓動彼
國輿論要求彼國政府冀於此次會議協助我國
而我反以淡然處之外人其謂我何英國政黨向分
進化保守兩派現進化黨當國該黨政治家多熱心
禁煙者倘我趁此機會提議專賣經萬國會員多
數贊成然後與英極力磋磨彼屈於公理終有就範
之日縱目前或不能辦到亦可為日後舉行之基礎
若再過一年彼國即屆組織新內閣之期設保守黨

當國則我國專賣一事更難望其贊成失今不圖

後悔莫及此就外交一方面所亟應提議者也我國奏

定禁煙各項章程各省疆吏奉行不可謂不力無如

幅員廣博一省百數十州縣一州縣地方數里百里綿長

莫及稽核綦難故所報禁種勸戒及給領牌照等事

率多有名無實若非舉行專賣以杜源節流恐再

過數年仍無效果議者每慮專賣稽查易滋紛擾

查政務處奏定章程凡銷煙之店吸煙之人均領牌照

如有不領照而私販私吸者從重懲罰各省奉行此項

章程必當嚴密稽查方能有效稽查私販私吸與稽

查私熬私賣同一事體何於彼不防滋擾於此獨多顧

慮耶故一行專賣則種土之戶不能匿報販膏之店不

能私銷買膏之人不能不逐漸減吸執簡馭煩實為禁

煙最善之法而且洋土藥合計年銷二十餘萬担價值約

二萬萬兩仿照日本台灣專賣章程於原價加二成發

賣除費用外尚餘二千餘萬兩以徐補稅釐之損失玉麟

等抵滬後接福州去毒社等各省戒煙會社来函及報
紙論說莫不延頸跂踵以希望此次會議提倡禁煙善
法為千萬黑籍生靈脫離苦海若一旦失其所望輿情
渙散志士灰心於禁煙前途關繫甚大此就内政一方
面亦應提議者也玉麟等奉
堂憲奏派充會議員宗旨原為研究善法報告
政府裁決施行並非一經提議即能作准惟是當會議
時必發出問題以為研究之目的設或噤若寒蟬不發

一議玉麟等一身之恥辱不足惜其如國體何其如輿論

何用特不忖冒昧將情節瀝陳伏望

諸公鑒及愚誠代回

堂憲可否准予相機提議或恐礙於回覆英使並無提

議之照會則俟英國勸禁洋煙會有專詞到公會時

玉麟等即據該稟以發議表明我國禁煙非專賣斷

難辦到以俟各國議員公評似此則提議於英人贊成

於各國我不過居表明之地位諒英使不能據為藉口是

否可行之處仰候

堂憲核示遵行再玉麟前上說帖共五條除設熱賣公

廠一條外餘均奉

堂諭照行未審將來能否遵照提議統希代請

堂憲示遵是荷感禱專肅敬請

均安統維

譽照不宣

諸公均此

唐國安
劉玉麟
徐華清　謹肅
吳籛誠

十二月三十日

滬字五號

敬再肅者正封函間適奉

尊處艷電敬領壹是仰見

碩畫周詳昌勝感佩玉麟等當相機因應遵照辦

理專賣必先專買英使處及一兩家捐勒價值一

節我國如果決定舉行專賣自當與英訂一專

約照前三年洋藥進口價值酌中擬一定價永不

加減自不必慮及捐勒至

度支部恐財政支絀一節似可毋庸過慮查香港

專賣由政府督查歸商人包辦我國如仿照辦法利

之所在人爭趨之我國富商巨賈在南洋各埠承辦

專賣者大不乏人只求

政府實力保護若輩必樂面祖國承允辦理此由商

辦不必慮及財政支絀也即仿照日本台灣辦法由官

專賣款項亦非難籌查專賣一事於原價加二成

發賣每年盈餘二千餘萬兩縱庫項支絀儘可與本

國銀行息借或本國各銀行不能立籌鉅款則與外

國銀行息借亦無流弊因此係生利事業田

政府擔保外人樂於信用斷無格外苛求況開辦之時

各處總批發人及零賣人必須交納保證金以領牌照

據鄭典史嘉謨上

度支部專賣保陳謂此項保證金以我國行銷數目

約計可收得二千八百萬元得此款以為周轉即息借外

款亦屬有限故此事只求英國就範不患款項難籌

此由官辦不必慮及財政支絀也愚昧之見未審

高明以為何如耳抑更有請者除專賣一事外將來開

會各國議員必有詰問之語當場應對貴於敏捷

倘於我國有益無損之事是否隨機應變抑或仍當

隨時電請

堂憲核示然後答覆并乞面明

電知以便遵守為感茲將美國擬定考查鴉片大略譯

漢錄呈

鑒覽再此次開會係屬萬國公同研究禁煙善法報告

各本國政府再行核定辦理並非即為決議之舉合併

陳明肅此再請

年安

　　　　　　　唐國安

　　　　　　　劉玉麟　再肅

　　　　　　　徐華清

　　　　　　　吳葆誠

另附鈔摺一扣

附片

鈔錄美國擬定考查鴉片大略恭呈

台覽

一鴉片發源之歷史

二洋藥

甲統進若干

乙分散何處

丙各種名目及其價優劣

丁發賣價值散賣價值

戊征稅

三土藥

甲如何種法各種名目優劣

乙總出產若干

丙每省出產若干

丁與洋藥比較力量如何

戊發賣零賣價值

己地稅若干統稅若干釐金若干

燈捐若干

四銷用

五稅釐

甲收洋藥稅釐

乙收土藥稅釐

丙中央政府所得若干各該省所得

若干

六禁煙辦法

甲政府與地方官之禁例

乙與論如何禁煙自治會辦法如何

丙戒煙藥方

丁總綱如何效果如何

七嗎啡

甲稅關報稅若干

乙私運若干

丙統籌辦法

八現在銷流情形

甲各省所報之大概

乙難辦之處

丙地方官示禁之後成效如何

九禁煙之 上諭與及地方官之告示

十將來用何法抵償所失之稅釐

十一各省地方能否禁止土藥出洋

十二鴉片為國民財政之損失

十三香港每日熱膏若干應用若干私運

入中國若干

以上各欵均已逐條撮要預備以待臨時公

同詳晰研究理合聲明

仁兄先生大人閣下 敬肅者前上滬字第八

號燕函計邀

台覽先後奉到

尊處宥江兩電並由 午帥轉到外度兩部及禁

煙大臣公電以專賣事窒礙難行飭知遵照等

語敬悉壹是此間會事自開議以來各國議員

將各該國調查鴉片報告書先後呈會旋即陸

續提議計共會議十四次直至初七日為末次會

議將各國提議各款由全體會員公評共計決

定九款即由各國會員報告各該國政府裁決

施行麟等於初七日曾將我國提議三款綱目

電達

左右其餘歷次議案及各國報告書均巳分別擇

要繙譯一俟譯畢再行彙案詳細報告此次

會議各國議員於禁煙問題均甚熱心研究

本會主席美國議員布倫德於我國提議尤

能竭力維持良堪嘉尚經此次會議將來逐漸
進行於萬國禁煙前途固有良好即我國禁煙
有關於國際交涉者亦可藉此次決定條欵以
為發議基礎庶幾逐漸進步就我範圍也麟
等才識譾陋專對無方於此次重大問題未能
一律解決實深抱歡尚幸隨時荷蒙
指示不致隕越貽譏耳再英美兩國議員已於初
八日取道漢口來京會晤時尚望慰勞一切以

答協助美意並請將以上各節代回

堂憲是所盼禱專肅敬請

均安諸維

答照不宣

附譯件清摺一扣

唐國安
劉玉麟
徐華清
吳葆誠

謹肅

滬字第九號

二月初十日

附收元年二月十五日收

謹將各國會議公決九款譯呈

憲鑒

一中國政府以禁除全國鴉片出產行銷之事視為重大

實力施行且與情協助得以日見進步故本會會員承

認中國之堅誠雖各處成效不一然已獲益不淺矣

二因思中國政府實行禁阻吸煙之例他國亦同有此舉

動故本會敦請各代表陳請各該政府於其本境或屬

地內體察各國情形逐漸推行吸煙之禁令

三本會查得鴉片之用除作醫藥外在會各國均視為

禁物而頒行嚴密條例使之逐漸銷滅因此本會承

認各國情形雖有不同惟應敦促各國政府借鑒別國

辦理之經驗考訂其取締規則

四查各國政府均有嚴屬法律其宗旨或直接或間接以

禁止鴉片煙暨鴉片質提製之品私運入國因此本會

會員聲明凡與會各國均有責任訂立相當之規例

以禁止鴉片煙暨鴉片質提製之品運往已頒行上

開禁例之他國

五查嗎啡之製售流布漫無限制早釀成巨患嗎啡痼

疾已露蔓延之象因此本會甚願力請各政府制定嚴

屬規則於其本境或屬地內以取締此項藥物之製售

流布及由鴉片中提製雜和之品研究其質偽若妄

用則與嗎啡毒害相同者一律限禁

六本會會員於組織上礙難按科學之理研究鴉片煙

及戒煙藥品之性質功用然深悉此項研究極為重要

故本會甚望各代表將此項問題陳諸各該政府酌定

辦法

七本會極力敦促凡在中國有居留地及租界之各國政府僑於各該居留地及租界之內尚未實行關閉鴉片煙館者須仿照他國政府已經施行之禁令參酌情形迅速舉辦

八本會會員敦促凡在中國有居留地或租界之國各代表須陳請各該國政府與中國議定條例禁止製造販賣內含鴉片煙質或鴉片提製品之戒煙丸藥

九本會會員勸勉各國代表陳請各該國政府凡在中國有居留地或租界者施行藥商專律於領事裁判權限之內俾該國之民有所遵守

清代外務部中外關係檔案史料叢編——中美關係卷　第六册·國際會議

敬啓者前上美字第十八號諒蒙

鈞鑒昨准美外部照稱美政府以天然物產最足寶現

在世界開通列國所產不少亟宜保存以資考察忖思

各國政府諒必共表同情兹擬聯合友邦在海牙保和

會將此事會同提議已飭駐京美使柔克義照會貴國

政府屆時派員赴會計當察覽用特知照請煩轉達

大部查核照允等語廷芳查天然物產各國均以為難得可

貴之物美政府倡議保存係為天地惜物起見似可照

允伏祈

代回

堂憲是所切禱專此祗請

勛安

　　　　　伍廷芳頓首　美字第十九號
　　　　　　　　　　　二月十九日

敬再啟者新任美總統於西三月四號蒞任前孟已將預

備情形畧陳一二茲於二月十三日即西三月四號巳刻

新舊總統同赴議院副總統以及各部大臣均隨之詣

議院後兩總統居中坐上下議紳與各國使臣並預其

列向章總統履任均在議院誓衆此次新總統在議院

所言大都有關於國際及東亞者可畧見其政策之宗

旨茲特譯就另摺錄呈查該總統向來推許我國頗有

愛我助我之意而尤以和平為宗旨昨二十一日酉刻

總統接見各國使臣及參隨人員屆時　延芳率同各員

前赴白宫晉謁總統晤廷芳時殷殷以中美睦誼敦好為

言前數年廷芳在美都與彼認識往來上年游歷中國

時廷芳適在香港重逢頗與浹洽握手之項即以舊交

相稱其人品性和藹誠懇可親嗣後中美交誼當更輯

睦可為預卜至其演說之詞論及外人入美禁例頗有

以美國官員例外苛待華工為不合公理之意又近日

美國西方嘉利科尼省自以美為合衆之國各省立例

可以不受中央政府節制因而議設特別之例苛待日人

日本政府大憤幾至決裂旋由前總統特諭該省議院

罷議而日本亦以自行禁工為詞始得轉圜今總統有

鑒於此恐因一省而陷全國於戰爭之險故發為議論

隱有所指蓋其用意以保守和平為主義也附譯錄一

件統祈

代呈

堂憲察核是禱專此再請

勳安諸惟

台照

廷芳再頓首

敬再啟者日前奉到

大部復致康格夫人函一件業已遵照轉遞矣再請

勛安

廷芳再頓首

駐美使臣梁來第十九號函

涵、附件 又六月廿六 入收

譯件一扣 坿十九號函

摘譯美總統達輔接任演說詞

國際政策

吾美國際政策常以增進平和為宗旨夫兵凶戰危無論

為勝為敗其效果每呈可怖之狀吾美非熟計夫此必不

輕易與人啓釁不特此也苟其事與一國之名譽利權無不

可相容之處則且以與戎為大戒必多方設法以期免啓釁端

所以凡屬保和弭兵之舉如海牙平和會及公斷條約等吾美

莫不深表同情視為解決國際爭端之要具

但事又有不可徒就一面着想者方今世界諸強莫不盛

修戰備磨厲以須則吾美亦當於軍備上求與彼立於同

等之地位苟不爾則人將乘吾不備蹈瑕抵隙以逞其欲

吾甯有幸乎此事理之甚顯著者若吾人猶不能洞見則

是黯於大勢眛於現情徒一愚騃之理想家耳

東方國際爭端或起於開放門戶問題或原因於他項事故

目下吾美對待之自問尚能固我利權於無缺凡有公平之

要素人莫敢不尊重之但若令人知我所謂保持利權者其

法不外以口舌文牘相辯難則必不能收如此之效

審是則凡海陸軍備暨守衛海岸諸費當視為吾國政府所

必應擔任之一事而不可徒藉口於財政一端而減輕之也海

陸兩軍欲求適用之吾美國家財力自問能供給之而有餘

而說者謂恐如此則危及共和政府與自由政體不知此皆

觩觢過應之詖實則並無絲毫之險也此又吾人所不應以

增加稅項為懼而藉口以求變更政策者

吾美政策自西班牙一役以後即已於世界各國中占有一有

勢力之位置此勢力維何即前此所未嘗見諸實行而後此

所當常常施用以保護我僑寓外國人民者吾美人民欲於

他國暫時居住若因種族宗教起見而為他人所歧視我國

家所當竭力維護以免其見凌受辱也

入境禁例

移住來美之亞人不能與美民同化業經訂定條約及法律或

由外交談判商定辦法以禁制其入境本總統深盼自茲以往移

住流弊日形減輕而兩國政府之間彼此能相讓當不致有無謂

之齟齬

凡外人無論隸何國籍享有條約上權利在吾國營謀合例

之生理應受法律保護者吾國當加意防護如有因種族感

情對於此項外國人妄起衝突者當按律懲治之

本總統令論入境事有不能不徑行揭示者即吾國聯邦政府

統轄權其間不免有一缺點是也夫我既與他國訂立條約允許

以法律保護其人民居住吾境內矣而又委其責於一省治或一

邑治之不受聯邦政府節制者政出兩歧辦理殊多棘手此誠

統治權中之一大缺陷所當急行彌補者

我國何難即以法律規定凡外國籍民據條約所享之權利聯

邦政府得以提出之於聯邦法院俾其有實行之效夫政府既

與他國訂約保護其籍民矣而遇有不能保護之時則又藉口

於責在不受節制之某省某邑以為解釋是則政府之力不

已自居於屢弱不振乎吾人有所承諾則必須自處於可以

踐諾之地位此事理之所必然者　查為合眾國各省財政自治原有不受中央政府節制之例

夫聯邦政府統轄權若經議院用法律規定而又有聯邦法院

以維持之則戰禍且可消弭於無形夫戰禍既如此即可消弭矣吾

國自必不能任聽一二處地方政府逞偏見之私辦理失宜致陷全

國於咎釁之險也

　國際貿易

本總統深冀新集之議院能重視吾美之國際貿易設法以鼓

勵振興之無論為東方為飛獵賓為南美洲其商務無不可增進

發達凡曾留意此事者當無不知之

吾美與飛島之貿易係採自由政策試觀棉花農具及其他製

造品之貿易即可見其收效之顯然南北美洲須有直接之航

路前總統暨外部大臣路持嘗請議院注意及之而路大臣且曾

至南美調查一切本總統極盼議院能採用郵船補助法以關此

航路也

歐洲商政持限制區別主義以抵制吾之輸入品而我農商工等

部有操縱其市場之責其重要當為有目所共覩吾國新稅則

不久將訂定深冀其最高最低兩稅率運用得宜則所謂限

制者將不患無法以消除之

巴拿馬運河於吾國東西兩部間之商業極有關係東西兩海

岸綫之轉輸將更形利便至於體量鉅大之商品其橫過大陸之

運費必因而大有變更若利益之最大者則此河實可以增進吾國
東岸與南美西岸間之商業而南美東岸之商場有與西岸以
鐵道接連者當亦可蒙其利賴也

附閏二月廿八日駐美伍大臣函

逕啟者接奉本國外部大臣函稱本國華盛頓省

之斯伯堅城地方定於西本年八月九號至十四

號等日舉辦民立農務凱會由官襄助該會員特

具請帖轉由外部大臣請中政府派員與會等因

相應函達

貴部王大臣查照轉請農工商部派員與會如允

派前往本國政府亦必樂於派員接待也特此泐

布即頌

日祉

美國使署　附洋文並請帖

柔克義啟　三月初一日

**AMERICAN LEGATION,
PEKING, CHINA.**

To FO No. 516.

April 20, 1909.

Your Imperial Highness:

The Secretary of State informs me that a National Irrigation Congress is to be held at Spokane,
Washington, from August 9th to August 14th of this
year.   This Congress is convened by the people with
the countenance and assistance of the Government.   The
members of this Congress now send through the Department
of State an invitation to the Chinese Government to
be represented at the Congress.

I have the honor to request that Your Imperial
Highness will hand the letter of invitation to the President of the Board of Agriculture, Industries, and Commerce.   If the invitation is accepted I shall be happy
to communicate the acceptance to my Government, which
will depute officials to receive the Chinese delegates.

I avail myself of this opportunity to renew
to Your Imperial Highness the assurance of my highest
consideration.

To His Imperial Highness
       Prince of Ch'ing,
             President of the Board
                   of Foreign Affairs.

權算司

呈為咨行事宣統年三月初一日准美國柔使面稱接

奉本國外部大臣函本國華盛頓省之斯伯堅城地方

定於西本年八月九號至十四號等日舉辦民立農務

漑田會由官襄助該會員特具請帖轉由外部大臣

請中政府派員與會等語希轉請農工商部派員

與會如允派前往本國政府亦必樂於派員接待等因前

來相應將原送請帖一分咨行

貴部查照是否派員與會之處希即見復以憑轉復美

使可也須至咨者　附洋文請帖一分

農工商部

宣統元年三月　　　　日

摘 第五七號　辰會　外國　入檔

咨外務部

宣統元年　三月廿六

宣統元年三月　　日

堂批閱定

為咨呈事接准

咨稱准美桑使函稱本年西八月在斯伯堅

城地方舉辦農務漑田會請派員興會等

語咨行查照見覆等因並附洋文請帖前

來查此案本部業經電請駐美伍大臣就近派員

屆期與會相應咨復

貴部查照轉復美使可也須至咨呈者

右咨

外務部

咨呈外務部　美國農務漑田會業電伍大臣派員興會由

堂批閱訖

宣統元年四月〔印〕

為咨呈事宣統元年三月初四日接准

咨稱准美㑺使函稱本年八月在斯伯堅

地方舉辦農務漑田會諮派員與會等

語附送洋文諮帖咨行見復等因當飛

三月初七日特發陽電咨稱駐美伍大臣

就近派員赴會益咨呈

貴部外案三月廿三日後准

咨稱准美㑺使面以美政府居保全北美

天然物產擬在華盛頓設立大會詢問中

政府是否派員赴會等語鈔錄原咨

行查核見復等因後於三月廿八日特發陽電

電咨稱駐美伍大臣就近派員赴會去後

茲准電稱頃電悉美前總統於西二月

在華盛頓招集各有㑺特倡議間設

天然物產會館由外部刻亦奏明籌先

許㑺未據在海牙會議現未有期前准

陽電已派駐波爾洞代理領事梅伯顯

屆期勅近赴會等因電復前未相應咨呈

貴部查照特後美使可以續玉請咨呈者

右咨呈

外務部

農務司趙〔押〕

咨呈外務部准從大臣電復天然物產會館未定期農務漑田會已派員赴會由

此錄美華政見未圖

逗在墨美國與墨西哥坂拿大為保住

此美天地物產在華國頃設立大會

現造各國公的願此該會意旨立一傑在

物產之會是以美政府擬本去居云未

可此有三國即立此會如此各國意見

相同六蜜店設法保存益應此有殘缺

及如廢棄之物產必須各方補足益

云若天下人同保世間之天然產不僅

利於本國且與天下名國利益共之即

如肥沃土地滋養食料一節石但與該

黑人民衛生有闊即與別國培植店

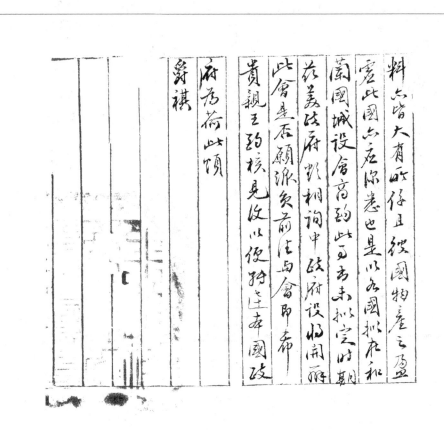

料六皆大有畋保且從國物產之盈

霍此國六店原巷也是以名國拟在私

蘭國城設會商約此正本未拟定時期

茲美政府即相詢中政府設此開辦

此會是否願派員前往與會即希

貴親王約核見收以便將達本國政

府為荷此頃

舜祺

照復美柔使美開保全天然物產會商部
已電咨駐使就近派員由

行　行

外務部左侍郎聯

外務部右侍郎鄒

四月　　四月
　　　　　　　　　
　　　　　　　　
日　　日

和會司

呈為照復事前准

來咨以

貴政府為保全北美天然物產擬在華盛頓設立大會

詢問中政府是否派員與會等語本部當即咨行農

工商部去後玆准復稱三月二十六日已電咨駐

貴國伍大臣就近派員並准電復

貴國前總統於西二月在華盛頓招集各省總督似

議開設天然物產會飭由外部知照各國如蒙允許

將來擬在海牙會議現未有期咨請轉復等因前來

相應照復

貴大臣查照可也須至照復者

宣統元年四月

復美桑使函天然物產會候有會期再派員與議由

行　　　行

外務部左侍郎聯　　　　四月

外務部右侍郎鄒　行　胃十六日　　日

復美桑使函

前准

来函以

貴國政府擬設立保存天然物產會現已約

請各國擬在和蘭國城高酌此事尚未擬定

時期茲詢中國政府設將開辦此會是否

願派員與會即希見復等因查

貴國倡設斯會於保存物產實有禆益中國甚

願與會俟接有開會准期再行派員前往與議相應

先行函復

貴大臣查照轉達

貴國政府可也此復順頌

日祉

全堂街　　　　　　　　日

宣統元年四月

清代外務部中外關係檔案史料叢編——中美關係卷 第六冊·國際會議

**AMERICAN LEGATION,
PEKING.**

To F. O. No. 544.

July 2, 1909.

Your Imperial Highness:

Under the instructions of the Department of
State I have the honor to extend to Your Highness' Gov-
ernment an official invitation from the Government of the
United States to participate in the Fifteenth International
Congress on Hygiene and Demography, to be held at Wash-
ington, September 26th to October 1st, 1910.

The International Congress of Hygiene and Demography ranks among the most important of international
scientific gatherings. It comprises distinguished representatives of many and diverse professions which are
more or less connected with governmental administration,
and it is therefore thought that representation at the
Congress by official delegates would not be without advantage to the Chinese Government. Your Highness will re-
mark that the date set for the meeting of the Congress
is more than a year hence. The Government of the United
States will learn with much pleasure of the acceptance of
this invitation by Your Highness' Government.

I avail myself of this opportunity to renew to
Your Imperial Highness the assurance of my highest consideration.

To His Imperial Highness

Prince of Ch'ing,   Charge d'Affaires.
      President of the Board
            of Foreign Affairs.

逕啟者茲接美外部大臣函囑於西曆一千

九百十年九月二十六號起至十月一號止

在華盛頓舉行第十五次萬國衛生延壽會

各國僉謂研究衛生實為最要之事每次

開會各國所派與會者均為官場名望素

著之員

中政府派員與會於中國亦甚有益開會

期尚有年餘如

美國使署

中政府樂於派官與會美政府定必欣悅

也此頌

日祉

　　　　　費勒器啟五月十五日

函復美費署使軍醫會派員與會由

行　　　行

外務部左侍郎聯

外務部右侍郎鄒　〔押〕

五月　〔押〕　〔押〕

五月二十八日

日

復美費署使函

逕復者案查

貴部軍醫會派員一事前准

柔大臣來函業經咨行陸軍部去後茲准復稱查

有軍醫學堂監督唐文源軍醫總局正軍醫官徐

英揚堪以派往與會除飭該員等屆時前往外應咨

復等因前來相應函復

貴署大臣查照轉達該會知悉可也順頌

日祉

全堂銜

宣統元年五月　　日

民政部為咨覆事前准咨稱接准美費署使函稱

西歷一千九百十年九月二十六號起至十月一

號止在華盛頓舉行第十五次萬國衛生延壽會

中政府派員與會於中國甚為有益美政府亦必

欣悅等因前來查衛生事宜為貴部所注意此次

美使函請與會應否由貴部派員前往以資研究

抑即就近知照出使大臣派員與會較為簡便等

因准此查美國此次舉行萬國衛生延壽會我國

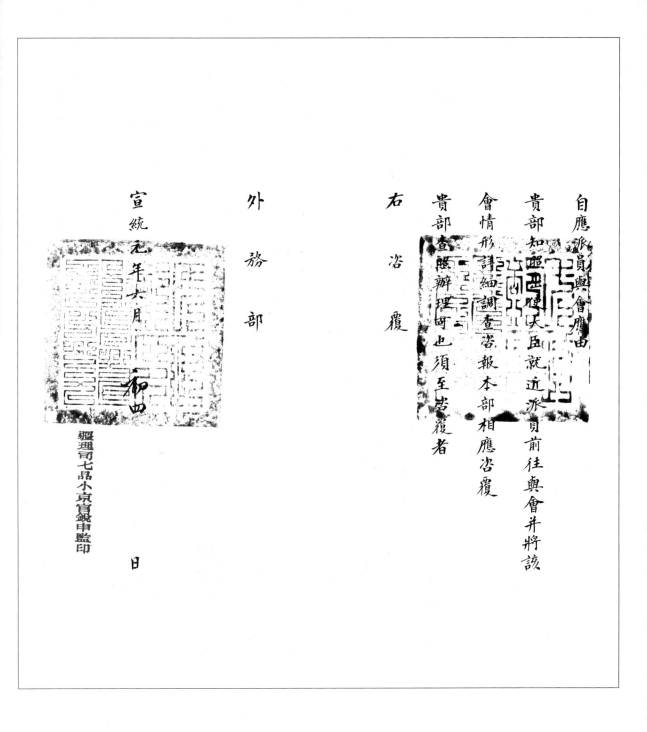

自應派員與會應由

貴部知照駐大臣就近派員前往與會并將該

會情形詳細調查咨報本部相應咨覆

貴部查照辦理可也須至咨覆者

右咨覆

外務部

宣統元年六月　　日

辦理司七品小京官鎮申監印

清代外務部中外關係檔案史料叢編——中美關係卷 第六冊·國際會議

函復美費署使美開萬國衛生延壽會屆時
派員與會由

行　行

外務部左侍郎聯　　六月　十　日

外務部右侍郎鄒　　六月　十　日

函復美費署使

逕復者接准

函稱西歷一千九百十年九月二十六號起至

十月一號止在華盛頓舉行第十五次萬國

衛生延壽會請派員與會等因本部除

咨行使美伍大臣屆時派員與會外相應函復

貴署大臣查照可也順頌

日祉

宣統元年六月　日

函致美費署使陸軍部派唐文源
等赴軍醫會轉行各關放行由

行　　　　行

外務部左侍郎聯　　　　外務部右侍郎鄒　行

　　　　　七月　　　　七月十三日

日

致美費署使

逕啟者所有

貴國本年舉行軍醫大會請派員與會一事

准陸軍部咨稱現經札派軍醫學堂監督唐

文源軍醫總局正軍醫官徐英揚屆時前往

與會茲該員等定於西八月三十一號即中曆

七月十六日由上海乘太平洋郵船公司蒙古

輪船前往希照會

美國駐京大臣轉行美國沿海各關卡於該員

等到關時查照放行等因相應函達

貴署大臣查照電請

貴國政府轉飭關卡於該員等到境時查照

放行可也順頌

日祉

堂銜

宣統元年七月　　　　　　　日

清代外務部中外關係檔案史料叢編——中美關係卷　第六冊·國際會議

美外部通告駐美各員預上海禁煙會各邦致美

國外交官文聲明奉行美國禁煙議會了

附丁家立上

崑大人書

聯美商局頌報平譯呈

九月廿三月
已抄送
禁煙會

美館漢務參贊丁家立上梁尚書 西九月十二日即十月二十五亦 將外部

敬啟者東館代辦費勒照命家立

茲來通告一件附呈

釣鑒以便奉國禁煙議會開會之前中美

兩國先行立換意見費代辦家立請

閱

貴大臣明日下午先否在署因有一二公事

面談故也

丁家立敬啟

美外部屢舉行禁國禁煙議會通告駐紮

暨預上海各國禁煙調查屬久邦之美國

救國禁煙調查屬之於一九寅九年二月二十

外交官文 一千八百寅八年九月一日自華盛頓行

六 為上海傳議美政府觀於該屬郵政之統

果實深滿思即擬照提偶禁煙事宜之領袖

之意亦以該屬郵政屬其廣尚美政府人民均以

此等缺果多由久國保國之代表對於形題

度常寬宏呀行

美政府深柔鴉片問題之宪大之生虞販賣呀

舍終濟趣以未之事要並觀於關係終濟久國

同心共濟該屬決定俟歐皆贊卾於東方久國

整久該國境內垂屬我屏陳寒此則美政

府陳居感勆者也

擥美國各員在本國調查禁煙事宜之根告而

知鴉片煙害陳閱於范律賓屬外界甚憂

延於本國境內此由中華人旅美之眾多

一由本國與東方商務之切近一電運入鴉片

下

製造焉此以之無限也

放美國之對於禁煙問題亦特出於愛之心

抑亦有物之願之趣味生為本國議院擬據上

海救國禁煙屬未聞前之調查特訂法律也

美國上下議院會訂定自一九寅八年四月一節

以政凡輪入久种鴉片煙醫一鴉片貿製變化

之此均作屬背法律論並其該久种鴉片煙

醫鴉片之續調製變化之此亦均預備存此而屬

醫藥之用者有按照畔布屬士部大臣訂定

之規則軍（入九九此軍）入者須按照現在及此

沒之法律完倘稅餉

且有更欺瞞業背法律輸入久种鴉片煙醫

鴉片貿調製變化之此亦助輪入之心則知該貿

屬犯禁鈍敢於眂藏唐則無論屬首為

洗一枕將于鴉片克公銷毀科犯罪之人

自五千元至五十元不筆之罰金並二年內

之拘禁或二者並科并褢判遵背此章

時尚查得被若研有鴉片印作居犯罪之進
撥陸凡被光納問陳審宦申辦洗卿
觀此法律不知陳作醫藥之用外鴉片一概整
此入口兩束國政府不久必須續行訂立法律
以便時鴉片煙照鴉片質調製變化必反成癖
病此喜加莫印度麻等類之製出深布歸聯
邦檔查
益美國並凡麻煙之邦若欲將邨立法律
收平實敦捧深鴉片流毒心控制該貨
隆之同情合作序必要矣
心之多少不為功欲控制該貨隆以之多少則國

原夫上海萬國禁煙調查廣之略以立止
美國政府知行公支布說觀於販賣此各鴉片
之結果此乃平時由久主明國通同議訂即締
貼賣掃除吃食之華程故提議倡立一案
團禁煙議會以便燒商該問題對於久國
之情形如無辦制並訂立一案國遵守之
條約俟於英政府之意心為久國永分武后決

定舉動之前須將鴉片貿易實情及鴉
片吃食結果詳細調查一方無下手此則
調查廣之辦法似此議廣展得計兩美國
亦心議廣所能得之資料處不足據以無
決定辦法因即政變前議於一九零六年
年終同問係該問題之久邦提關證立
一萬國禁煙調查廣以驗究鴉片問題以於
枢約財政造德立法矢情形
久國政府末後乃決定於一九零九年正月
一乎立上海舉行萬國禁煙調查廣然
考欲顯貴店
德宗景皇帝大事之故之屬去二月一乎乃於
聞廣玉二十六字聞廣總名代表將鴉片問
題久才面切實調查以研究政決定以下
之佳款
一中國政府以素隆全國鴉片出產行銷之事
視為軍大實力於行且與情協助得以以
見彼步故束會會員承認中國之堅訓期

九霄雲外動不一而足皆莫不俯首

二因思中國政府實行禁吸煙之新代國
弥同有此舉動故本會敦請各代表陳請
深布政府於本境或屬地內俟察各國
久該政府於本境或屬地內俟察各國
情形並酌擬施行禁煙之禁令

三本會查明鴉片之用除作醫藥外並無益於
國計視為毒物而須行嚴密偵伺使之逐
漸銷滅因此本會承認各國情形雖有
不同惟應敦促各國政府儀鑑別國力量

醫藥之用者有按照現今各國大臣訂定
之規則運入或此運入者須按照現在及此
凡有真欲瞞藏背法律輪入各種鴉片醫
鴉片貿調製變化之品或輸入此明知該貨
居范業而散於收藏者臟唐則與論首為
洗一枕將于鴉片充公銷毀科犯罪之人
其有真欲瞞藏背法律輪入各種鴉片醫
自五千元至五十元不等之罰金或二年內
之約束或二者並科並審判遵背此章

八 各會之員務於各國代表陳請之該國政
府及在中國有居留地或租界者施行
蓋商手律於顧了裁判權限之內傳
該國之民有應遵守

叭陛時未曾正式聲明與調查唐案
已提及承認以止公決條欽無論於何道德上
有何可要之關係條此久國復將公決條
欽及問像久問題訂立一國際徑約則期滿
立明興論之欲計

美政府深悉鴉片問題之重要提倡鼓
勒不當限於一隅應按照上海議决條欽辦
理故此居上海萬國禁煙調查唐公决之條
欽必須得有國際之允非於行因此美
政府擬任海牙或別處選擇相宜日期
舉行萬國禁煙議唐並預唐團委派一
員武一員以止事以能將上海公决條欽望于
結果訂成約章之全稿 美政府依據若
禁烟調查唐之辦法暨平公决條欽試擬定

商事件如下

一 先國應訂立同一之法律章程取締鴉
片煙暨鴉片質提製點之產製深市

二 凡煙國祇將鴉片（軍）輸之此岸應限制
午敷月

三 設法在開行之各禁止鴉片暨鴉片質
提製點（軍）往禁平入口或欲粜平入口或欲
取締平入口之國

四 此國軍往彼國之鴉片及鴉片質提製
品應將不准出口總數互相告知

五 各國郵便電應訂立洋郵約審送鴉片
及鴉片質提製品之章程

六 限止民取締罌粟之種植暨致向不產
煙之國樹藝煙種抵敵中國印度減少之敷

七 左中國有居留地或租界之夬政府應左
其領事裁判權限代內旅行各該國
藥商手律於各該國人民

八 現左鴉片貿易既依附而行之國際約

九、凡國訂立關於鴉片生産貿易條約凡
違背者各國應施行同一之刑法

十、凡此國運往彼國之鴉片煙包應置於同
一之記號以便認識

十一、販運鴉片並監督鴉片提製照之人應給券
國互相搜查
執照

十二、凡鴉片疑有裝載違禁鴉片之船只名
國互相搜查

十三、凡販運鴉片煙之船只應設法禁平掛
用不應常之旗號

古、應設立一國際會以便施行所訂之
國際條約

美政府並不欲將該會之範圍預先審定
亦不欲擬不容更改之議與美政府
自信以上所擬各欵至少能供初議之
基礎故現今要請各預會國審核上列條
欵並將禁煙問題之別方面該國視為特別

重要者表于意見於未開會之先互相研擬
如貴大臣所駐國之政府贊成以上所擬各
欵則預會諸政府希於本年十二月十五日或一
號以前將于意見及易擬辦法函換則房
益多矣如此則必特縮短會議時日並可
使美國政府按照各國意見辦法預先擬
就一定章程

因此務希貴大臣將此訓令轉達駐國之
外部大臣並請于選派代表一員或一員以
上于以協議締結條約之全權與此函關
先聞視該政府對於按照上海禁煙調查會
之結果另立一禁煙議會贊成與否

署理外部大臣 史 慶慶 啟

China

IN REPLY REFER TO
FILE NO. 774.

INTERNATIONAL OPIUM CONFERENCE.

DEPARTMENT OF STATE,

Washington, September 1, 1909.

To the Diplomatic Officers of the United States
  Accredited to the Governments which were Represented
    in the Shanghai International Opium Commission.

Gentlemen:

The Government of the United States has learned with
satisfaction the results achieved by the International
Opium Commission, which concluded its labors at Shanghai
on February 26, 1909. In the opinion of the leaders of
the antiopium movement much has been accomplished by the
Commission; and by both the Government and people of the
United States it is recognized that the results are
largely due to the generous spirit in which the representatives of the Governments concerned approached the
subject.

The Government of the United States appreciates the
magnitude of the opium problem and the serious financial
interests involved in the production of and trade in the
drug, and it is deeply impressed by the friendly coopera-
tion of the Powers financially interested and the desire
as expressed by the resolutions of the Commission that
the opium evil should be eradicated not only from Far
Eastern countries, but also from their home territories
and possessions in other parts of the world.

During the investigation of the opium problem in the
United States by the American Commissioners, it became
apparent that, quite apart from the question as it affects

[9-3-1909-100.]

the Philippine Islands, a serious opium evil obtained
in the United States itself; that this was primarily due
to the large Chinese population in the country, to the
intimate commercial intercourse with the Orient, and to
the unrestricted importation of opium and manufacture of
morphia.

Thus, the interest of the United States in the opium
problem is material as well as humanitarian, and, as the
result of the investigations made before the meeting of
the Commission at Shanghai, the Congress of the United
States passed the following legislation:

Be it enacted by the Senate and House of Representatives of the United States of America in Congress assembled,
That after the first day of April, nineteen hundred and
nine, it shall be unlawful to import into the United States
opium in any form or any preparation or derivative thereof:
Provided, That opium and preparations and derivatives
thereof, other than smoking opium or opium prepared for
smoking, may be imported for medicinal purposes only,
under regulations which the Secretary of the Treasury is
hereby authorized to prescribe, and when so imported shall
be subject to the duties which are now or may hereafter
be imposed by law.
Sec. 2. That if any person shall fraudulently or
knowingly import or bring into the United States, or assist in so doing, any opium or any preparation or derivative thereof contrary to law, or shall receive, conceal,
buy, sell, or in any manner facilitate the transportation, concealment, or sale of such opium or preparation
or derivative thereof after importation, knowing the same
to have been imported contrary to law, such opium or preparation or derivative thereof shall be forfeited and shall
be destroyed, and the offender shall be fined in any sum
not exceeding five thousand dollars nor less than fifty
dollars, or by imprisonment for any time not exceeding two
years, or both. Whenever, on trial for a violation of
this section, the defendant is shown to have, or to have
had, possession of such opium or preparation or derivative
thereof, such possession shall be deemed sufficient evidence to authorize conviction unless the defendant shall
explain the possession to the satisfaction of the jury.

It will be observed that this Act excludes from the
United States opium except for medicinal purposes. It is
not unlikely that the Government of the United States may

at an early date enact further legislation to place the
entire manufacture and distribution of medicinal opium,
its derivatives and preparations, and other habit-forming
drugs like cocaine and Indian hemp, under federal super-
vision and control.

The United States, however, is not itself an opium-
producing country, and in order to make its laws fully
effective and stamp out the evil there should be control
of the amount of opium shipped to this country. To this
end it will be necessary to secure international coopera-
tion and the sympathy of opium-producing countries.

In the original despatches which led to the calling
of the Commission, the American Government considered the
time had come to decide whether the consequences of the
opium trade and habit were not such that the civilized
Powers should take measures in common to control the trade
and eradicate the habit, and the suggestion was made that
there be an international conference to consider the question in its international bearing, and if feasible to
draft an international agreement.

As, however, the Government of Great Britain inti-
mated that procedure by way of commission seemed better
adapted than a conference for an investigation of the
facts of the trade and the consequences of the habit preliminary to any action by the Powers jointly and sever-
ally, and inasmuch as the material placed before the conference might be insufficient to arrive at definite recommendations, the United States modified its original
attitude. Therefore, in the latter part of 1906, the Government of the United States approached several of the
Powers more particularly interested in the question for

an international commission of inquiry to study the scientific, economic, moral, and legislative aspects of the opium problem.

It was finally agreed by the Governments concerned that a commission should meet at Shanghai on the 1st of January, 1909. The Commission met on February 1, having been postponed out of respect to the late Emperor and Dowager Empress of China, and adjourned on February 26, 1909. After a thorough and searching study of the opium question in all its bearings, the Commission adopted the following resolutions:

Be it resolved:

1. That the International Opium Commission recognizes the unswerving sincerity of the Government of China in their efforts to eradicate the production and consumption of opium throughout the Empire; the increasing body of public opinion among their own subjects by which these efforts are being supported; and the real though unequal progress already made in a task which is one of the greatest magnitude.

2. That in view of the action taken by the Government of China in suppressing the practice of opium smoking, and by other Governments to the same end, the International Opium Commission recommends that each delegation concerned move its own Government to take measures for the gradual suppression of the practice of opium smoking in its own territories and possessions, with due regard to the varying circumstances of each country concerned.

3. That the International Opium Commission finds that the use of opium in any form otherwise than for medical purposes is held by almost every participating country to be a matter for prohibition or for careful regulation; and that each country in the administration of its system of regulation purports to be aiming, as opportunity offers, at progressively increasing stringency. In recording these conclusions the International Opium Commission recognizes the wide variations between the conditions prevailing in the different countries, but it would urge on the attention of the Governments concerned the desirability of a reexamination of their systems of regulation in the light of the experience of other countries dealing with the same problem.

4. That the International Opium Commission finds that each Government represented has strict laws which are aimed directly or indirectly to prevent the smuggling of opium, its alkaloids, derivatives, and preparations, into their respective territories; in the judgment of the International Opium Commission it is also the duty of all

countries to adopt reasonable measures to prevent at ports
of departure the shipment of opium, its alkaloids, derivatives, and preparations, to any country which prohibits
the entry of any opium, its alkaloids, derivatives, and
preparations.

5. That the International Opium Commission finds that
the unrestricted manufacture, sale, and distribution of
morphine already constitute a grave danger, and that the
morphine habit shows signs of spreading: the International
Opium Commission, therefore, desires to urge strongly on
all Governments that it is highly important that drastic
measures should be taken by each Government in its own
territories and possessions to control the manufacture,
sale, and distribution of this drug, and also of such
other derivatives of opium as may appear on scientific
inquiry to be liable to similar abuse and productive of
like ill effects.

6. That as the International Opium Commission is not
constituted in such a manner as to permit the investigation from a scientific point of view of antiopium remedies and of the properties and effects of opium and its
products, but deems such investigation to be of the highest importance, the International Opium Commission desires
that each delegation shall recommend this branch of the
subject to its own Government for such action as that Government may think necessary.

7. That the International Opium Commission strongly
urges all Governments possessing concessions or settlements in China, which have not yet taken effective action
toward the closing of opium divans in the said concessions and settlements, to take steps to that end, as soon
as they may deem it possible, on the lines already adopted
by several Governments.

8. That the International Opium Commission recommends
strongly that each delegation move its Government to enter into negotiations with the Chinese Government with a
view to effective and prompt measures being taken in the
various foreign concessions and settlements in China for
the prohibition of the trade and manufacture of such antiopium remedies as contain opium or its derivatives.

9. That the International Opium Commission recommends
that each delegation move its Government to apply its
pharmacy laws to its subjects in the consular districts,
concessions, and settlements in China.

Although no formal declaration was made, it was a
matter of discussion and was recognized by the Commission
as a whole that the foregoing resolutions, however important morally, would fail to satisfy enlightened public
opinion unless by subsequent agreement of the Powers they
and the minor questions involved in them were incorporated
in an international convention.

Impressed by the gravity of the opium problem and the desirability of divesting it of local and unwise agitation, as well as the necessity of maintaining it upon the basis of fact as determined by the Shanghai Commission, the United States deems it important that international effect and sanction be given to the resolutions of the International Opium Commission, and to this end proposes that an international conference be held at a convenient date at The Hague or elsewhere, composed of one or more delegates of each of the participating Powers, and that the delegates should have full powers to conventionalize the resolutions adopted at Shanghai, and their necessary consequences. The Government of the United States suggests as a tentative programme, based upon the resolutions and proceedings of the International Commission, the following:

(a) The advisability of uniform national laws and regulations to control the production, manufacture, and distribution of opium, its derivatives and preparations;

(b) The advisability of restricting the number of ports through which opium may be shipped by opium-producing countries;

(c) The means to be taken to prevent at the port of departure the shipment of opium, its derivatives and preparations, to countries that prohibit or wish to prohibit or control their entry;

(d) The advisability of reciprocal notification of the amount of opium, its derivatives and preparations, shipped from one country to another;

(e) Regulation by the Universal Postal Union of the transmission of opium, its derivatives and preparations, through the mails;

(f) The restriction or control of the cultivation of
the poppy so that the production of opium will not be
undertaken by countries which at present do not produce
it, to compensate for the reduction being made in British
India and China;

(g) The application of the pharmacy laws of the Governments concerned to their subjects in the consular districts, concessions, and settlements in China;

(h) The propriety of restudying treaty obligations
and international agreements under which the opium traffic
is at present conducted;

(i) The advisability of uniform provisions of penal
laws concerning offenses against any agreements that the
Powers may make in regard to opium production and traffic;

(j) The advisability of uniform marks of identifi-
cation of packages containing opium in international
transit;

(k) The advisability of permits to be granted to ex-
porters of opium, its derivatives and preparations;

(l) The advisability of reciprocal right of search
of vessels suspected of carrying contraband opium;

(m) The advisability of measures to prevent the unlawful use of a flag by vessels engaged in the opium
traffic;

(n) The advisability of an international commission
to be intrusted with the carrying out of any international
agreement concluded.

Without attempting to prescribe the scope of the
conference, or to present a programme which may not be
varied nor enlarged, the Government of the United States
believes that the foregoing suggestions might properly

serve as the basis at least for preliminary discussion, and invites a formal expression of opinion not merely upon the topics outlined, but an enumeration of other aspects of the opium problem which may seem of peculiar importance to any participating nation. The United States considers it important that an exchange of views take place as early as possible before the meeting of the conference.

If the programme, as outlined, meets with the approval of the Government to which you are accredited, it will be highly serviceable that on some subsequent date-- for example, on or before December 1 of the current year-- the participating Governments exchange their views, together with such recommendations and observations as occur to them. This course will not only facilitate the work of the conference and materially shorten its labors, but enable the Government of the United States to prepare in advance a definitive programme based upon the suggestions and views of the participating Governments.

You are therefore directed to transmit a copy of this instruction to the Minister for Foreign Affairs of the Government to which you are accredited, and at the same time to request that a delegate or delegates be appointed, furnished with full powers, to negotiate and conclude an agreement, provided that the Government to which you are accredited is favorable to the idea of an international conference for the suppression of the opium evil, as the result of the inquiries of the Shanghai Commission.

I am, Gentlemen,

Your obedient servant,

Alvey A. Adee

Acting Secretary of State.

迳啟者茲因各國向有定章每屆五年開會一次酌商

各國刑律及改良監獄等事上次曾在奧國開會今年

又屆會期本國政府擬定西十月二號起在本國京師

照章開會七日其各國會員名單須先於西二月宣布

特囑本署大臣孟達

貴王大臣轉詢

貴政府是否派員與會即希

貴部先行咨商該管部院委定

美國使署

見復茲奉上英文冊一本內係會中應商各事即希

查收是荷此泐順候

日祉 附洋文並書一本

費勒器啟 十二月十五日

AMERICAN LEGATION,
PEKING.

To F.O.No. 31?.   January 25, 1910.

Your Imperial Highness:

It has long been the custom to hold International Congresses at intervals of five years at the
capitals of different countries to discuss questions
connected with Criminal Law and Prison Administration.
The last meeting of this Congress was held in Austria,
and by invitation of the United States Government the
next meeting will assemble at Washington on the 2nd.
of October, 1910, and will continue for one week.
          I am directed by my Government to extend an invitation
to Your Highness's Government to be represented at the
International Prison Congress by delegates. As it is
considered important that the list of delegates should
be made up not later than by the end of February next,
I beg to request Your Highness to refer this matter to
the proper authorities for their early consideration.

I avail myself of this opportunity to renew to
Your Highness the assurance of my highest consideration.

                                        Charge d'affaires.

To His Imperial Highness, Prince of Ch'ing,
          President of the Board of Foreign Affairs.

Enclosed   One Pamphlet "The International Prison
          Congress, Its Origin, Aims, and Objects."

二二一

作

大理院為咨呈事准外務部咨稱宣統元年

十二月十五日准美賞署使函稱各國定章

每屆五年開會一次酌商各國刑律及改良

監獄等事上次曾在奧國開會今年又屆

會期本國政府擬定西十月二號起在本國

京師照章開會七日其各國會員名單須先

於西二月宣布特囑本署大臣函詢貴政府

是否派員與會即希咨高該管部院妥定

見復茲奉上英文冊一本內係會中應商各事

希查收等因應否派員赴會之處相應將原

送英文冊飭員譯漢沿行貴院查照酌核見復

以憑轉復該使等因前來查各國開會酌高刑

律及改良監獄等事既經該使函詢是否派員

與會自應選定通曉中外法律人員派令赴

會以崇

國體本院查有候選知府法律館纂修本院刑

科推事金絡城法政科進士法律館纂修本院

候補五品推事李方均於中外法律具有心得

且皆精熟西國語言文字可以直接與議相應

開送銜名並譯成英文咨呈

科推事金絡城法政科進士法律館纂修本院

候補五品推事李方均於中外法律具有心得

且皆精熟西國語言文字可以直接與議相應

開送銜名並譯成英文咨呈

貴部查照轉復至該二員出洋費用及應否

具奏之處再行續商辦理可也須至咨呈者

右 咨呈 計銜名壹紙

外務部

宣統貳年正月　　　日

柒

候選知府　Expectant Prefect
法律館纂修官　Compiler of the Bureau of Law Revision
大理院刑科推事　Justice of the Supreme Court
金　紹　城　Kunpah T. King

法政科進士　Doctor of Law
法律館纂修官　Compiler of the Bureau of Law Revision
大理院候補五品推事　Assistant Justice of the Supreme Court
李　　方　A. Leefong Ahlo

復美費署使函

逕復者上年十二月間准

函稱各國酌商刑律及改良監獄等事上次曾

在奧國開會今年又屆會期本國政府擬定西

十月二號起在本國京師開會七日特囑本署

大臣函詢是否派員與會希咨商該管部院

妥定見復等情當經本部咨行法部大理院酌

核去後茲准法部咨復查有京師高等檢察

廳檢察長徐謙奉天高等審判廳一廳丞許

世英堪以派往赴會旋又准大理院咨復查有

候選知府法律館篡修本院刑科推事金絡

城法政科進士法律館篡修本院候補五品推

事李方均熟悉中外法律及西國語言文字可

以直接與議各等因前來相應函復

貴署大臣查照轉達

貴國政府可也專此即頌

日祉

堂銜

宣統二年正月

一二三

欽差出使美墨秘古等國大臣張　　　為

咨呈事案照准

大部咨開宣統元年十二月十五日准美費署使

函稱茲有本國聾人會發起意見擬自本年西

八月五號起至十二號止在本國移羅拉多地方開
（科羅拉多）

各國聾人大會請屆時派員赴美襄助會中各

事附送英文請帖及大會應商條款單希即查

收等因本部查美國明年在科羅拉多地方開各

國聾人大會應由駐美出使大臣酌量在就近領事

館派人赴會相應譯錄原送請帖及條款單咨

行查照辦理等因承准此本大臣查美國科羅拉

多地方與紐約相近屆時應派紐約領事楊毓瑩

及通譯侯良登前往赴會藉資考察除札派遵

照相應咨覆為此咨呈
外

照相應咨覆須至咨呈者

大部謹請察照須至咨呈者

右　咨　呈

外　務　部

宣　統

　　　　初十　日

外務部

北京

劉大人寶森勛啟

Registered

SHANGHAI
No. 400

H. E. Liu Yuk Lin,

Waiwupu,

Peking

H. E. Tang,
Imp. Tele. Admin.
Shanghai

PEKING
MAY

Copy

3rd May 1910

His Ex. Lin Yuk Lin,

   Waiwu Pu,

      Peking.

Dear Mr. Lin,

    I beg to acknowledge receipt of your letter of the 26th ult. quoting a letter from Mr. Chow Tze-yee. I have brought the matter to the notice of the Editor, but we do not find in the remarks referred to anything to the detriment of China. It is surely through some misunderstanding that any such interpretation has been given to the paragraph which distinctlyximxxximxxxxxxxxxxxxxxx implies that the discontented lamas are discontented because they do not know how China has done her best for them.

    If the quotation in your letter is intended to imply that that the information is not correct and that therefore the conclusions drawn are not based on reliable foundation I would point out that at the present time we are compelled to rely upon the information published in our contemporaries. We have suggested before that the only way in which we can be put in possession of satisfactory news is by having it supplied to us direct from Peking by a duly qualified person who knows exactly what is true and what is not true and can therefore inform us of such at the earliest possible moment. It is most important that the world should be informed at once of the truth in all important matters. Very much depends upon the first impression that the world gets and in order to produce the proper impression it is necessary that the Chinese side of every question should be put before the world at the earliest possible moment. In order to do this I would propose that Mr. Tong Kai-son be instructed to keep us informed by telegram of all important developments. If he were authorised to keep us informed by telegraph and arrangements made for the transmission of his telegraphs to us at press rates we would of course bear the expence thereof. At present we are compelled to trust to outside information, often dirived from predjudiced sources, and almost always derived from ill-informed sources. The plan which I have suggested will obviate all that.

    I need hardly assure of our desire to serve China's best interest. In order to do so Captain Kirton is now in London, at great expence to us, pushing the interests of the paper and bringing it to the notice of London editors of importance. I enclose for your information a proof page that is to appear in the London Graphic" concerning "The National Review" and the claims of China, and I also enclose a copy of a letter received from him which shews that he is devoting himself to the furtherance of our interests in London. He will shortly proceed to New York where he will conduct a similar campaign on our behalf. The policy of "The National Review" is fair for China and if we are kept informed of the facts we are quite capable of putting those facts before the public in such a way as to benefit China to the best advantage. Your chief need at the present time is accurate information and if we can secure that we can carry out in the fullest possible way what we believe to be the wishes of the Board. We hope the above explanation will be found satisfactory.

    Yours Faithfully,

       Y.C.Tong.

Copy

Adelphi House, Strand,

London,

12th April 1910.

Y.O.Tong Esq.,

Shanghai,

My Dear Mr. Tong,

An appointment with the Editor of "Commercial Inte,legence" tomorrow at 11a.m., will prevent me from writing at the last moment of mailing so I do now.

Herewith you will find the full page from THE GRAPHIC, which has not yet appeared but which I am given to understand will come out in this week's issue. I regret to say that I have had this in my possession for over a week and could have sent it to you, as it is, some time ago. The fact of the matter is that newspapers printers here are big dam fools. Shanghai has no monopoly of such. This was sent me -- several sheets -- as a Proof, and I correctrd it in certain particulars. But word came that the printers had cast the plates already and that it was impossible to changr anything. Being very keen to get this magnificent Ad. I made no kick, but there are certain things in the "Interview" which should have been expressed differently. The tittle to the picture is altogether wrong, of course, and altogether there is too much of Mr. Kirton. Also there are certain other things in the letter press which I do not like, but we must be thankful for small mercies, and anAd. of this sort it is impossible to place a value upon. I am having a thousand pulls of it and it will be sent round to all potential advertisers together with our own pamphlet the proofs of which I have just corrected. I enclose an uncorrected proof of the same just for your advance information.

Yesterday I has a long interview with F.A.Mackenzie, of THE TIMES and the DAILY MAIL. He is the author of "The Tragedy if Korea", the book you read when we were at Mukden. Marlowe, the Editor of the Daily Mail, told him to come

to me, but we are also old friends, having been together during the Russo-Japanese War. I am entertaining him to our House Dinner at the Club next Saturday Night.
He is writing up our "interview" and will send the proofs along just now. In fact
I hope to get the interview of the Daily Mail published on or about the smae day
as that of THE GRAPHIC. I have also given "The Daily News" a lot of stuff. On
Thursday at noon I have an appointment with the Editor of the Daily Chronicle. I
am also fixing up with the Daily Telegraph and the Morning Post and other papers
too numrrous to name. This is harrowing work. The London is a most fearful bird
to get hold of, however well you know him personally. You ask Ridge about this
sort of thing. By James, these fellows look at minutes like at ten pound notes
and you have to be quick and handy with your tongue.

I am sorry to say that there is no chance of giving Lectures in this country
just now. Easter came so early, and Easter is the close of the Lecture Season.
with all the good in the world my old chums of the Lecture Agency could not fix
up any engagements for me. I do not feel justified in incurring the risk of great
loss by trying to run them myself, besides, this newspaper propaganda will pan
out much better. You will tumble to what this all means. Of course I have put
a little sugar around so as to get them to bite, but I want to do everything possible
to SECURE THE FUTURE OF THE REVIEW, and to get as much advertising support from
these busters as we possible can. We don't want to be hanky panking around with
Ads. worth a gew dollars only. We want Ads. that will not only pan out well for
us but will be kept in the paper for a good long time. Thus we go to the best p
people, and the biggest firms.

It will not be necessary for me to point out what all this work means for the
more political and influencr side of the paper. Every newspaper on this side
will know about us now.

PROGRESSIVE CHINA AND THE OPPORTUNITIES IT OFFERS
A TALK WITH MR. WALTER KIRTON. BY WENTWORTH HUYSHE

The name of Walter Kirton will be familiar to the readers of THE GRAPHIC as that of one who helped to keep them well informed during the progress of the South African and Russo-Japanese Wars, which latter he followed attached to the staff of General Kuroki. After the close of the Manchurian campaign Mr. Kirton went to China, and, becoming interested in that marvellous country and its people, travelled extensively there, and made the acquaintance of many of the leading men.

Having remained in the Far East for several years, Mr. Kirton has now returned to England for a brief holiday. Hearing that during his stay he had established an important newspaper enterprise in China, and feeling sure that his experiences in that country would be interesting to English readers, I called upon him the other day for a little talk on the subject. I started it with a question as to his journalistic achievement and its connection with the awakening of China.

"This is my position," said Mr. Kirton, who has that way of going straight to the point which stamps the man of decisive ideas : " I am the managing editor of the *National Review* (China), which is now the recognised national organ of the Chinese Empire. The Empire, as you know, is a huge agglomeration of all sorts of parties and schools of thought, and in speaking about China it is difficult to differentiate between these parties and their interests ; but, in spite of certain necessary limitations involved by this fact, the *National Review* is the authoritative organ of the Chinese Empire. It is printed in English, because it is impossible for the outside world to read Chinese ; but a Chinese edition is now in course of being established. It will be the duplicate of the English edition."

" And what is the policy of the *National Review* ? "

" To give the world the truth upon Chinese affairs, especially in their international application ; to assist and encourage by all possible means the development of the Chinese Empire on lines consonant with its ancient history, its dignity, the magnificent character and genius of its people, and with the enormous dormant power and wealth of the country. Similarly, and as regards the relationship existing between the Chinese and British races, our policy is one of conscientious sympathy, with a desire to consolidate interests already established on lines of mutual reciprocity and esteem. This effort may be regarded as one of the symptoms of the great change taking place in the Celestial Empire."

" And since you have been in England you have been struck, I dare say, with some of our Western difficulties which may beset the path of Chinese progress. Is there any real vitality in that progress so far ? "

" The vitality is beyond question. Apart from any concrete evidence I may be able to give you, it must be obvious that, following upon the precedent of history, a movement directed by men of the highest intelligence and intellect, who are animated by a patriotism the natural outcome of a prolonged national existence, and educated in the greatest centres of Western learning—this movement not only possesses great vitality, but must ultimately succeed in its object."

" And that object is——"

" Broadly speaking, to graft upon the ancient civilisation of China (a civilisation which has stood the test of centuries) all that is best in Western civilisation. The promoters of the movement are determined to avoid those fearful incidences of Western civilisation which are observable in every great city of England and America. With the object-lesson which may be learned by any student of humanity in the course of a few minutes walk through the byways of London and other great towns, it may easily be imagined that Chinese statesmen shrink from adopting in their entirety methods which have led to such deplorable results."

" And of course your paper is helping in this ? "

" Yes ; and insisting that in China economical development by the people and for the people must proceed hand-in-hand with political reform."

" And you have met with support from the Chinese ? "

" I am glad to say we are now being supported not only by the most influential classes of the Chinese themselves, but by the best elements among the residents in the Treaty Ports."

" But I dare say you did not always find this so as regards the latter ? "

" Well, of course, once upon a time our policy aroused considerable antagonism, and I was referred to in more or less uncomplimentary terms as a ' pro-Chinese.' But now all that is changed, and foreigners, especially the Anglo-Saxons, are coming (if, indeed, they have not already come) to recognise that our policy is sound ; and that, after all, co-operation and not antagonism between the races is the real secret of the prosperity of all concerned. With mutual understanding of each other's characteristics, friendship between Chinese and British should be, and will be, quite easy on both sides. And such friendship is all the more natural and possible, because the two races are animated by a high sense of honour. Both of them, so to speak, ' play the game.' "

" And you have seen the growth of this friendly feeling ? "

" The part that it has already played in Chinese affairs is most striking. English is now the secondary official language of the Empire, all official correspondence with

THE COVER OF MR. KIRTON'S CHINESE REVIEW
Which is now the recognised National Organ of the Chinese Empire.

foreigners being conducted in that language. Why, even the paper upon which official Chinese communications with foreigners are written bears the English equivalent of the Chinese characters and the date at its head. And I may say by the way that English typewriters are in use in every Yamen (Government office) of the Empire. I need hardly tell you what an immense advantage has thus been secured to Anglo-Saxon interests in this, the greatest potential market of the world."

" You spoke, just now, of the concrete evidences of the vitality of the Progressive movement. Will you give me an instance ? "

" I think perhaps the most salient of these is the action taken in connection with opium. It is impossible to go fully into this question, but I can only state that this evil (and there can be no question of its being an evil) is being eradicated at a rate which can only be termed remarkable. To put the matter into few words, opium-smoking is now regarded in China as the depth of ' bad form,' and its growth, cultivation and abuse are sternly discouraged, if not prohibited, throughout the Empire. It must necessarily take several years before the ultimate aim will be achieved. I need only mention fiscal considerations and the impossibility of a sudden readjustment of an industry which has yielded a vast revenue to the State and income to numbers of the predominant class in China—the agricultural class."

" And will alcoholic liquors, do you think, eventually supplant opium ? "

" I am of opinion that liquor, in its cruder forms and uses, will never be acceptable to the Chinese. And here I would strongly advise those who appear invariably to associate the Chinese with opium and who are responsible for the more or less active opium propaganda in this country, that the party of progress is fully alive to the baleful influence of this curse, and is capable of carrying out its programme unaided. And I would also suggest to them that the money so expended could be used to vastly greater advantage in London, where, in the course of a few minutes, I have just seen more drunken people than I have in five years in China, either from opium or alcohol."

" To return to what you said just now, that China offers the greatest potential market in the world."

" Well, you need only glance at the map and the figures that show the area of the Chinese Empire is over four millions of square miles, and that its population numbers something like four hundred millions, to realise the truth of that. But when to this is added the knowledge that this enormous area and population constitute a *commercial unit*—long past the pioneering stage—which is now awakening to the knowledge of the necessity for national media of development in every national and human connection ; and when, further, it is realised that not only is China the richest and most extensive cultivated country in the world in the agricultural sense, but that its mineral wealth exceeds that of any other known homogeneous area in the world, it must be obvious that China will shortly become the greatest customer for the commodities and conveniences of the West."

" And Great Britain will come in for a share of this great business ? "

" To secure their share of the huge volume of business which in the near future must accrue from this source, the British people have only to give evidence of their sympathy with the Chinese in their great effort towards National Reform ; to maintain the high standard of commercial and industrial honesty which has generally distinguished them in the past ; to avoid giving cause for offence by arrogating a superiority which has little if any solid foundation in fact ; and, generally, to treat the Chinese on a basis of reciprocity and with a mutual consideration for each other's idiosyncrasies. It may not be generally known, but I can assure you it is a fact, that, unlike certain other Oriental races, the Chinese are intensely reciprocal."

" Do you not think that in the past, although, as you say, British dealings with China have been characterised by honesty, British interests in China have been neglected ? Have we made the most of our opportunities ? "

" Generally speaking, British interests in China have in the past suffered through the action of irresponsible exploiters and concession-hunters, who have regarded China as a happy hunting-ground in which they could procure valuable rights for little, if not absolutely no consideration. I can assure you that that day is dead—as dead as Queen Anne—and that it is now impossible for anyone to obtain any franchise from the Government and people of China without giving in return an adequate consideration. In many cases, unfortunately, these exploiters have been able to pull the diplomatic strings in their favour, and this has resulted in a very justifiable suspicion on the part of the Chinese authorities of all ' foreign' enterprise. While Great Britain has done very well in China, and still maintains her lead in the overseas commerce and its collateral industries established at the ports, there is no doubt that these interests are capable of a much wider extension, provided that Great Britain recognises her responsibilities towards China and the Chinese people."

" And the relations between China and Japan ? Can you give me your views on them ? "

" In view of the apparently unshakable loyalty of Great Britain to the alliance with Japan I prefer not to touch upon this matter further than to refer you to the history of the past two or three years, which will speak for itself to any unprejudiced student of world affairs. Suffice it to say that the perpetual aggression to which China has been subjected has left an indelible impress on the minds of her people. "

CHINA—THE GREATEST MARKET OF THE WORLD.

Dedicated to *BRITISH BUSINESS MEN*
by the *Proprietors of*

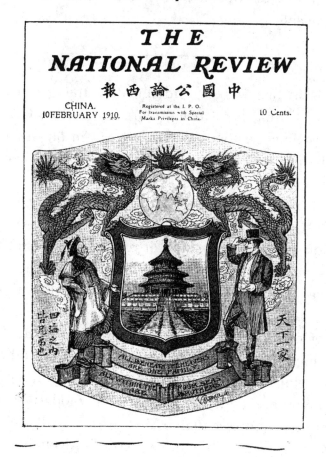

清代外務部中外關係檔案史料叢編──中美關係卷　第六册・國際會議

CHINA—The Greatest Market of the World.

" No part of the world contains, or has ever contained, greater possibilities for profitable business enterprise than does China, but—you must be enterprising."

These words of one who is, undoubtedly, the greatest business authority on China, Sir Robert Hart, Inspector - General of the Imperial Maritime Customs, should be graven on the memory of every British business man and writ large in every counting-house.

China is the most populous and the richest country in the world. Some FOUR HUNDRED MILLION people—a quarter of the population of the earth—inhabit an area of slightly over *Four Million* square miles, an average of 100 per mile. These people are not savages. On the contrary, they are in a high state of civilisation, which, in many respects compares most favourably with that of occidental countries. Certain practical disabilities, however, have been, and are, associated therewith, chief amongst them being the absence, generally speaking, of those methods, conveniences, and commodities of modern existence which, while familiar and essential to Westerners in all their applications and incidences, are but now becoming known to the Chinese.

This great homogeneous Empire is now emerging from that state of segregation in which it has remained for centuries. Following upon what we may term the initial pioneering era of restricted intercourse with western peoples, which may be said to have terminated with the Russo-Japanese War, the events of the past few years have not only given birth and strength to a movement of unparalleled magnitude towards reform of existing conditions and a remodelling of ancient usages, but have demonstrated—beyond possibility of cavil—that this movement must proceed upon economical lines. It is growing rapidly in momentum, in spite of inevitable but temporary reactions, and, following the course of every progressive movement known to history, it cannot possibly be extinguished by any forces that may be directed against it. Proof of the inherent stability and wealth of this great country, now in the throes of that great political upheaval which is affecting the whole of Asia, is forthcoming from the records of the Money Market. Imperial Chinese securities, without exception, are quoted above par.

Perhaps the most significant practical demonstration of the vitality of this desire on the part of China to fall into line with other nations is the existing and ever-increasing demand for the means and methods, the conveniences and commodities of occidental civilisation, and this opens up a field of enterprise to the enterprising business man such as hitherto has never come under his purview. Over 400,000,000 purchasers and consumers await his economical and commercial propaganda! These millions require, or will ultimately require, those conveniences, commodities, and luxuries YOU are capable of supplying, and when once YOU have impressed upon them the fact that YOU are able and willing to meet all their requirements, have created, aroused, and stimulated their appetite, and have secured or elaborated your business connection

4

with them, the possibilities of this market are simply staggering in their immensity.

AGRICULTURE.

Authorities with whose opinion no business man can be at variance or now afford to neglect state that the natural wealth of China transcends that of any other country. Hitherto the chief, and practically the only, source of national wealth to be exploited, in any considerable degree, has been the surface of the soil, and the bulk of the people are essentially agriculturists. Their methods and efforts in this connection are open to immense improvement, and agricultural machinery, appliances and commodities of every description, together with their corollaries, will ultimately be required in huge quantities. The figures before quoted alone afford ample evidence of the richness of the soil and the consequent ability on the part of the inhabitants to discharge their financial obligations.

COMMERCE.

Many millions of Chinese are engaged in trade and commerce, and a large and ever-increasing number of industrial enterprises and factories, operated under modern or semi-western conditions, have been established—mainly at existing centres of trade—throughout the Empire. Many more are required and myriads more will be established ultimately. The commercial probity of the Chinese is well known and requires no comment on our part. Their business acumen is very great and they take full advantage of their opportunities. Similarly they are intensely reciprocal, and anyone who treats them fairly and squarely will reap a golden harvest. In this connection we wish to correct what we are given to understand is a common impression among British business men, to the effect that Chinese traders are of lax morality in their appreciation of trade-mark and kindred regulations. Far from this being the case, the Chinese appreciate the value of a "Chop" (private or trade mark) enormously, and guard its rights most zealously and to the best of their power. The absence of a trade-mark law is, however, conducive to a certain amount of instability in this connection, but this state of affairs is in process of rectification. In the meantime it is possible to secure ample protection by registration in the Board of Industry Works and Commerce. It is part of the business policy of the *National Review* to assist all legitimate efforts to this end, and we place our organisation at the disposal of our clients.

RAILWAYS.

Many miles of railways have been constructed and opened during the past few years. Some thousands of miles are now either in course of construction or projected, and many more thousands will be required to provide means of communication between these millions of people, satisfying their extraordinary penchant for travel, and furnishing them with transportation for their milliards of tons of products and requirements. All railways in China are national undertakings and are controlled by the Imperial Board of Posts and Communications. The realm of finance and engineering contains no more lucrative opportunities than those afforded by this gigantic field of exploitation.

6

MINING.

With the exception of a few widely-scattered coal and iron mines and an infinitesimal number of primitive workings of other deposits, the mineral resources of China are at present undeveloped. The politico-economical movement referred to before must develop in this direction. The Government of China is actively preparing for an era of mining enterprise, and whatever form the arrangements made, or to be made, may take regarding the financing and development of this great national asset, the fact remains that an enormous amount of money will have to be spent upon modern machinery and mining appliances, as well as for mining and contingent supplies of every description. The new mining regulations of the Chinese Empire have already been drafted, and their promulgation is expected daily.

The history of Great Britain and her Colonies, to say nothing about any other part of the world, demonstrates that mining is one of the most powerful levers in the upraising of the standard of wealth and consequent spending capacity of a community.

COMMUNAL AND "MUNICIPAL."

A considerable demand for appliances and facilities necessary to communal life and comfort already exists throughout the Empire and is becoming augmented rapidly.

Electric lighting has made phenomenal strides during the past two years. Peking—the Metropolis ; Nanking—the Southern Capital; and many other cities now possess electrical lighting installations. The provincial capital of Manchuria—Mukden—was lit up by electricity for the first time during the writer's visit in December last. The advisability of securing a "day load" for these generating plants has commended itself to the authorities, and every effort is now being directed towards that end. There is now a large demand for small motors and machinery suitable to the thousand and one industries — small and great — in which these most industrious people engage.

Tramways, waterworks, and other "municipal" undertakings are coming into ever-increasing favour. As an illustration of this fact, British-built steam-road-rollers are already in use in the above-named cities.

Spinning, weaving, and all textile machinery, of every description, and for plants of every grade of capacity, is most urgently required. Builders of primary motors, such as gas, petroleum, oil, and kindred engines, also windmills, machine tools and mechanical appliances for use in the numerous trades, callings and crafts of these millions have an enormous future before them in China.

The use of vehicles of all descriptions — carriages, motor-cars, bicycles, jinrickshas (the small, coolie-drawn, two-wheeled carriage of the Orient), &c., has increased phenomenally during recent years.

With these lines we must, perforce, content ourselves and conclude this section. Suffice it to say that every appurtenance of western civilisation is marketable amongst these myriads of people.

EDUCATIONAL, SCHOLASTIC, AND LITERARY.

The educational movement in China possesses an intense vitality. Schools on modern lines are springing up throughout the length and breadth of the land. To the scholar in China all things are possible. For instance, scholarship is the highest qualification for appointments in the service of the State. The demand for everything in this connection, while already large, is rapidly increasing, and will ultimately prove enormous.

GENERAL.

The general standard of living among the people of the country is becoming more elaborate daily. A considerable demand for personal and domestic appliances and commodities has sprung up, and is increasing rapidly in sympathy with the economical developments in progress. Similarly, the demand for articles and facilities of a character pertaining to or verging upon the luxurious is already considerable, and the appetite for such only needs cultivating and stimulating to enhance that demand to an enormous extent.

POSSIBILITIES OF BRITISH ENTERPRISE.

The low tariff on imports—5 per cent. *ad valorem*—combined with the pre-eminent position initially secured by British commercial effort in the Chinese Empire, is extremely favourable to British commercial enterprise therein. English is now the secondary official language of the Empire. But in view of the extremely active commercial propaganda of your great competitors — a propaganda into which politics enters largely — it behoves you to impart a vastly greater degree of energy to your undertakings than has been evidenced hitherto. The old China is a thing of the past. The new China has arrived, but many conservative " old China hands " are loth to acknowledge the fact, and attempt to pursue the

even tenor of their way along the old, old lines. New times demand new methods, or a re-casting of the old, and the present is
not only the most auspicious time for instituting such methods,
and thus getting in "on the ground floor," but, in view of the
strenuous competition of others, it is imperative that if full advantage is to be taken of the unexampled opportunities now presenting themselves your programme should be put into execution with
all possible speed.

The conduct of a commercial campaign in China very much
depends upon the line you are engaged in or wish to push. There
are, however, certain general principles governing commerce with
the people of that country which have a comprehensive application.

1. The Government of China, while theoretically a combination of the democratic with the despotic, is practically patriarchal,
and is vested, to all practical purposes and in its general application to the country at large, in the Mandarinate, the literary or
educated (as distinct from the illiterate) classes. The Government
maintains a more or less comprehensive control over all development, industrial and commercial enterprise. The Guild also is a
very powerful factor in Chinese commerce. Thus it is essential,
generally speaking, to secure the good-will of the influential classes
and recognised institutions in connection with ventures in which
the rights or interests of the body-politic are involved. In a corresponding degree this principle applies, in a declining scale, to
every undertaking and every transaction throughout the country,
especially those in which "foreigners" are concerned or interested. A compensating advantage of this amenity is the increased
security afforded. Consequently, it is necessary to exercise a certain amount of what we may term semi-political *savoir faire* in combination with your more purely business policy.

10

2. In China a great deal depends upon the familiarity of the inhabitants with your " Chop." This has a comprehensive application. Your business, your name, your firm, the enterprise with which you are connected, the article or commodity in which you deal—in fact, almost everything pertaining to you — is known by the " Chop." An essential preliminary to remunerative business in this wonderful market is to get your " Chop " known and respected. This entails considerable expenditure of time and money, as the Chinese are naturally conservative in such matters, but when once success is achieved, the returns will be proportionately great.

3. Active representation and judicious publicity carry as much weight in China as elsewhere. The practice of giving sole agencies to firms at such a distance and leaving your interests entirely in their hands is not to be commended, especially in connection with advertising. There are, of course, certain exceptions to this ruling; but, generally speaking, the time has passed for this negative form of representation. Your competitors have already realized this fact in a very marked degree.

4. Integrity and good workmanship, combined with fair prices, will always command commercial success with the Chinese, other things being equal.

In conclusion, we beg to emphasize the fact that *The National Review* (China) organization does not confine itself to academic professions of faith. We have discarded the more or less archaic programme aforetime associated with newspaper enterprise. We believe in attempting to translate into practice the creed we preach. *The National Review* is now the recognized organ of the Chinese Empire, and its influence upon and connections with those who may be regarded as the mainsprings of national progress and economical development are such as to render it the most potent lever in the great operation of opening up to western influences a country of such vast possibilities and containing so many opportunities for extraordinarily profitable business to the enterprising British business man.

In the event of your desiring to avail yourself of this organization, we beg to inform you that the undersigned representative of the Proprietors of *The National Review* is now in London, and may be consulted by appointment.

The National Review (China),
(Signed) WALTER KIRTON.

Address : *The National Review* (China).
Adelphi Chambers,
Strand, W.C.

Telephone : 14647 Central.

London & County Printing Works, Drury Lane, W.C.

一切摺內聲明所需經費擬咨商外務部度支部

李方前赴美京萬國刑律監獄改良會並調查

三庭推事金紹城法政科進士候補從五品推事

大理院為咨呈事查本院奏派候選知府刑科第

入會會金　　　　　　　　共約四十兩

照相費　擬將各國法庭監獄

　　　　規則彩照以作模範

共銀三萬五千三百八十二兩

購書費

調查開庭辦法

聘請法文繙譯　在美國聘請報

　　　　　　　酬約一千兩

酌核辦理等因奉

旨該衙門知道欽此欽遵在案現在該員等預備起

程事宜應將所需經費比照法部酌量減省開

具清單咨呈

貴部請即核定賜覆以便咨商度支部核辦

可也須至咨呈者

外務部

右咨呈　計清單壹件

宣統貳年肆月　　初陸　　日

監印官彭□□

預算經費清單

計開

薪俸項下

會員　係奏派人員比照二等參贊月薪發給　二人　每人月薪四百兩　八個月計六千四百兩

書記官　照一等書記官　一人　每月三百兩　八個月計二千四百兩

治裝項下　按照一個月薪俸

會員　二人　八百兩

書記官　一人　三百兩

川資項下

由北京至日本輪船

會員　二人　一百六十兩

書記官　一人　六十兩

由日本至美國輪船

會員　二人　一千兩

書記官　一人　四百二十兩

由美國至歐洲輪船

會員　二人　五百兩

書記官　一人　二百十兩

由歐洲至北京火車

會員　二人　一千兩

書記官　一人　四百二十兩

旅費項下　歐洲各國車費往來均在內

住美國四十日

會員　二人　每人每月以美金二十元　計約合銀四十二兩四錢　三百九十二兩

書記官　一人　每月以三十四兩計　一千三百六十兩

住歐洲英法德比奧匈荷意日葡俄等國每國十日共約計

一百日

會員　二人　每人每月以英金三鎊　計約合銀二十五兩五錢　五千一百兩

書記官　　　一人　每日約二十兩五錢　　二千零五十兩

住日本二十日

會員　　　　二人　每人每日約十兩計　四百兩

書記官

書記官　　　一人　每日約八兩計　　　一百六十兩

交際項下

美國全體會員宴會二百人中下等膳每人美金
十元約合銀十七兩　　　　　三千四百兩

請大臣宴會　　二十人　上等膳每人美金二十
五元約合銀四十三兩五錢　　八百五十兩

預備項下

聘請法文繙譯　在美國聘請報
酬約一千兩

調查開庭辦法

購書費

照相費　擬將各國法庭監獄
規則彰照以作模範

入會會金

共銀三萬五千三百八十二兩

共約四千兩

大理院為咨呈事查本院奏派候選知府刑科第

三庭推事金紹城法政科進士候補從五品推事

李方前赴美京萬國刑律監獄改良會並調查

一切摺內聲明所需經費擬咨商外務部度支部

10

咨呈

欽差出使美墨秘古等國大臣張　爲

咨呈事案照前承准

大部咨以美國本年西八月五號起至十二號止在科羅拉多地方開
各國聾人大會請屆時派員赴會等因本大臣原擬派駐紐約顧事
楊毓瑩通譯官侯良登屆時赴會當經咨呈在案現查科羅拉
多地方與金山為較近應即改派駐金山總顧事黎榮耀通屆時會
同通譯官歐陽祺前往赴會以資考察除扎行外理合備文咨呈為
此咨呈

大部謹請察照施行須至咨呈者
右　咨呈
外　務　部

宣統二年四月　　　　日

粘捌

仁

逕啟者前經

貴部將京師高等檢察廳檢察長徐謙

等前往美國赴監獄改良會經過各國之

護照一紙并嚴志誠運柩回滇取道香港

安南等處之護照一紙均請簽押蓋印前

來茲本大臣業將二照簽蓋妥協專函附還

望祈

貴部轉交該員等持執前途可也泐此順頌

日祉　附護照二紙

馬士理啟　中四月二十七日　西六月初四日

大理院為咨呈事本院奏請遴派刑科第三庭推事金紹城候補

從五品推事李方等前赴美京萬國刑律監獄改良協會並就便

將各國法庭規制審判辦法詳細調查一摺奉

旨知道了欽此欽遵在案茲據該推事等稟稱此次奏派本係專為

赴萬國監獄協會而設自應先行赴會再行調查各國司法事宜

擬於西曆十月二號赴會畢後歸途所經英國法國比國荷國瑞國

丹國與國德國俄國日本國等均逐細詳加調查應頗行知照本

國駐使以資接洽等語查該推事等擬赴各國既屬歸途所

事由係調查所必及有應由駐使詳加指導並通知各該國政

府務期考知司法改良實際及一切相關事宜以資借鏡而便

取法相應咨呈

貴部查照轉咨可也須至咨呈者

外務部

右咨呈

宣統貳年伍月貳拾叄日

咨法部沈其昌出洋兔扣資俸礙難照

辦由

行　行

外務部左侍郎鄒

署外務部左侍郎曹

外務部右侍郎胡

六月　日　科　六月　日　免　尤

和會司

呈為咨復事准

咨稱本部奏派高等檢察廳檢察長徐謙等赴

美國萬國監獄會查有法政科舉人分部員外

郎沈其昌堪以派充一等書記官會同前往業

於上月十四日起程兹該員沈其昌掣分外務

部惟本部札派在前自應補行咨明查出洋人員

向章免扣資俸該員奉差出洋事同一律因先

期啟程未及到部應否以吏部文到之日作為

該員到部日期准其免扣資俸請煩查照轉咨

吏部等因前來查向章凡出洋免扣資俸皆係

奏調人員該員沈其昌尚未到部即由

貴部派充書記官隨同出洋與奏派出洋者不同

所稱免扣資俸一節礙難轉咨相應咨復

貴部酌核辦理可也須至咨者

　法部

宣統二年六月

卜　咨呈

欽差出使美墨秘古等國大臣張　為

咨呈事案照本年六月初五日承准

歌電內開美使函稱本年西八月十四號至二十號在華盛頓開第六次

萬國語言會請派員赴會等語屆時由尊處就近派員入會另咨

達等因兹於七月初八日又承准

大咨事同前因並附鈔該會規則一紙當經本大臣札派美館一等

書記官伍常三等通譯官盧炳田屆時入會除俟事竣再行報告外

理合備文聲復為此咨呈

大部謹請察照施行須至咨呈者

右咨呈

外務部

宣統二年七月　　　日

敬啟者本軍現派軍醫科監督游敬森前往美國赴
軍醫會並往英日德法義奧等國考查軍醫事件前
經鈔奏咨行在案惟該員祇通英文於日本等國
語文素不諳悉若無通譯人員偕同辦理殊多窒
礙用特函達
貴部敬祈分電出使各國大臣於該員到後准在
使館借用譯員襄助一切至該員旅行日期擬於
中歷八月到日本十二月到德法義奧等國
合併附陳專此奉懇敬請

　台安

載　濤
載　搢　頓首

清代外務部中外關係檔案史料叢編——中美關係卷 第六冊·國際會議

清代外務部中外關係檔案史料叢編——中美關係卷 第六册·國際會議

Registered

外務部 北京

顏大人勛啟

(s)

His Excellency, W. W. Yen,

Wai-wu-pu,

Peking

R NGHAI 1696

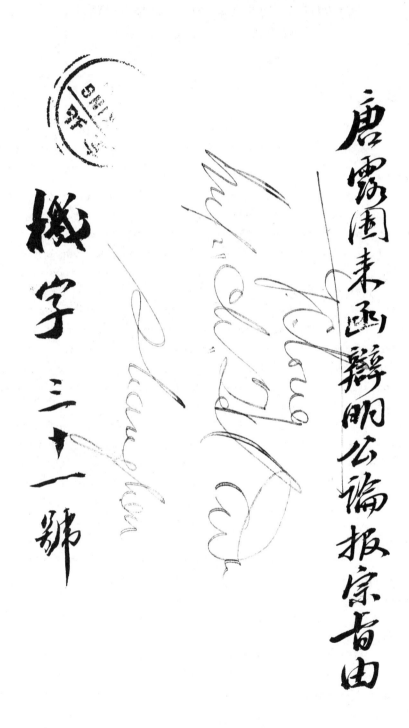

唐露園來函辯明公論報宗旨由

機字三十一號

IMPERIAL CHINESE TELEGRAPH ADMINISTRATION.

Shanghai, 27th December 1910.

His Excellency W. W. Yen,

    Wai-wu-pu,

      P E K I N G.

My dear Dr. Yen,

        I beg to acknowldge the receipt of your despatch dated
19th December and to inform you that I handed the same to Capt. Kirton
for action and report. He tells me he has replied direct to you and I
trust that it will be found satisfactory. We are struggling under great
difficulties and I can only ask you to extend us your consideration and
to soften matters as much as possible. Now that Capt. Kirton has returned
I am sure that there will be little if any cause for comment on the work,
although the path of newspaper work appears to be strewn with rocks and
thorns, and no man can escape them always. I have great pleasure in giving you the above information. As you will doubtless remember, on the
receipt of the subvention from the Government and after the most careful
consideration of all matters in connection with this newspaper and publicity work, in which Kirton is an acknowldeged expert of metropolitan
reputation, it was decided that a portion of the amount could be most
advantageously expended in sending Kirton to Europe and America on a publicity mission. He left here last February and travelled via the Eastern
route to Europe, thence to America, and out across the Pacific. At every
place he touched he got into communication with our officials, with pro-
minent people of all classes, and publicity organizations and newspapers.
He has interviewed many scores of public men in the most influential pos-
itions around the world, including President Taft, Mr. Roosevelt, Mr. Knox,
Sir Edward Grey, Ambassadors, Members of Parliament and Congress, the
Editors of the great newspapers, the heads of the great news organizations
and publications whose good offices are essential to China. He has also
placed the case for China before many financial and commercial magnates
and men-of-affairs, Chambers of Commerce, Institutes, and kindred organizations and societies. His efforts have been seconded by our Ministers
and Consuls abroad in the various places he passed through and he has
worked like a horse in the interests of China. I do not wish to crack up

my own man but I say that in Capt. Kirton we have a man who not only deserves our confidence in every way but who is invaluable to China. He has sacrificed everything to doing this work and he works like a hero. I cannot indicate a quarter of what he has done, all I can say is that we now have a chance of doing work that will be worth more than any money to our country, and that Kirton's work only needs backing up to produce results such as will completely convince everyone concerned as to the value of this sort of work when conducted by a man like Kirton. It is not every country that can command the services of a gentleman whose status and reputation gives him easy access to the greatest and most influential-ly placed people throughout the world and I for one think that China is most fortune in this respect.

I am sending Kirton up to Peking directly he has got things into shape here. A huge amount of correspondence and business has already resulted from his mission, but he is getting through with it and I hope that he may be able to come up in a week or so. He will then give you an account of all his doings and also shew you how we have fulfilled our trust in the matter of the subsidy.

Wishing you compliments of the Season, I remain,

Yours very sincerely,

J. Cloug

興澤唐元港政章京顏惠慶函
逕啟者接奉西十二月十九號
來函誦悉一切當將原函交克爾登大尉閱看楼
攜克此云業已逕行回覆
免諸美洲茅歷患艱難趣計退
洞鑒為望華
曲意周金為籌司爾登現已西過振務甚難得一途枝
著様芒荊綀密布當前匯趨避各難今克爾登
業已四縣歟詳審可補息美當軫恤
費新津賬之時原議曾提出著平作為克
宋登氏縣應歐美就費克氏手西二月間限者
東路並歐由中國員接治一切而與各界有
勢力者六相聯絡又雲往渴各國執政諸公善
綹綹塔克德羅斯福外相諾克司葛東電
以及外交議負大振主葦根社領
中國情實至狀況敷陳軍與財政商務偉人

商務總會及其他有力會社剴切數陳彼六
雲澤本團使領之助為以裨中國元
洪益不以克爾登而已之私人而遍為揄揚但以
克此之寄腹心而住事豪使誠不勞觀敷
計禪中中國實敷譯引華淺鮮
附撙欸叔實敷為我已可宜乘此
計禪起正日科程揫候精之就綹波即書命
有可此美彼自考察四沒信件事實撙集
爾登晇為之事振須假以援手助則敦果
書書
當書
武當起正日科程揫候精之就綹波即書命

其北上大約旬日可心振京屆时微室錄将出差
咸績展託陳
師表
左右心四報不重慶之一微年肅此敬請

时視

外務部

咨呈

法部為欽奉華寧派政廳案呈本部奏

派赴美萬國監獄政良會徐謙等回京

報告一摺於宣統二年十一月二十一日奉奉

旨依議欽此相應刷印原奏清單咨呈

貴部遵照可也須至咨呈者

右　咨

　　呈計原奏清單壹本

　外　務　部

宣統貳年拾貳月　拾貳　日

監印官

一應　之件

附件

法部奏派赴美第八次萬國監獄改良會會員報告書

法部謹
奏為前派第八次萬國監獄會會員赴會事竣歸國具呈報告
書謹據情代奏摺繕單仰祈
聖鑒事竊據京師高等檢察廳檢察長徐謙法部參議上行走奉
天高等審判廳廳丞許世英呈稱謙等於宣統二年正月二
十六日經法部奏請派往美國赴第八次萬國監獄會並就
便考察各國司法事宜奉
旨允准並將啟程日期奏報在案謙英遵於五月十四日偕續經
奏派隨同赴會之外務部員外郎沈其昌法部主事羅文莊
束裝出都取道西比利亞首至俄京次由俄而德而奧而義
而法而比而和而英先事考察各國官府無不敦睦邦交特
派專員導引恭觀接待既極殷勤指示亦復懇切而德意志
尤為優異調查所得舉凡法部之組織審判之階級監獄之
規模及與司法有密切關係之感化事業司警察兩制度之
均已略領其大凡及八月渡大西洋至美與會會期中歷
八月二十九日開始先十日美政府特備專車派員在紐約
迎候各國會員導觀各處法院與監獄觀畢齊赴華盛頓謁
見總統后八月二十九日即西曆十月二號會期假南北美
洲會館計到會者三十有五國各國國家所派會員
及以簡人之資格與婦女之參入者百有五十一人會制分
總會與部會議會場計議決定議案分四部以
刑罰為第一部監獄為第二部豫防犯罪幼年保護為第三
第四部每日午前部會討論午後合議於總會歷時七日解
決問題十有三得交欵目共六十有九於九月初六日問

一

會而會事竣伏念此行關係於改良司法之前途至重且遠
謙英等學識淺陋膺茲重寄敢不兢兢刻入會期遲既無五
年之豫備考察日淺又無累歲之研求心得幾何更增慚悚
第達中外之奧通新舊之郵使者之責義無可辭僅就所知
者分具報告報告兩種一日第八次萬國監獄會報告書一日考
察司法制度報告書會事報告計分六節欲知此會之情狀
當先明監獄會之所由生當先溯監
獄改良之創始故以萬國監獄改良會冠首而萬國監
獄會之沿革次之第八次萬國監獄會之概況會場演說及
議案與閉會後之豫備又次之篇末繫以按語謙英等意
見以為應行進取之方法辦理之手續皆備為考查報告
計分五類日司法部制度日審判制度日監獄制度日感化院
制度日司法警察制度逐類各加按語比較異同斟酌取舍
努堯之獻雖無補於高深然河嶽之容必不棄夫流壞伏乞
聖明垂鑒並請將兩種報告書
飭交資政院憲政編查館修訂法律館民政部法部酌量採擇以
期實行仍請將監獄會報告由法部通行各省督撫照法
司轉飭各屬俾一般官吏人民知監獄事業影響於社會甚
鉅羣相從事於改良則獄制日善斯犯罪日少人格日高而
幸福日增矣除考察司法制度報告書容俟擬就再行續陳
並各國所贈及所購圖式書籍咨交法部編繹用費冊報另
遂度支部備查外理合懇請代
奏前來臣等查閱報告書所紋監獄改良之緣起會事之沿革
此次開會時之狀況言簡而明所述之演說與議決之議案

二

詳慎周密慮遠思深所擬按語亦皆動中窾要切實可行應

請

飭交臣部及資政院憲政編查館修訂法律館民政部分別參酌

採用總期見諸事實不至徒託空言仍分行各省督撫提法

使俾得輔助進行以收監獄改良之效除考察司法制度報

告書容俟該檢察長廳丞擬呈再行具奏外理合將第八次

萬國監獄會報告書恭繕清單伏乞

皇上聖鑒訓示謹

奏宣統二年十一月二十一日具奏奉

旨依議欽此

三

御覽

計開

第一節　萬國監獄改良之緣起

謹將京師高等檢察廳檢察長徐謙法部參議上行走奉天

高等審判廳廳丞許世英所具之第八次萬國監獄會報告

書照繕清單恭呈

監獄制度泰西各國在十七世紀以前或粗陋荒敗而不足

論或殘慘貪酷而不忍言自十八世紀時有英國之博愛家

約翰華爾德氏出始倡議改良氏蓋世界改良監獄之泰斗

也氏生於千七百二十六年卒於千七百九十年數十年間

專以改良監獄為事業嘗五游歐亞著書立說鼓吹當世並

屢散家財以助之於是朝野耳目為之震動英國議院遂提

出法案決定改良監獄是為萬國改良監獄之嚆矢繼其後

而實行者則為美人千七百九十六年創設分房監於片蘇

巴尼亞州之非拉的爾肥亞行晝夜分房之監禁法即世所

謂片蘇巴尼亞制是也千八百二十年米的苦州創設新監

獄於窩不倫行晝雜居夜分房之監禁法即世所謂窩不倫

制是也兩制皆以分房為主要所異者前則晝夜分房限

極嚴後則晝間授以相當之工作並許其室外之運動惟夜

間寢臥必使之獨居畫間組織雖有等差而其注重教誨使囚徒

改過遷善出獄後復爲社會良民之目的則同兩制各有責

理至今猶相持對抗兩存其說

美國既實施改良之事蹟名譽乃轉及於歐洲各國遂羣起

相師英國爲始德法及大陸諸國體之咸派專使調查新制

四

各以所見歸報本國有善片蘇巴尼亞制者有善窩不倫制
者於是片蘇巴尼亞制行於英近制行於歐洲大陸近
百年來或以理論研究益深眞理日出獄則之良
否幾視爲國際上競爭之事業千八百四十六年德人密梯
梅惠爾玉盧斯比人特披亞和人司林格爾法人毛盧苦爾
托夫英人華托和司陸悉耳等開萬國監獄會於蘭苦科爾
托提出議案其最滋紛議者則爲分房制之利害
而終以最多數之意見決定片蘇巴尼亞制然爲善而分房制
之學說遂騰於士夫之口而見諸實際荷蘭比利時尤爲
完備風潮所至遠及日本日本自明治二十六年第二次改
正監獄則發布後雖未能驟行片蘇巴尼亞制然已參酌歐
美諸國之精義行階級之制矣（階級制者以分段而執行其雖居者假出獄也　如一犯人一種三年監禁之刑初年使居分房第二監六箇月或內一年實他改過遷善則使階級制之終級制此則間階級制獄是爲終級）

會者殆不可思議也

第二節　萬國監獄會之沿革

尚屬幼稚時代日事講求所至皆有監獄協會以討論其學
理而調查其實況將來各國監獄之進步其裨益國家與社
此則使階級制現今各國尤以改良監獄之事

監獄改良自十八世紀以來各國既已次第著手成效大著
有美人瓦晋司者監獄學大家也發議宜創立萬國監獄會
斟通各國風俗習慣政治法律使日趨於大同於是代表美
國政府使於歐洲游說各國所至歡迎萬國監獄會於是成
立千八百七十二年第一次會議開於倫敦各國政府及各
國監獄協會咸遣委員到會者三百四十人而以箇人之資

五

格與婦女之參入者亦實繁有徒是爲萬國監獄會之起源
以後定期每五年開會一次千八百七十八年第二次會議
開於斯脱克夫俄爾到會者二百九十八人千八百八十五
年第三次會議開於羅馬到會者二百三十四人千八百九
十一年第四次會議開於聖彼得保到會者七百四十八人千
八百九十五年第五次會議開於巴黎到會者八百十七人
日本派員入會自此始千九百年第六次會議開於布魯悉
耳千九百五年第七次會議開於匈牙利到會者日益增多
千九百十年第八次會議遂開於華盛頓
溯自萬國監獄會成立迄今已三十八年其創設宗旨則在
聚集各國法律家慈善家以及執掌於審判監獄之官吏使
各就經驗所得討論其利害斟酌其異同而刑罰改良與豫
防犯罪及幼年保護制度亦均在範圍之內計分四部推闡
益精其初影響甚微如風起秋蘋之末其後則蓬蓬勃勃淹
蓋一世各國政府且咸就會議所得見諸施行而國家文明
進步亦賴以扶助於是萬國監獄會遂爲世界所注重而我
國特派專員入會則自第八次始

第三節　第八次萬國監獄會之概況

萬國監獄會雖發自美人而前七次開會均在歐洲千九百
五年美國議院提出議案邀請政府通知各國第八次會議
開於華盛頓各國咸悅於是美政府預備美金二十萬圓爲
會場用費定於千九百十年十月二號即中歷八月二十九
日在華盛頓開會
先期十日美政府派員在紐約迎候各國會員導觀各處監

六

獄及審判署後齊赴華盛頓九月二十九號各國會員在白
宮謁見總統塔夫脫氏會長愨德生代表達頌詞總
統答畢一一握手爲禮美國監獄協會即於是日假紐維拉
旅館爲會場各國會員亦皆加入由事務所發給徽章每人
代價美金五圓萬國監獄會徽章亦同
十月二號萬國監獄會開始各國國家所派會員及以簡人
之資格與婦女之參入者計百有五十一人假南北美洲會
館爲會場首由美國總檢察大臣代表總統演說次由第七
次會長匈牙利人別離代表全體致逑答辭再次則會長愨
德生宣布開會自十月二號起每日午前分四部研究第一
部刑罰改良問題第二部監獄改良問題第三部預防犯罪
制度第四部幼年保護制度午後四部合議晚間自由演說

（七）

通用法英德三國語言四號六號美監獄協會與美政府公
讌萬國會員至八號閉會共計七日解決議案並決定第九
次在倫敦開會公舉英國監獄協會會長拍拉士爲會長於
是散會所有各國到會人數按照會場所用英文字母排列
之次序列表於後

地名	人數
美利堅	五十三
阿眞丁	一
奧大利亞	二
比利時	二
英吉利	七
次拿大	三
中國	八
哥倫比亞	一
古巴	三
芬蘭	一
法蘭西	六
德意志	三
希臘	四
西印度海梯	二
加地馬那	一
荷蘭	九
罕都那司	一
匈牙利	七
意大利	四
日本	四
奈巴利亞	一
盧森堡	二
墨西哥	二
新南威爾士	一
挪威	一
坤斯蘭	一
俄羅斯	九
三藩多	一
暹邏	一
西班牙	三

（八）

瑞典　一

瑞士　三

突尼斯　一

土耳其　一

維尼斯允拉　一

第四節　會場演說

十月二號開會時先由美國總檢察大臣代表全國行開會
禮並代表總統致迨頌詞其略曰今日代表總統歡迎各國
會員來至美京深爲榮幸此會雖係美國於三十八年前創
始然在美國開會實係第一次先是一千九百零五年三月
三號由議院函請總統要請本年在華盛頓開會故今日得
有第八次之會議當初此會倡議之目的在欲知各國監獄

九一

制度及其成績並考求各國法律與執行方法推而至於預
防犯罪幼年保護制度亦共同研究綜其大要不外四端而
利益廣被實有不可以言語形容者其故因會場雖非立法
機關而影響所及能使立法者採取議論見諸施行近年來
各國刑罰主義由重改輕因殘忍變爲仁慈皆受是會之潮
流有以洗濯而陶鑄之即偶有用重刑取懲一戒百之意者
然其要義非如古時刑罰徒使觀者一方面之畏懼而已蓋
欲使身受者自畏而不敢再犯也總之改良刑罰問題皆以
預防犯罪爲基礎諸略言改良之歷史從前刑罰與監獄種
種設施皆係報復與威嚇凡懲治一犯祇欲令平民警
畏不顧因徒之痛苦故殘虐貪暴史不絕書自十八世紀英
國有約翰華爾德及伯露利亞氏出目擊黑闇情形著書

立說使上下議院派員調查逐漸改良始得文明之效果今
日公會即謂爲約翰華爾德氏等之所賜可也自有公會以
來各國監獄競爭改革犯人在監時勤加教誨使其改過自
新出獄時又有保護協會與之天接代爲謀生使其能自存
活不再爲非且於幼年犯罪者特設幼年監受感化院以
教養之此皆受公會之所賜也即以美國論受公會之所賜
者亦復不少自前年政府派員調查全國監獄後重新改建
者已有八所本京又購地六千餘畝敝建築感化院去年三月
議院又將刑法修改並擬定假出獄及免因保護等法實行
於可倫比亞諸會員參觀本國各處監獄甫歸當知所言之
不謬如是則此會之進步不已滿足乎然而尤有一言進之
監獄至於今日建築已極美備管理方法已極完全待遇犯

十一

人已極優異無可訾異但恐看守人不能如法管理則種種
流弊因之而生是宜多設協會以濟其窮夫如是而監獄之
能事乃盡云云
次由會長慈德生演說其略曰
今日承各國會員厚意置慈德生於最關緊要最有名譽之
地位不勝榮幸之至今日爲第八次監獄會開幕之初萃各
國之大公平家大慈善家而聚處一堂其樂何如諸會員或
從東方或從西方來至阿美利加少年之民主國當極爲歡
迎美國與世界交通東有大西洋西有太平洋今從東方來
者羨其爲文明發達最早之邦從歐洲來者羨其爲改良進
步之先鋒從非洲來者羨其競爭改革之新造諸會員之
大學問眞經驗若明證照物巨細不遺在上古中古時此明

鏗早已發現至今日得諸會員而放大之其鏗愈巨其光愈
明諸會員來蒞聚會蓋專為一種目的而來目的維何即社
會公敵是也此社會公敵既思立嚴密法制使無可逃一方
面仍當許其自新冀為良善人皆云公正心與慈愛兩種心不
能並立其實不然有罪必罰是公正心而慈愛即寓乎其中
如漫無限制濫用慈愛則非徒鼓勵身受者之依賴心久之
且恐助長其為非貽害於社會而慈愛心終不能遂故公正
與慈愛並立始能達完全目的方今世界大同無論何種人
類皆係同種當研究此共同問題近有分種界國者皆
者目光錯誤不能從哲學上觀察之所致也故今日所重要
係即聚合萬國學者之心思才識推出一種真理可以通行
於全世界真理一出則雖各國風俗略有等差辦法小有出

十一

入而精義流通終可以貫徹無礙有人云感化罪犯非法官
之責任乃慈善家之義務以為法官者祗應依法科斷執
行者亦祗應按罪懲罰殊不知倡此議者皆係古時報復與
威嚇主義其亦不思之甚也假使犯人在監時受
種種不良之待遇出獄時身體較平時瘦弱思想較平時惡
劣技藝較平時蠢拙匪獨此也而沾染惡習向犯竊罪者
必復為盜向係初犯者必至再犯此時實慈善家以義務恐
不勝其煩且不夫刑法制度至於今日餓斃刑早
已全廢死刑亦少身體刑亦已停止所注重者自由刑耳而
美國現時所注重者又在自由刑中之一種所謂不定期刑
是也不定期刑者何即就諸會員公同之意見公認之學理
而尋思之諸言諸會員所公認者一幼年犯罪者須另寄感

化院釋放年限以能否改悔為斷二因精神病犯罪者須另
置精神病院釋放與否亦以已否痊愈為衡三因犯輕罪者
須交保人擔保不付監獄以全其名譽四因徒能改悔者須
令之假出獄五職業犯罪者其有期限須交政府所派公正人
酌定最長年限以此等人最有危害于社會也以上五端諸
會員共同之意見即美國所行之不定期刑之是否確
當未敢審問時或貌知然保護社會改良罪犯之宗旨則一也
何以言不定期刑之當注重也蓋被告人之性在法庭流
露往往非其真相假如其人性質本善當審問時或偶失檢
束法官因而誤會判之以重罪又如其人性質本惡當審經
時或貌為馴謹法官因而誤會判之以輕罪及至入獄後經
典獄官看守人教誨醫師等平時體驗其惡真相軒豁呈露

十二

斯時若將良者而釋放歟苦其期間未滿將惡者仍監禁歟
苦於法律所無此中困難情形當亦諸會員所深悉以今日
世界法官學問深邃心術公平本不患有此流弊惟犯人性
質變態百出法庭少時之觀察不若監獄多時之體驗深望
諸會員乘最大公正心以為之解決也此外尙有重要事件
則預防犯罪與幼年保護之法此兩種問題係正本清源之
道恆人云本固者枝自榮源清者流自潔深望諸會員悉心
為之考究也以上種種問題必當分部討論後
仍須各部會議各將心得宣示大眾交換智識庶幾不致隔
閡況各部問題彼此均屬相通各會員尤須存謙退之學理
採集眾見以趣合真理此即本會所祝望者也法律之良否
當以真理為斷不必問與各國憲法合與不合與不必問與各

國定制合與不合不必問與各國風俗習慣合與不合須破
除各種成見獨往獨來切實研究真理方出諸會員萬不可
為種種成見束縛在此七日中專精討論以期副此最大之
責任方今世運變遷日新月異種種法制悉當與世運相推
移即如從前法制人人皆以為是者至今日人人皆以為非
如斯變態真不一而足諸會員當恍然悟也第八次監獄會
今日開始宜努力猛進勿怠勿忘云云
附述萬國會員謂見總統演說其略曰今日深喜在
斯地接見諸會員更喜諸會員所經營之事業日益進步既
如刑法改良自英國維羅伯扶斯及魯密雪兩氏出各國咸
次第減輕監獄改良自英國約翰華爾德氏出各國亦次第
變革至今日而刑法監獄兩問題已為世界所注重精益求
精即以美國論亦嘗著手研究曩曾游觀全國監獄覺理想
仍超過事實尚須再加整理期與理想相合雖然美國從事
於監獄者亦已非一日間有所得深願諸會員參觀而質證
之今日諸會員來茲聚會討論刑法改良與監獄改良諸問
題實為各國文明進步之真據從此日見發達將使全世界
人類皆享文明幸福將使已犯罪之人滌除舊染復為良民
實惟諸會員是賴云云

第五節 議案
會議大體組織分總會與部會部會決議後提出於總會更
求總會之審定而問題於是解決所有議案分部列後

第一部 刑罰改良問題
第一問 不定期刑如與刑學原理不相違背則何等罪犯

十三

及何等案情方可適用若何設施方無窒礙適用時可否
於判定刑罰後作為附加刑
決議 從前定期刑法應保存不廢惟幼年犯罪及累犯
並有精神病者方可引用不定期刑但不定期刑名詞方
既泛範圍太廣適用時恐生弊端當附添三種條件方
可適用其條件列後
甲 幼年犯罪者適用不定期刑時必須予
乙 累犯者必係釋放出監後確與社會大有危害方
以相當之教育
丙 當適用不定期刑時須臨時採用假出獄制度
可適用不定期刑
此外定期刑中亦有四種當審判定刑時仍在定
丙 期刑外附判不定期刑至刑期滿日臨時酌定適用
與否四種人如左
甲 定最長期監禁者 例如二十年三十年 之禁監
乙 習慣犯罪者
丙 以犯罪為營業者
丁 犯罪原因非由外界感觸乃其人有一種犯罪特
性者
此四種人皆與社會危害甚大頗難望其自新故必須
附加不定期刑其判斷權以審判官警察官監獄官
醫官行政官五部分之人組織臨時法庭公同酌定
當開臨時法庭時須獨立判斷不得受外界搖動

第二問 本國人在外國犯罪經外國審判廳定罪如逃回

十四

本國是否應照外國所定之罪辦理

決議 一本國人在外國犯罪經外國審判廳定罪如逃

回本國應照外國所定之罪名辦理惟仍由本國審判

廳按照本國刑法判令施行

二外國人在外國犯罪經外國審判廳定罪如逃至第

三國亦可由第三國審判廳按照法律辦理

三凡犯人經法庭判定後如逃出境外無論至何其

原定判詞皆有效力

四各國須立約訂明如此國所定罪名他國必須認可

如此國欲知犯人一切案情求他國詳查者他國必

盡情相告

五應設立萬國法律事務所綜理各國通行法律及審

十五

判與偵察事宜

以上五條國事犯不在其內

六凡犯人經法庭認許假出獄後無論至何國皆當認

其有假出獄之自由

以上第三條第五條第六條應俟下次會議時決

定作爲萬國通法

第三問 凡預防多數人聚合犯罪起見應否定幫同犯罪

人特別罪名

決議 一凡幫同預備犯罪之人如定特別罪名似與刑

法精神不合

二近日聚合同謀犯罪之人日益加多凡係同謀犯罪

者審判官應有權加重治其罪

第二部 監獄改良問題

第一問 近世感化院制度應根何良法方爲合宜犯人入

院應否分年歲等級應否將少年犯罪及不改過之犯入

別監視入院後是否俟其惡性全化日始行釋放

決議 一凡犯人無論年齡如何及再犯累犯總宜令其

改過遷善不可存絕無希望之心

二凡犯人在監禁時須從懲戒及感化兩方面著手

三凡感化犯人須並用智育體育德育三種使其出院

後足以自立

四感化院期限以長期爲宜比之短期釋放後或至再

犯爲有益且可養成完全人格

五感化院既定長期必須兼用假出獄制度惟出院時

十六

必經臨時法廳認定出院後必須有合宜之人隨時

監督

六凡幼年犯罪者應當有特別管理法其法如左

甲 幼年犯罪應付感化院者其期限之長短由審判

官臨時酌定不必拘定法律總以幼年人何時可以

改變性質爲斷

乙 長期之犯如於刑期未滿時確能改悔自新經臨

時法庭許其出院則原判決之審判官亦當認可不

得異議

丙 凡幼年犯罪者候審時應與短期監禁人分別場

所不得合在一處

第二問 能否將假出獄制度更加改良何等官吏可以判

定假出獄

決議 一假出獄制度當有一定法罪凡罪人在監須滿
最短期之監禁刑方能施行假出獄無論何人皆有享
受假出獄利益之資格
二有判定假出獄之權者即臨時法庭之官吏惟出獄
後仍須隨時監督如察其不能改悔仍可隨時拘引
入獄
三假出獄制度施行後政府須設一定官吏監督假出
獄之人如一時未設專官地方慈善會亦可受政府
委託管理此事惟犯人行爲如何須隨時報告政府
四所有永遠監禁及非假出獄罪犯皆由審判廳獨立
辦理與臨時法庭無關臨時法庭不得干涉

第三問 監獄建築之大小何者爲宜小監獄之犯人應否
一律工作
決議 一全國監獄分散各處宜立一專部統轄全國專
管各處監獄事宜全國監獄皆當聽其號令
二監獄中犯人無論刑期長短無論大小監獄皆當令
其作工
三宜立大監獄可容多數犯人庶可經營大工比多
立小監獄較爲有益
四如不能多立大監獄則小監獄中亦必令犯人從事
小工作不可使之閒居
五大監獄中經營大工作組織必求完備須以此種監
獄與工業學堂一律看待此種監犯出獄後可令其

十七

爲小監獄中之執事人
六監獄官中至少須有一人深通工業可以指揮一切
第三部 豫防犯罪制度
第一問 猶豫執行制度有幾國已經實行其成績如何應
否再行推廣
決議 一猶豫執行制度各國刑法多經採用成績雖佳
必須附三種條件方爲有益
甲 猶豫執行之罪犯必使其不得擾害社會
乙 罪犯得享猶豫執行之優遇者必確信其人不必
監禁即能自行改變
丙 猶豫期間必須有人隨時監督
二猶豫執行制度應行推廣惟各國均須特設專官專
管監督猶豫執行之犯人

第二問 防止浮浪無職業者辦法應照第七次議決案辦
理
決議 防止浮浪無職業者有何善法
附 第七次決定案以多設游民習藝所爲主
犯人監禁時其家族應如何設法安養
予工資分作二分一分交其家族俾得養贍一分俟出
監時令作爲營生資本
第三問 一所有監犯在監作工應照其所作工業高下酌
給工資其法雖善各國尚難實行即如美國
二監獄犯酌多一時亦不能辦到惟慈善會及監獄協會
宜負此義務不可令犯人家族失所

十八

三監犯酌給工貲既可保護其家族復能使囚徒出獄
後可以自立其關係至爲重要第照目前情形槪難
辦到宜請各國政府就此問題各發意見俟下次開
會再議

第四部　幼年保護制度

第一問　幼年犯罪是否用普通刑事法科辦如不用普通
刑事法應以何法爲善

決議　一幼年犯罪者當特別辦理不得以普通刑事法
科斷

二審判幼年犯罪者當照下列各條辦理

甲審判官當有心理學社會學之智識方能通曉幼
年人之種種習慣及其性情

乙幼年犯罪者亦適用假出獄制度出獄後必有特
定之人監督惟此監督人當法庭審問時必須到庭
聽審俾深知其犯罪原因

丙當未審判之先必須令深通心理學社會學之醫
生詳細考究其犯罪原因密告於審判官以助其審
判

丁當發覺受拘捕時其腦筋必隱受傷損是宜以
別法令其到庭不可拘捕

戊拘留場所當與成年人分別審判時間亦當與成
年人距離

第二問　年齡太稚者犯罪既不宜收入監獄知識未開亦
不宜途入感化院應以何法管理

十九

決議　應多設幼稚園多教手工令其心有所繫仍須多
設運動場俾其性情活潑

第三問　在大城鎮之幼童應用何法約束以防其游隋犯
法

決議　一法律應明定三種辦法

甲　幼童犯罪者父母當負其責任

乙　有不顧家族之人法律應強迫令其扶持家族

丙　父母有惡習教育不良者應將其童稚移入
感化院令受相當教育

二應多設演說場講演家庭教育使有子女之父母來
聽並勸令教堂同演講至報館著作亦當注重家
庭教育以鼓吹世人

第四問　私生子應否設立專法辦理如設立專法應以何
法爲善

決議　一管理私生子應有兩種辦法

甲　明定法律專條保護私生子

乙　應令慈善會多著淺近之書散布社會使人知私
生子之害令其自悟並注重德育令無遺譏之男女
皆知自重庶可漸次斷絕

二明定法律保護私生子雖一時社會情狀不能與正
當婚姻所產之子一律看待必當漸次平等

三判定私生子歸何人管理應以私生子將來利益爲
斷或歸其父或歸其母或歸其親族鄰里皆可

四私生子判定歸何人管理後如歸其父管理其母亦

二十

當幫同扶養如歸其母管理其父亦當幫同教育

五凡女子私通受孕後往往有墜胎者有將私生子致死者有墜落爲娼者此種流弊皆當豫爲保護之法宜有多人幫助慈善會辦理其辦法亦分三種

甲 女子私通受孕後應由此種人妥爲照料不令墜胎不令將私生子致死並量爲伏助不令墜落爲娼

乙 女子私通受孕後應調查私生之父令其負調護責任

丙 女子雖私通生子一切看待仍當平等遇有疑難時妥爲指導

第六節 閉會後豫備

二十一

第八次萬國監獄會議案既已決定十月八號閉會於是宣布常會章程由各國政府派常會委員每國一人五年中聚會一次或二次會期會地臨時酌定專任調查本國刑罰監獄與慈善事業之報告並提出下次總會之議案於開會前一年交齊擴充本國之學說增長全國之名譽皆常會委員之希望擴充各國大都以常會委員爲赴會會員其經費由各國擔任出費多寡以人口計每百萬人年出美金五圓中國以四萬萬人計歲費美金二千圓據會長懿德生云各國人口無多於中國爲費太鉅時似可酌量減少至加入常會奧否亦由各國自定惟必在閉會後第二年四月以前由政府通知本屆會長或第九次會長其進行機關即寓於常會而第八次萬國監獄會於是告竣

二十二

謹按監獄制度與刑法審判二者有密切之關係監獄不良則行刑之機關未完善而立法與執法之精神均不能見諸作用無論法律若何美備裁判若何公平而刑罰宣告以後悉歸於無效故監獄立法審判三者之改良必互重並行始能達法治之目的增人民之幸福泰西各國自十八世紀改戻刑法審判以來而於監獄一事即一日趨重計日考其組織或以男女而分之爲男監女監或以年齡而分之爲幼年監成年監或以性質而分之爲已決監未決監或以罪名而分之爲重罪監輕罪監或以規模而分之爲大監獄小監獄或以區域而分之爲總監獄分監獄或以經費而分之爲中央監獄地方監獄或以形式而分之爲十字形扇面形星光形或以制度而分之爲分房制雜居制階級制論其要旨則皆採用懲戒感化兩主義使犯人各事工作受教誨冀其改過自新稽其實效則囚徒出獄後大都能自改悔能自生活復爲社會之良民而犯罪之人數日益減少是監獄之職務極爲繁難監獄之學問極爲精密監獄之良否影響於國家人民者至深且遠監獄之優劣關係於世界評議者至重且鉅故入其國觀其國獄制度向未嘗其國家進步之遲速人民知識之高下中國監獄制度沿至隋唐鼇定專刑名五等無監禁之刑法既用報復主義流傳至今未能盡革而監獄遂專以羈留未決之犯其建築則卑污草率其管理則殘慘貪酷流弊所之致使在監時有傾家蕩產瘐斃囹圄之憂出監後有沾染惡習犯罪增加之患邇者

清代外務部中外關係檔案史料叢編——中美關係卷 第六冊·國際會議

朝廷洞鑒此弊改徒流等刑爲工作創設罪犯習藝所以收容之
近又採取新法創設模範監獄於京師及各省城而府廳州
縣之監獄亦限於五年內一律成立是行刑學之講求已爲
全國所注重然而監獄法尚未頒布則建築管理諸事勢必
各異其制各殊其形破碎支離不獲收統一之效又況從前
舊監概未改革種種需索苛暴情狀有令人不忍言者外
觀世變內察國情若獄制不善終不能與各國躋於大同謹
竭一得之愚獻著手改良之策一此次議決之案宜採用也
查萬國公會雖非立法機關而每次解決問題各國多見諸
實用此次議案請由資政院憲政編查館修訂法律館法
部分別探擇以便施行一監獄官吏宜養成也查歐洲各國
任用獄官之法雖有不同而其必由學習而來則一如德之

二十三

用軍人義之用學生和比之二者並用要皆於未受職前使
之修養練習試可乃用義更使之爲終身官應請由法部創
設監獄學堂於京師並轉商學部通飭各省法律學堂添設
監獄學一科以期宏造人才一監獄協會宜倡也查監獄
協會之性質有二一係研究學理一係調查東西各國
斯會多如林立亦多以法部大臣爲名譽會長誠以學問日新
月異愈求愈出且恐美觀守人不能奉法得會員調查而報告
之其弊乃揭法戾意美觀於美總檢察大臣之演說益可深
信應請由法部擬訂協會簡章通行各省督撫提法使勸令
設立以期補助進行一監獄制度宜酌定也查獄制近分分
房雜居階級三者自美國創立片蘇巴尼亞監獄後學者輩
相推重英比二國全國施行惟以建築之費較鉅故他國未

能盡改分房有用晝雜居夜分房之制者有用先分房次雜
居終付之假出獄者以中國現時情形而論若全國盡建分
房監獄財力實有未逮應請由法部通行各省於建造監獄
時內分分房雜居兩部以免紛歧一俟新刑律宣布後即可
用假出獄之法而行階級之制一監獄形式宜規定也查歐
美各國監獄之形式或用十字與一字或用扇面與星光荷
蘭新建之哈爾倫監獄則又形如橢圓似羅馬二千年前之
鬥獸場名目既多理論亦異然詢之學者僉謂看守之便利
費用之節省光線之通明空氣之充足仍以十字形爲宜故
監禁二百人以下者宜用十字形二百人以上五百人以下
者宜用雙十字形即世所稱星光形也獄司官宜重視也查全國監獄監督
省照辦以示整齊一典獄司官宜重視也查全國監獄監督

二十四

之權雖操於法部大臣而奉大臣之命令以贊助指揮者則
在司官司官學識之有無即監獄良否之所繫歐洲各國有
法部者無不特設司遴選有學問有經驗者爲之中國雖
於監獄學尚少專科而在外學成歸國與已經設立模範監
獄之典獄官似不無練達之才應由法部速調到部優加廉
体責令見功以期提挈綱領一感化院宜速立也查感化院
之意義係輔助監獄權力之所不及歐美各國大都收留幼
年犯罪與不受家庭教育及家庭教育不良並浮浪乞丐者
良以幼稚之童血氣未定最易遷移若寄之於普通監獄必
至耳濡目染相習爲非根本不端枝業必敗易日蒙以養正
即是此意或者曰中國古時所設之濟貧院育嬰堂等近時
所設之教養局等何莫非感化院之相似殊不知我之所設

者偏重在養又不僅限於幼年人之所設者係教養並重且
純爲幼年之感化各國從經費上之區別有國家與地方之
分然觀其設置凡學科工藝以及田園花木無一不備幾如
一最新之村落觀其男女無一不性天活潑如小學校之學
生而朝士大夫以及慈善宗教各家方且孜孜不倦日求擴
充斯爲預防犯罪正本清源之道應請由法部或民政部先
行創設感化院於京師以爲之倡一面通行各省令地方官
切實講演多方勸導俾士紳均得從事斯業以期培養人格
一保護事業宜勸設也查刑罰之執行固屬於監獄官吏而
所以終其刑之執行使犯人出獄後有以生存而不至再犯
者則社會之責任是即保護事業之所由生詳而論之蓋由
私人公立一會凡犯人釋放時保護會即與之交接或給其

二十五

衣食或給其居住或給其職業或給其資本或借貸其器用
或假予其旅費如斯之類不堪枚舉要而言之凡於免囚之
便利無一不代爲謀也歐美各國此會甚昌日本亦有免囚
保護法以我國現時人心而論其對於出獄者嫌忌之不暇
違云保護然而監獄未改以前實難責以義務若自茲以往
日增斯擔負重應請由法部或民政部創設一免囚保護
而觀念不變竊恐免囚終必爲害於社會則獄費
通告通行各省令地方官喻戶曉並令各報館大加鼓吹
俾得輪灌知識於一般人民以期慈善普及以上八策除第
一策係此次議案外餘皆爲改良監獄之要事亦皆爲各國
已行之良法已著之成績儻不急起直追匪但內政不修抑
恐第九次赴會時無以見重於各國也今世界文明尊崇

人格刑法一事已有主張去死刑之議荷蘭則已全廢比利
時則置之適用之外其他各國雖未刪除而引用之案歲不
常有人格愈高犯罪愈少刑罰愈輕各國之日事討論者全
在自由刑之問題而監獄乃執行自由刑之場所遂爲刑法
之主科自十八世紀以來競先改革日求進步中國雖遠處
東隅而大勢所趨日接日屬斷不能翹然立於風氣之外又
況各國強行領事權於我國其藉口亦每在刑法審判之
獄之不良又況海牙和平會抑中國爲三等雖以海陸軍不
能振興亦以法律積弱而領事裁判權之朝鮮當未歸併以前經
拒回領事裁判權而領事裁判權以撤中國有四千餘年之開
法典普設審判而領事裁判權乃叢爾之遷邏尚能改正刑法
化二十餘省之土地四百兆之人民乃受此無公理之待遇

二十六

不平等之名譽一日不去即國人忍垢蒙羞痛心疾首之一
日今者新刑律草案猶未議定民商各法尚待調查訴訟法
亦未完全監獄法亦甫告竣將來縷議頒行若不將從省報
復威嚇之主義概行滌蕩若不將徹去領事裁判權之宗旨
公同抱定竊恐拘牽新舊不成法令愈多政治愈增繁
擾外強日進程度日見距離匪惟不能自立抑且不足圖存
立法司法如此推而至於行政亦何莫不然方今世界立國
之道皆本於大同主義舉凡風俗習慣政教法制已漸趨同
一之勢故曰國因之他國必從而推廣之蓋交通便利國際頻
新法也此國創一公會也一國和之各國群起而趨附之行一
繁風氣所之幾如水之匯海山之歸獄而不可遏抑主動者
強被動者弱不動者亡縱觀歐美各國得斯道者無不勝失

斯道者無不敗當可恍然悟也美前總統盧斯福有言剗除

村落思想德皇維廉第二有言破除家族主義國之存立其

在斯歟其在斯歟

二十七

BUREAU INTERNATIONAL
DE
L'UNION POUR LA·PROTECTION
DE LA
PROPRIÉTÉ INDUSTRIELLE.

————◄►————

Berne,le 1er avril 1911.

Adresse télégraphique:Protectunions,Berne.

Annexes envoyées à part.

Circulaire No.132/512.

Aux Administrations spéciales des Etats,membres de
l'Union internationale.

Aux Gouvernements non unionistes invités à prendre part à la
Conférence de Washington.

Me référant à ma lettre-circulaire du 23 mars 1911,No 131/450,
j'ai l'honneur de vous envoyer par ce courrier 3 exemplaires du
document suivant:

Conférence de Washington. Documents préliminaires.

Observations et propositions de l'Administration de la France.

Ce document fait suite aux fascicules I - X ,précédemment
expédiés.

En vous priant de vouloir bien m'accuser réception de cet envoi,
je vous renouvelle, Monsieur le Ministre ,l'expression de ma très
haute considération.

Bureau international

de l'Union de la Propriété industrielle,

Le Directeur,

Au Ministère des Affaires étrangères

de l'Empire de Chine,

P é k i n.

保護工業萬國公會辦事處來函

逕啟者三月二十三號寄奉之信敬祈

詧納茲又寄呈華盛頓會集之豫訂文件

三卷係法國提議修正之案即續另寄一

二十冊後伏布

收閱盂盼

見覆順頌

日祉　　件另寄

　　　總理簽名　　瑞士都城發

　　　一千九百十二年四月一號

逕啟者茲因數年前外國設立一會譯名萬國遇旱

益農會該會意旨係將各國所有缺雨田地設法令

其豐收雖為民立之會本國政府甚為重視今據該

會書記由本國外部送來一函係萬國遇旱益農會

自本年西十月十六號起至二十號止在美國科羅

拉多地方開辦第六次大會特請

貴國派員前往茲將該會原信函送

貴部希為轉送農工商部查照即望

日祉附洋文函件另封

見復是荷順頌

美國使署

嘉樂恒啟 五月十三日

AMERICAN LEGATION,
PEKING.

To F. O. No. 91.

June 9, 1911.

Your Imperial Highness:

     Several years ago a society was organized call-
ed the International Dry Farming Congress. The object
of the Society is to devise means to increase the product-
iveness of the arid regions in all the different countries
of the world. Although this Congress is a private organ-
iz-ation the American Government regards it as important
and therefore the Department of State has instructed me
to forward to the Board of Agriculture, Industries and
Commerce an invitation from the Secretary of the said Congress to send a representative to attend the Sixth Annual
Session of the International Dry Farming Congress, which
will be held at Colorado Springs, Colorado, from October
16 to October 20, 1911. I beg to request Your Highness'
Board to transmit the invitation to the Board of Agriculture, Industries, and Commerce, and to favor me with a reply.

     Iavail myself of this opportunity to renew to
Your Imperial Highness the assurance of my highest consideration.

                    American Minister.

To His Imperial Highness
    Prince of Ch'ing,
        President of the Board
           of Foreign Affairs.

入收

致柯爾樂稅司函　美國特派員照

頃奉本月三號　惠書迅即作復我

政府以此次鴉片會議為全權會議凡各

團特派員均有畫諾全權但不得出本

國憲限之外譬如美國使庫須得總統

同意上議院協贊中國此次特派員須

如徑前馬關條約庚子和約李鴻章而

得之全權此全權或給予梁大臣一人或

令与伊同事共有之均無不可會議之時

儻可隨時電商北京政府議定之後特

派員俱有簽押全權重言以申明之梁大

臣須得便宜行事全權儻會議時此等

全權有不妥委北京政府仍可更改

12

16

Editorial Name List of Volume VI

Chairmen of Committee:	Hao Ping
	Hu Wanglin
	John Rosenberg
Deputy Chairmen of Committee:	Li Yansong
	Wu Hong
	Hu Zhongliang
	Xu Kai
	Pei Likun
Members of Committee:	Liu Yuxing
	Wang Zhiwen
	Liu Hefang
	Zhang Jingwen
Chief Editors:	Hao Ping
	Hu Wanglin
	John Rosenberg
Executive Editors	Hu Zhongliang
	Xu Kai
	Pei Likun
Deputy Chief Editors:	Liu Yuxing
	Wang Zhiwen
Editors:	Wang Zhiwen
	Liu Hefang
Digital Editors:	Li Jing
	Ye Bin
Assistants:	Qi Yinqing
	Li li
	Wang Ning
	Zhang Jingwen
	Venus Cheung

A SERIES OF DOCUMENTS ILLUSTRATING THE
DIPLOMATIC RELATIONS BETWEEN
CHINA AND FOREIGN COUNTRIES
IN THE QING DYNASTY

CORRESPONDENCE BETWEEN CHINA AND THE UNITED STATES

VOLUME VI

INTERNATIONAL CONFERENCES

THE FIRST HISTORICAL ARCHIVES OF CHINA
PEKING UNIVERSITY, CHINA
LA TROBE UNIVERSITY, AUSTRALIA